Threading the Bible
New Testament

Threading the Bible
New Testament

Requests for information should be addressed to:
Duranno Press, 95 Seobinggo-Dong, Yongsan-Gu, Seoul, 140-240 Korea.

ISBN-10: 89-531-1253-7 03230
ISBN-13: 978-89-531-1253-7 03230

Printed in Korea.

Threading the Bible
New Testament

B. J. Moon

Duranno

Contents

Forward I

Behind the Scenes of the English version preparation

During my five-year tenure as a Foreign Diplomat in both Washington, D.C. and New York, I had the privilege of being invited as the guest speaker at Revival Gatherings or Bible Seminar events held by Korean churches on approximately over 150 occasions. On these visits I learned about the difficulties confronted by resident pastors in dealing with the English Ministry within the local Korean churches. The common concern among all pastors was that college students as well as youth groups (1.5 generation or 2nd generation of Korean Americans) did not read the Bible. I was even more alarmed by the fact that these young adults had no interest at all in knowing the Bible.

If this situation continues it is probable that in about 10-20 years Korean churches will become like many American churches. Big buildings with only handful elderly people in regular attendance. My heart was compelled to do something about it. With that in mind, I had the vision to translate my book entitled "Threading the Bible" into English so that the 1.5/2nd generations could read the English version of this book and gain an understanding of the Bible. Simultaneously, at the suggestion of numerous pastors who also realized the remarkable recovery of passing on the faith of respective parents to the next generation, the birth of translating the Korean version to English was activated. Through God's grace, Young-Hee Park, who was given a bilingual gift and was also a member of the Leaders Bible Study Group that I was leading at the time, volunteered to take upon the task of translating the book. With her commitment and dedication, the whole process took 8 months and has finally come to reality at this point of publication.

In spite of what occurred behind the scenes, now that the book is published in English it is my desire and hope that Christians throughout the world will benefit in their understanding of the Bible from Genesis to Revelation. This book was written in attempt to assist the reader to capture and follow God's message with interest, enthusiasm and grace. Especially in the 21st century, many people are losing hope in the future because of economic crisis, but I pray that through this book my readers will realize the only hope to overcome hardship and difficult situations in the world is to hold on to God's Promise (the good news) Ultimately, recovering vision for a prosperous future.

My deepest gratitude in Christ to Deacon Young-Hee Park for her diligence in translating this book with the passionate love of Jesus. I would also like to extend my thanks to Dr. Chang-Woo Lee and Deacon Tim Yoon for their assistance in this project and to Dr. Won - Ho Jhe for his help in the reviewing and editing process.

I give all glory to our Lord Jesus!

Elder
B. J. Moon

Forward Ⅱ

Until All Our Churchgoers are Changed with the Word of God

In spite of being a Christian from birth, a big blow of realization hit me at the age of 40 when I was working at the Korean Mission to the United Nations in Geneva, Switzerland. The big blow was my lack of knowledge of the Bible.

Upon my return to Korea, I was determined. Without missing a day, my feet automatically led me to Onnuri Church as soon as I got off from work. Obviously, there were many relatives, friends, and classmates that I wanted to spend time with since I was living abroad for quite a number of years. But I wrestled off all those temptations and instead spent my days attending and even setting up various types of Bible study programs at Onnuri Church. I literally ran after each study groups available at the church. Then one day in the fall of 1994, my eyes caught the wording of an ad on the wall: "Strategy Pursuit of the Bible in 40 Days-Capture the Threading of the Bible!" My heart was totally captivated. I was overwhelmed when I read this ad and exclaimed, "This is it! It's exactly what I need." I couldn't help myself but to think God had prepared this seminar for me. I was desperately yearning for a deep and abiding study. A study that was systematic and organized for easy understanding. The expectation and joy was difficult to hide so I immediately registered for the seminar.

Then later I was diagnosed with stomach cancer. God made me hold on to Him by bringing me near to the valley of death. It was during this time the Holy Spirit was poured onto me, giving me the gift to teach the Word of God. With the encouragement of God's guidance, I started my first Bible seminar of "Threading the Bible" in Beijing, China while going through my cancer treatments. The seminar took place wherever my feet led me. Reflecting back, almost 10 years have flown by but if feels like only yesterday.

My heart stops and my mouth speechless by God's amazing love poured onto me through the Holy Spirit. God has transformed me into a person waking the dawn with shedding tears of prayer each morning. It has become a joyful mission for me to alert the believers in teaching them to begin each day with early morning prayers at church before going out to the world.

In early 2005, with God's grace I was able to hold a 'Threading the Bible' seminar in New York where thousands of people gathered after attending respective Sunday services from various churches. Unfortunately, many other religious institutions strongly opposed it because of my occupation as a government official. The Bible study lasted 5 weeks. At the urging of many people yearning to understand the Bible, this has prompted me to put together a 'reference' handbook that could be used alongside the Bible. Most Christians have been encouraged to study the Word of God, yet many have not been shown how.

I thank God for giving me an opportunity and enabling me to widen the scope to spread the Word of God through this project. The importance of it was proven by a letter received from a man who was serving a one year term in prison in Korea. During this time he had read the Bible 20 times in 8 months and was about to complete his 21st reading in a week. He wrote in his letter that the Bible was difficult to comprehend and confessed that in spite of reading the Bible numerously he felt no significant impact at all. Instead, it made him more frustrated than ever. While going through moments of turmoil, he came across my book *Early Bird Christians* and found out about the Bible study with a twist--a methodical approach for easy understanding. He was asking for help in understanding the Bible so that he could explain to those in prison. A prisoner who did not believe in God approached him being fully aware that he was reading the Bible day and night and threw him a question, “Do you feel at peace when you read the Bible?” His response was, “Quite honestly, I don’t know.” He felt that he had missed his opportunity in evangelizing this prison mate and felt greatly frustrated. I was convinced that if I wrote a tutorial book on Bible study it would be of great help in assisting those who find themselves in unpredictable situations.

I have been approached by publishers frequently in the past and my excuse was that time was not on my side. But through the works of God, I find myself doing something that was unthinkable. Fortunately, Duranno Press was kind enough to consolidate all the notes taken from my previous studies which I was able to organize it from time to time. Again, I praise God for His grace.

My primary goal is to emphasize each individual's ability to read the entire Bible so that they may experience God's love and grace. Furthermore, for the readers to be able to realize and know what the 'good purpose' (Philippians 2:13) is all about. Needless to say, there are many Bible study materials available. I believe the Holy Spirit will lead and help those who yearn for a deep understanding and abiding relationships with God to live out the truths. God will reveal Himself to them so that they will discover new ability, strength and confidence.

Regardless what level of faith or whatever situation a reader may be in, I pray that through this book, all churchgoers and believers may be able to read the 66 books of the Bible with ease along with the grace and inspiration of God. I earnestly hope that this book will not only ignite the readers' attempt to know God but also allow them to challenge the ongoing questions and puzzling quests raised and interact with the Bible. May each reader experience the existence and grace of the Holy Spirit to guide his journey into the spiritual world.

I want the readers to use this book as a reference guide so that when reading the Bible, each individual may hear the voice of God by applying the truth to our life. In His inspired Word, God has given us everything we need to know about life and godliness. I look forward to the days ahead that from all parts of the world, praise will be given to God for His grace and glory.

I owe my gratitude to Reverend Jin-So Yoo (Presently Senior Pastor at All Nations Church in Los Angeles) for teaching me such an insightful 'formularized' Bible study. My deepest gratitude to Reverend Yong-Jo Ha (Presently Senior Pastor at Onnuri Church in Seoul, Korea) for his continued support in enabling me to deliver the Word at the church and always being there for my spiritual guidance and growth. I thank, in the name of Christ, Reverend Chun-Soo Lee (Presently Senior Pastor at Inchon Sansung Baptish Church) for teaching me the structure of spiritual theology. Without a doubt, it would have been impossible to transfer my lecture notes to a book if it wasn't for these precious people. I also want to convey my love to my wife, Jong-Sook Park, for her dedicated prayers during my lectures and most importantly, for her sharp and impeccable commentary feedbacks never failing to remind me to focus on alignment with God. Additionally, I want to thank the staff members at Duranno Press and Deacon Shin-Hee Han, for her drafting work. Lastly, I would like to thank Elder Byung-Ik Lee of the Ezra Missionary Group who helped me wrap up this project from my official government assignment in New York.

I hope that this book will help future generations of readers to understand the Bible afresh.

I give all glory to our Lord Christ!

Elder
B. J. Moon

ALEXANDER THE GREAT AND THE QUASI KINGDOM OF JUDAH

Daniel 7-12

The prophecy of Malachi that before the coming of the great and terrible day of the Lord, Elijah the prophet would come is fulfilled by John the Baptist and Jesus who came into the world after 400 years have lapsed since Malachi proclaimed. Theologically, this 400 years period of silence is referred as the 'intermediate of the Old and the New Testament' which sets the background of the New Testament. In addition, it also clearly shows us how the history of the world that we live in now is grafted into the Bible. The message of the intermediate portion could also be interpreted as the answer to the following question: "Why did the Messiah specifically have to come at that time and at that place?" Let us look into how God worked for 400 years to prepare the coming of the Messiah.

THE PROPHECY OF DANIEL

What Sort of Things Happened During 400 Years?

The book of Daniel is divided into two parts. The first six chapters relate to the historical events in Babylon, covering the span of the nation's exile while the remaining chapters (7-12) record four distinct visions of future events that is to occur given to Daniel.

God had already prophesied the future events that will happen after Malachi the prophet. Through Daniel's visions and dreams, the great purpose of God's world view of history and the reason for sending the Messiah at such specific time was revealed. Particularly Daniel's visions and reams were about the progressive link to the birth of Christ - Babylon becoming Persia, from Persia to Greece and from Greece to Rome.

The story of King Nebuchadnezzar's dream is told in Daniel chapter 2. The idol that appeared in King Nebuchadnezzar's dream consisted of different materials; the head was made of fine gold, its breast and arms of silver, its belly and thighs of bronze, its legs of iron and its feet partly of iron and partly of clay. The king was greatly alarmed by the stone that was cut out of the mountain without hands which struck and crushed the statue on its feet of iron and clay. God revealed the dream to Daniel as well as its meaning which is summarized as follows:

The head made of fine gold is Babylon under King Nebuchadnezzar's reign. The breast and arms of silver meant that a foreign kingdom of Persia would destroy Babylon. The belly and thighs of bronze indicate that another forceful country, Greece, would destroy Persia. And lastly, the legs of iron and feet partly of iron and clay meant that a bigger country, Rome, would rise and destroy Greece. The fact that the feet were partly made of iron and clay foreshows that the Roman Empire would be split into two empires (east and west) but ultimately the stone that was cut out from a mountain (Son of Man, Christ) would crush these four kingdoms and restore God's kingdom. (Daniel 2:37-45) More detailed explanation will follow in Daniel 7.

The Vision of the Four Beasts_Daniel 7

Daniel saw a dream and visions of four beasts coming up from the sea. First, a lion with the wings of an eagle appeared but his wings were plucked. Then a bear rose up on one side with three ribs in its mouth between its teeth. Next, another beast resembling a leopard with the four wings of a bird on its back and four heads surfaced. The fourth terrifying and mighty beast had large iron teeth with 10 horns.

Daniel was distressed with the visions and began to ask, "What is the meaning of these visions?" and the angel gave him its interpretation. The four beasts symbolized four successive empires. Even though the angel did not mention the exact names of the countries, we can easily gather information from Daniel 2 and 8 that the four beasts represented the following countries: Babylon, Medo-Persia, Greece and Rome.

The aged lion was Babylon (it is said that the ancient flag of Iraq was the wing of an eagle). The bear was Persia and the three ribs symbolized the neighboring countries. This vision was about Persia attacking Babylon and taking over Syria up to Egypt. According to this vision, the region of the Middle East was unified for the first time during the Persian Empire.

The next beast of a leopard with four wings and four heads was the Greek Empire. King Darius III of the Persian Empire who had unified the Middle Eastern territory had plans to conquer the European side but was defeated by the swift leopard of the Greek Empire. The power of Europe had drastically occupied Asia Minor.

Alexander the Great and his power did not last long as revealed in the dream. (God's messenger, Angel Gabriel provided interpretation of the ram and goat in Daniel 8.) The 'four horns' were the divided kingdoms upon his death.

The fourth beast with iron teeth which was devouring, crushing and trampling down the remainder with its feet was the Roman Empire. According to the prophecy of the dream, the Roman Empire conquered the world. The little horn (the 11th horn) that came out in the midst of the ten horns possessed with eyes indicated Emperor Nero who persecuted God's people.

The most significant climax of the vision is on the dominion of the 'one like a son of man' — Jesus Christ, who would come in the cloud to save the saints from great persecution, inaugurating His eternal conquest and victory.

Obviously, the dream is focused on the first coming of the Messiah at the time and simultaneously, the vision is also related to the distant future ? the end time when the suffering will be finally over upon the 2nd coming of Christ who will come in the greatest glory in the midst of the angels' trumpets. God revealed all that is to happen to Israel and their exile in Babylon through a dream and interpreted it to Daniel.

Vision of the Ram and Goat_Daniel 8

The vision of the ram and the he-goat appears in Daniel 8 which focuses on the second and third empires. The two-horned ram which symbolizes Medo-Persia is superseded by the swift-footed goat, Alexander the Great's Greek Empire (Persia, today's Iran). The 'great horn' means Alexander the Great himself.

We have seen the works of God through the period of exile in the Old Testament - a war was sparked between Iran and Iraq; and the hands of Babylon (Iraq) was tied up through King Cyrus's victory (Iran) for His people to return to their homeland, Jerusalem. We are able to know that God raised King Cyrus by anointing him to fulfill His plan. (Isaiah 45:1-2) Through God's providence, Persia ruled over Asia Minor for about 200 years after occupying Babylon. But the king of Persia's ambition was not yet satisfied. Eventually King Darius III attacked Greek which was under the powerful king, Peter the Great in Macedonia and ultimately, collapsed miserably in front of Greek's young upcoming king, Alexander the Great.

After the great horn was crushed (Alexander the Great died before his time) at the young age of 33, the 'four horns' that followed thereafter (the four Greek kingdoms), especially the fourth horn, the Syrian Seleucid empire persecuted God's people severely.

Visions of the Northern King and the Southern King_Daniel 11

The issue of who will conquer the land of Canaan (where the people of Israel lived) is explained in detail in this awesome vision. During the period of the book of Daniel, Canaan was ruled over by two parties: Greek's northern king, the Selucid dynasty of Greek in north and the Ptolemaic dynasty of Egypt in the southern part of the land. Struggle for power over this region continued on from this point on. Even though the king of the south held the control over the territory for a long time, a vision foretold how an evil king from the north would appear and suppress Jewish religious practice and the Temple rituals while persecuting people in Israel. The prophecy of this vision which was shown several times by God actually becomes a reality. According to the vision, the baton of power was passed on from Seleucid dynasty to Antiochus IV. In the history, the exactor of tribute was Seleucus IV, who was shortly succeeded by his brother Antiochus IV, the persecutor of the Jews. Antiochus attacked Jerusalem and desecrated the Temple trying to pull the roots of the believers of God.

This is the context of the prophecy and the background of the Old Testament preparing for the coming of Christ. We are able to confirm the prophecy through the changes that took place in the history of the world. How awesome is this! Let us give our praise and glory to our Almighty God.

THINGS THAT HAPPENED IN THE ACTUAL HISTORY OF THE WORLD

Fall of Persia and the Entry of Alexander the Great

As Daniel's vision is interpreted, Persia falls into the hands of the Greek empire after having ruled over Asia Minor for approximately 200 years since Babylon. In order to pursue his ambition to conquer the world, the Persian king Darius III crossed over the Mediterranean and continued battles with Peter the Great of Greece. Taking advantage of the time when Greece was not strong yet, the Persian King Darius III initiated the battle in the sea and eventually advanced to Europe through land. This offense made the Greeks act defensively, but on the other hand, severe casualties in Persian military force were also inevitable. At this time, the son of Peter the Great, Alexander the Great came into the picture and defeated the Persians (B.C. 333). The Greek/Hellenistic rule suddenly rose into power. Alexander the Great won victory after victory and it was said that there were no more worlds to conquer. This event not only made Asia's power decline but for Europe, it became a milestone for them to advance to Asia for the first time.

Alexander the Great was more than a legendary general. He became a king at the young age of 20 and as Daniel's vision indicated, he surely was a lion with the wings who rapidly charged towards Asia both by land and sea. His army easily consumed Egypt and Syria like a spark of a fire, destroyed the Persian kingdom (majority of the Middle Eastern region today) and advanced up to India, conquering Asia. Historically, this was the first encounter of the east and the west but sadly, the first meeting was through a bitter battle.

Alexander the Great is famous for his victorious battles over Asia. But most of all, besides the fact that he had created the empire in Eurasia, he was also a great scholar. He was Aristotle's best pupil and had the heart not simply the urge to conquer the land but to spread Greek ideas (Hellenism) and Greek culture wherever he went. Who is Aristotle? He is the famous Greek philosopher, scientist, mathematician, physician and medical scholar — the originator of higher education of politics, social studies, humanities, science that we study in our world today. (Note: But as Christians, let us not forget that Apostle Paul referred to these as elementary levels of knowledge.) Apparently, Alexander the Great, who was to succeed Greece as a king, wanted Aristotle to be his private teacher but Aristotle refused each time according to a western reference book.

Setting aside his pride, young Alexander was eager to learn from Aristotle and asked him, "Whatever your wish may be, it will be granted if you agree to be my teacher. What is it that you want?" Aristotle was studying geometry and was drawing a triangle at the time and said to the Prince Alexander, "I do have a wish. I'm drawing a triangle right now and you're creating a shadow so please step aside." This is actually a famous incident. In any event, Alexander the Great became an Aristotle's favorite pupil who spread the ideas of Hellenism throughout the world, influencing even us today.

Alexander the Great was obsessed with a sense of duty to spread Greek ideas and culture believing it would make the world better. There is even a saying that if a person had the same degree of passion as Alexander's in spreading the Word of God, half of the world probably would have been conquered. Just as Ottoman (Osman) Turkey had asked the world to choose whether it be a sword or the Koran when conquering the world, Alexander the Great, on the other hand, attacked and killed people claiming that they are cannibals and justified it that it is what one must do for the sake of civilization and enlightenment. For this reason, many people were slaughtered by the swords in Asia, yet, Alexander the Great felt no remorse. Through him, Asia and Europe became one. It was during Hellenistic age that Greek influence was most widely felt and continued to spread. Through Alexander the Great, the Hellenism entered Asia and the scholastics spread widely from the west to the east.

Threader: Alexander the Great thought that he had conquered the land with Hellenism but the gospel of Jesus which started from Jerusalem in the East has been spread throughout the ends of the earth as commanded. 'But you will receive power when the Holy Spirit has come upon you; and you shall be my witnesses both in

Knowledge Search 17

Ideology of Hellenism

All of our thinking mechanism today is based on the influence of Hellenism of Alexander the Great. The studies of the world is based on the ideology of Aristotle. The characteristics of Hellenism are based on self-focus, individualism and logic, which are totally the opposite of Hebraism that is based on God in the center, relationship and experience. The ideology of Hellenism makes you think the opposite of God and thus, the Bible becomes difficult to understand.

The Hellenism which began in the period of Alexander the Great (B.C. 300) has been influencing the world greatly even today. Among many, one of them is the Olympics. Therefore, certain conservative gospel-oriented denominations raise a question on the Olympics. Physicality of human body is emphasized in the Olympics. "How high can a human body jump?" (High Jump) "How long can a human body run?" (Marathon) Basically, it's all about 'who is better.' It appears quite healthy at the first glance but actually, it is an activity originated from the ideology of Hellenism, merely letting human become animalized.

The ideology of Hellenism was rooted from the spirit of Satan and it progressed even into a point where anthropomorphizing invisible God. The Greeks treated their god just like a human being. Some of you may have read the Greek myths where gods become lovers to each other like humans and commit adulteries and so forth. The Greeks brought the god down to the human level and humans were brought down to the level of animals.

When the spirit of Satan is at work on people, man focuses only on filling an animalistic instinct. It blocks people from having any interest in spirituality. Under the name of rationalism which is based on the ideology of Hellenism, people reject the world of spirituality.

Jerusalem, and in all Judea and Samaria, and even to the remotest part of the earth.' (Acts 1:8) Where is the end of the earth? This was a time when people believed in geocentricism (Ptolemaic theory) and they thought the sea ended somewhere; so in their mind, Savannah (Spain) was the 'end of the earth.' It is why Apostle Paul said 'I will go on by way of you to Spain.' (Romans 15:28) But actually, the globe is round so when the pilgrims shipped out from England and arrived in America, the gospel started circling around the earth: from England to America, from America to Korea, then from Korea to western part of China. The gospel travels continuously towards the west and eventually, when Jerusalem recovers the gospel, it will be the last day for mankind.

For this reason, Alexander the Great is not only famous historically but biblically an important person as well. Even now the two ideologies: Hellenism and Hebraism are being challenged. The world we live in is a spiritual battleground between the gospel and the Hellenism.

The Ptolemaic Empire and Seleucid Empire

Alexander the Great had plans to conquer the eastern part of Babylon (today's Iraq) and the entire world but died young due to malaria at the age of 33. Upon his death, the Greek Empire that connected Europe and Asia for the first time ever was divided. Just as Daniel's vision (Daniel 7) indicated, a strong 'horn' (Alexander the Great) appeared momentarily. And as it disappeared, the 'four horns' (the four Greek kingdoms) surfaced thereafter.

The world history covers all four kingdoms but we will focus on the two powerful kingdoms that greatly impacted Israel the most. These are the two kings that appeared in Daniel 11: 'the kings of the south and the north' ? the Ptolemaic and the Seleucid Empire who ruled over Syria.

The Ptolemaic Empire_B.C. 303-B.C. 197

The land of honey, Canaan - Palestine is the most crucial key point of the world. The power to conquer the world had to cross over the land of Palestine. The Ptolemaic Dynasty who was governing Egypt took over the land of Palestine first. Struggle for power continued between the kings of the north and the south (Ptolemy). Seleucus (king of the north) was defeated continuously by the king of the south and at each retreat, he attacked Jerusalem and desecrated the Temple.

The Ptolemaic Dynasty is the Greek Empire of Egypt. The famous Cleopatra came from this lineage. The Ptolemies (the Greek kings of Egypt) controlled Palestine for about 100 years (B.C. 303-B.C. 197). During this period of time, the customs and ideas of the Greeks formed an important part of the life and culture of Palestine. The Ptolemies chose Alexandria as the capital of Egypt and made it the holy ground of Hellenism. The center of studies on the rich culture and ideologies of Europe and Asia at the time was in Alexandria not Paris. The Greek architecture changed the appearance of many towns where Greek style gymnasia, theatres and stadiums were built everywhere. Museums were built to store the ancient scriptures as well as cultural treasures of the east and the west.

The Ptolemaic Empire left behind a historically great achievement during this period. The Hebrew Scriptures were translated into Greek (known as the 'Septuagint') for the large colony of Greek-speaking Jews who lived in the city Alexandria. The Ptolemaic Empire requested for approximately 70 rabbis in Jerusalem to be sent to Alexandria for the translation work. Eventually, 72 people, 6 from each of 12 tribes were sent and they produced the Bible of the 'role of 70 people.' Later, as Greek became an official language of the world just as English is an International Language today, an explosion of translations followed thereafter. Especially as Luther translated the Bible into German, it provided a turning point to the foreigners, giving them an opportunity to read the Bible.

The Seleucid Empire_B.C. 197-B.C. 164

Later on, the Seleucid Dynasty seized Palestine and ruled for approximately 30 years (B.C. 197-B.C. 164). To fulfill the dreams of Alexander the Great, King Seleucus carried out a forceful rural enlightenment movement to change the ideology of the uncivilized cannibals to logical and cool-headed rationality. He ruled violently and oppressed the religious practices in order to make Palestine completely absorb Hellenism. An evil king like him does not last long. The history records that Seleucus IV, who succeeds his brother Antiochus IV, was the most vicious one in persecuting the Jews. He desecrated the Temple, suppressed the Jews for keeping the Sabbath and burnt the books of the Law (Torah). Eventually, Jewish patriots started a resistance movement to overthrow the oppression of the Syrian ruler Antiochus IV.

Quasi Jewish Kingdom_Hasmon Dynasty

Independence by Whirling of an Iron Hammer_Revolution of Maccabees

The oppression on religious practices became stronger because of Antiochus IV. The Jews continued to enter the Temple even if it was prohibited so in the end, it came to a point where a pig's head was tied in front of the Temple and they were asked to bow and kiss the pig's head before entering it.

The resistance was led by an aging Maccabaeus and his five sons for the liberation of the Jews from the foreign ruler. Maccabaeus was not a Levi so actually he could not become a high priest but it was only possible since the movement happened at a disorderly time period as they(Israelites) were returning from the exile. Therefore, his descendants were able to become the office of ruler and high priest. The passion of Maccabaeus was remarkable who died a year later since starting the resistance movement and his third son, Judas took over the baton after him. Judas earned a nickname 'Maccabee' since he had a skill of whirling an iron hammer 'maccabee.' Maccabaeus and his companions attacked the Greek soldiers guarding the Temple by whirling the maccabee through underground movements and successfully restored the Temple in Jerusalem. This is referred as the Maccabees Movement.

Shortly after, the Seleucid Dynasty fell in B.C. 164. The Jews thought they had won because of their successful resistance movement with their whirling of iron hammers. But we know that it was possible through God's guidance and providential protection.

The Jews who had won a brief period of freedom under the Maccabees were very soon subjected again, this time by the powerful Romans. The Roman general, Pompey overpowered the Greeks and gradually paced towards the east.

And the oppression of the religious practices ended when Antiochus IV died in battle against General Pompey. At this time, the Jews celebrated the 'Hanukah' (Dedication/Festival of Maccabees) for the first time commemorating the restoration of the Temple. The name 'Hanukah' came from the fact that the Temple was restored in B.C. 164 and to this day, it is one of the most important ritual practices of the Jews.

The Dynasty of Hasmon was born sometime later and the Israelites thought that 'now' is the time - 'let us be independent.' They were not the descendants of David as promised through the Law of the Old Testament and the prophets. But, they voluntarily placed themselves into kingship of Israel strictly on their own. Yet amazingly enough, the Hasmon Dynasty lasted for 100 years from B.C. 164 - B.C. 63.

It is astounding that even though it was for a short period of time, for the first time in 400 years, a Jewish Dynasty had existed since the Northern Israel and Southern Judah had completely fallen in B.C. 586.

Entry of the Pharisees

The Maccabees movement was originally started to recover the faith of God. Once the Hasmon Dynasty was raised, the people turned their interest into politics. The movement they started for God initially prompted them to fall deeper into Hellenism in the end. They found the Olympics (the symbol of Hellenism) was interesting after all. The Hasmon Dynasty built a round stadium in front of the Temple in Jerusalem. It is said that the high priests of the Temple hastily conducted sacrificial offerings and went to the stadium to watch the races - just like people today who attend early services at church and quickly go home to watch a game on TV. You can still see the remains of the stadium if you travel there.

The faithful Jews started to oppose people who were neither the descendants of David nor the descendants of the Levis, making their own dynasty and promoting Hellenism. The Pharisees were born during this time. The word 'pharisee' means 'to oppose' and this name was given by the Hasmon Dynasty. The Pharisees believed in the Law and resurrection. They also thought they were the best believers of God. The Pharisees who studied the Word of God more than anyone else since they wanted to live according to it had failed to recognize Jesus as the Messiah and opposed him the most.

Conquest of Rome

The crucial point of downfall for the Hasmon Dynasty was due to power struggle. The last queen of the Hasmon Dynasty had two sons who were fighting over the kingship. The two sons ended up concluding that General Pompey of Rome would be the best judge to see who would be the next true worthy king for the Hasmon Dynasty. At their invitation, the Roman soldiers came and took over Jerusalem without a battle. Pompey put the two sons behind bars. This is pretty much the end of the Hasmon Dynasty.

All along, Pompey had keen interest in taking over Palestine realizing that it was strategically an ideal territory. Nevertheless, he did not force himself to conquer it but waited until the people of Israel approached him to say, 'Please help us, General Pompey' because he remembered the words of Alexander the Great who saw the holiness of the high priest and said, 'I have no idea who the Lord God is but these people are truly holy.' Alexander the Great saw the holiness of God that he had never seen before from anywhere through the high priests of Jerusalem.

REASONS WHY JESUS HAD TO COME INTO THE LAND OF THE PALESTINE DURING THE ERA OF THE ROMAN EMPIRE

Jesus had to be born during the era of the Roman Empire in the land of Palestine and fulfill the promise of the Old Testament. In this chapter, we will review why it had to be so and build up the backbone of the New Testament. The bulk of the New Testament is largely divided into the periods of Jesus Christ and the Holy Spirit.

WHY THEN IN THAT PARTICULAR TIME PERIOD AND LAND?

HEROD THE GREAT

The period of the Roman Empire begins as General Pompey marches into Jerusalem in B.C. 63. Later, upon seizing the government of Rome, Julius Caesar appoints Antipas II, an Idumean, as governor of Judah in B.C. 47. This was the beginning of Herod's ruling kingdom.

Herod, the second son of Antipas II was appointed as governor of Galilee in B.C. 47 at the age of 25. It was him, who ruthlessly gave orders to slaughter all boys of the age of two, upon hearing the birth of the king of the Jews from the Magis from the East. He swept away all the bandits surrounding the areas of Galilee and successfully defeated Antigonus, a strong remnant of the

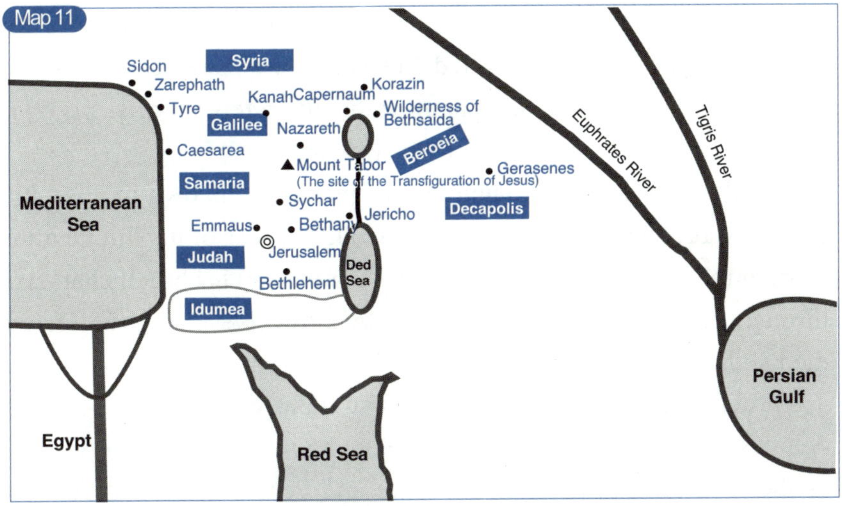

The New Testament Period: The reason why Jesus came to Palestine was to fulfill God's promise with Abraham and David. Prophet Micah had already prophesized the birth of Jesus in Bethlehem and through Prophet Isaiah it was proclaimed that Jesus was to be the root of Jesse and a descendant of David.

Hasmonean dynasty. He was a skilled military strategist in dealing with hostile military groups. After his father Antipas II was murdered, Herod secured his claim to the throne as the first tetrarch king of Judah in B.C. 40 with the support of Emperor Augustus. In B.C. 37, Herod took the role as sole ruler of Judah upon defeating the Parthians, who were occupying Jerusalem, at the time while getting rid of Antigonus.

Herod the Great played a significant role in maintaining a delicate friend and ally relationship between the Romans and the Jews revealing his superb diplomatic skills. Herod's crowning achievement was building a port city in the Mediterranean and called it, Caesarea Maritima, in honor of the emperor. He rebuilt Samaria and the city of Jerusalem as well as actively constructing Hellenistic theatre and an amphitheater. Last but not least rebuilding the Temple in Jerusalem was among his most ambitious architectural project that began in B.C. 20 which was completed after his death.

Herod the Great was not a pure blood Jew but Indumaean successors to the Edomites which made him a half-Jew. In order to be favored by the Jews he married Marianne, a Hasmonean princess. However, due to tension and paranoia, he ultimately murders his own family or whoever was a threat to his throne.

He killed his wife, Marianne out of jealousy, his own mother, his two sons, brother and grandfather as well. For fear of his throne after hearing the news of the birth of Jesus, he revealed his brutal character through his acts of massacre of toddler boys. (Matthew 2:16-18) Herod died at the age of 70 in B.C. 4 right after the birth of Jesus.

Threader: King Herod who executed John the Baptist → Herod Antipas → 2nd son of Herod the Great who reigned B.C. 2 - A.D. 39 as the tetrarch king and ruled Galilee and Perea. He is best known for his purported role when Jesus was brought to him under his jurisdiction by Pilate but mocks Jesus and sends him back to Pilate.

King Herod who beheaded James, one of the first 12 Apostles who died as a martyr. → Herod Agrippa I - the grandson of the first Herod the Great, and nephew of Herod Antipas. (This is the Herod that appears in Acts 12:1 where he is simply introduced as King Herod.)

King Herod who judged Apostle Paul. → King Agrippa II - the son of Agrippa I who heard the defense of Apostle Paul during his visit to Governor Festus in Caesarea. As a procurator upon hearing Paul's appeal he could not find any sin. (Acts 26:1-29)

Julius Caesar and Octavianus

The Failure of Julius Caesar and Cleopatra

Julius Caesar became the dictator of the Roman Republic in B.C. 49 after he assassinated Pompey, the great Roman general in Egypt. His name is well known today in spite of the fact that he reigned only for 5 years between B.C. 49 to B.C. 44 and lived a short life.

After boldly turning over the Roman Republic, Caesar was transitioning into the established dictatorship of the Roman Empire when a problem arose. Queen Cleopatra from the Ptolemaic Dynasty, which ruled Egypt at the time, had entered the scene. There is even an aphorism that "had Cleopatra's nose been shorter, the face of the world would have changed." In any event, a person's life and the world history had changed because of Cleopatra. Cleopatra intentionally approached Caesar, who was the greatest leader at that time, to make Egypt independent from the Roman Republic.

When Caesar almost came to complete the transition into dictatorship, he met Cleopatra and fell madly in love with her. Cleopatra demanded a lot of things from Caesar. In spite of Caesar having a queen already and a grown up son she demanded, "Invite me to Rome officially and promulgate me as an Empress of Egypt. Next, promulgate me as a queen of the Emperor Julius Caesar of the Roman Republic. And then promulgate our son as a prince of Roman Republic."

Is that a simple request? The Republican opponent clique still existed and his adopted heir Octavianus came forward and opposed harshly. Octavianus was totally flabbergasted. Out of nowhere, a strange woman appeared and was about to take away his position as the next Emperor of Rome. But Caesar granted everything Cleopatra had wished for. To what extent was her beauty to make this happen? Eventually, he was killed by the sword of his lieges, Brutus and uttered his last word, "Even you, Brutus!" which has become a world renown phrase.

Then Cleopatra flirted with Marcus Antonius, who was a friend and long time political supporter of Caesar, and made an alliance with him. Later on, Antonius and Cleopatra both committed suicide after their allied forces were defeated by Octavianus, son of Caesar, from the naval Battle of Actium.

Octavianus at this point had absolute authority and changed his name to Augustus Caesar and became the first emperor of the Roman Empire. Ever since then, there were no more wars, because there were no countries rebelling against the Roman Empire and Roman

Peace (Pax Romana) continued for a few hundred years. At that time the Roman Empire became the most powerful empire in the world.

Population Census of Rome

After uniting the kingdom, Emperor Augustus carried out a census of the population in the Roman dominion to find out how much taxes could be collected and how many men could be mobilized as soldiers. Accordingly, all Israelites were sent back to their home towns to report. Threader: Do you recall when God sent pestilence upon Israel killing 70,000 men while King David was conducting a population census in the Old Testament? The Roman Empire also enforced the population census to boast how big their empire was just like King David. "In those days Caesar Augustus issued a decree that a census should be taken of the entire Roman world." (Luke 2:1)

Mary and Joseph were legally married by Jewish customs even though they were engaged and did not live together. Mary had to follow her legal husband Joseph to Bethlehem to muster the Roman population census even though she was in the last month of pregnancy. Mary and Joseph left their farm village of Nazareth which was located westerly south of the Sea of Galilee and headed towards Bethlehem which was a seven-day journey riding on a donkey.

Among the 12 tribes, the tribe of Judah was the largest, so just imagine how many descendants there must have been. There were no rooms available since every tribe of Judah came in groups to Bethlehem. Mary and Joseph had no choice but to stay at a stable. In the midst of all this, Jesus Christ, the Son of God, who came as the Messiah, was born in Bethlehem away from Nazareth. Jesus fulfilled the prophecies of both Micah and Isaiah. "But you, Bethlehem Ephrathah, though you are small among the clans of Judea, out of you will come for me one who will be ruler over Israel, whose origins are from of old, from ancient times."(Micah 5:2) "A shoot will come up from the stump of Jesse; from his roots a Branch will bear fruit." (Isaiah 11:1)

Three Sects of Israel

There were three types of sects in Judaism at the time of Jesus: Pharisees, Sadducees and Essenes. However, all three parties did not comprehend the fact that Jesus came as the Messiah.

The Pharisees

First, the Pharisees. Threader: Rebelling against the Hasmon Dynasty heavily influenced by Hellenism, the Pharisees were law observing people and believed in resurrection. I have mentioned in the Old Testament portion that the name of "Pharisees" which means "against and to resist", was given by the Hasmon Dynasty.

Their meticulous legal observance of the Law and tendency to place higher value on rituals became a matter of a formality which resulted interpreting the Law literally. In a way, they had no choice but to be like that. The time had not come since Jesus was not crucified or resurrected yet. Therefore, they did not receive the Holy Spirit and only knew God intellectually. They regarded themselves as pure and godly people by knowing the Word of God. Jesus referred to them as "brood of vipers" and "whitewashed wall." The reason Jesus rebuked them was that He believed the Pharisees still had a bit of hope because they believed in resurrection. We must understand that God rebuked them for the purpose of urging them to repent and not for condemnation.

The Sadducees

Second, the Sadducees. 'Sadducees' means descendants of Tsadoc, who was the high priest of King David and King Solomon. They were not real descendants of Tsadoc but they named themselves as the descendents of Tsadoc. In fact, they were Hasmonean bogus high priests.

Being power-oriented people who were drawn to the riches and comfort, they placed great importance on gaining social power and authority by schmoozing. They also had the mentality of 'What more do you want? Enjoy life with all the pleasures of the world. What resurrection? Once you die, that's it.'

Realizing the Roman Empire had the core political powers such as diplomacy and national defense, the Sadducees believed they had practical power in religion throughout different regions. So, approximately 70 local elders got together and formed the Sanhedrin (the Jewish Supreme Council) which carried functions of an assembly, self-government and had dominant authorization. The Sanhedrin assembly system was approved by Persian King Artaxerxes to give the right of self-government to the people of Judah when Nehemiah returned to Persia after rebuilding the Jerusalem walls. With a false front as high priests with no faith, they pursued political power and worldly pleasures. Jesus did not show any hope in them.

The Essenes

Third, the Essenes. They were extreme pietistists who have left the world. This monastic sect of Essenes lived in deliberate isolation in the Qumran caves. They lived in piety and communal life by wearing white clothes and waiting for the coming of the Messiah. They occupied their time in the cave, writing the Word of God in a scroll. Their hand-written scroll of the book of Isaiah was discovered and is presently stored in the museum of Jerusalem.

Why that Time and in that Land?

Why the Period of the Roman Empire?

Why did God send the Messiah to the land of the Palestine during the period of the Roman Empire? First, the language was standardized. Rome unified the world's language into Greek rather than their native tongue of Latin. Why did God differentiate the incident of the Babel Tower from this aspect by allowing the Romans to conquer the world and unify the language into Greek? It was for the purpose of spreading the gospel to Jerusalem, Judah, Samaria and to the ends of the earth. The gospel was spread through Apostle Paul, an elite Roman citizen who spoke fluent Greek and learned the Law devoutly. Through his three mission journeys, Paul spread the gospel throughout the world.

Second, the administration was standardized. The Romans not only unified the language but also the administration as well. Today, one of the first things missionaries have to prepare are visas. In the days of the Roman Empire, visa was not necessary because most part of the world was under the rule of the Roman Empire. This was the reason why the Word of God was able to spread to the ends of the earth without any obstacles.

Third, the roads were connected. It is often said that "All roads lead to Rome." The Romans completed road system and expanded sea routes. There are still some roads found in Rome today paved with bricks on the surface of a road instead of asphalt. They also cleaned up the last Greek force pirates in order to expand sea route. The movie "Ben-Hur" was based on this background. (A brief glimpse of the scene: The Roman commander's ship that Ben-Hur was in gets hit by cannon shots from the pirates. As the ship is about to collapse Ben-Hur manages to save the life of the commander who was trying to commit suicide.) Apostle Paul was able to go anywhere and spread the gospel because the Romans dominated the sea route completely.

God had prepared a complete infrastructure so that the gospel be spread to the ends of the earth through the history of 400 years during the new silence period.

Why the Land of Palestine?

This is simple. It is because God had promised Abraham that he would be the source of blessing. Jesus came to Israel as the descendant of Abraham and David to fulfill His covenant with them. Through Micah's prophecy, the Messiah was to be born in Bethlehem and through Isaiah, the Messiah was to be the descendant of David and the root of Jesse. History well proves that without possessing the area of Canaan (whichever country it may be) a country cannot conquer the world from a geopolitical view. The same applies today. After the World War II, the Middle East and Korean peninsula were two tinder-boxes of the world during the Cold War era. In particular, the war the disputes in Philistine and North & South Korea issues. It was rumored that if any Administration or any Secretary of State of the USA failed to accomplish peace in the Middle East, the people would write them off as lack of competency to a certain degree.

Ever since the ancient times, one of the reasons that the land of Canaan has been continuously the center of world politics is because through God's promise with Abraham; He was going to make a great nation, give inheritance of the promised land and make him the father of all blessing.

Biblical scholars are in agreement that the end of the earth will come when the gospel goes into Israel, the true end of the earth. The Palestine issue cannot be resolved even if a prominent country and leader emerges as long as this issue is handled like the Old Testament: "eye for eye, tooth for tooth, hand for hand, foot for foot." (Exodus 21:24) It will not be resolved until the Gospel of Jesus spreads into Israel so that the Holy Spirit reach the hearts of the Jews.

THE FORMATION AND HISTORY OF THE NEW TESTAMENT

The Structure of the New Testament_27 books

The structure of the New Testament can be largely divided into

History Books and Letters. The History Books of the New Testament consist of 5 books in total which are the four Gospels: Matthew, Mark, Luke and John including Acts. The other remaining 22 books are Letters. But from the quantity standpoint, the 5 History Books are lengthier than the 22 Letters.

With the same concept as we have studied the Old Testament, we will also approach the New Testament focusing on the History Books first and treat the Letters like prophecies of the Old Testament.

The history of the New Testament can be largely divided into the period of Jesus Christ and the period of the Holy Spirit.

First, the period of Jesus Christ is mentioned through the four gospels. How did Jesus come to earth? What was the birth of Jesus and His childhood like? How did Jesus work His ministry on this earth? How did Jesus die on the cross, resurrect and ascend to heaven? All answers are dealt through the gospel.

Second, the period of the Holy Spirit starts from the book of Acts. "On one occasion, while He was eating with them, He gave them this command: "Do not leave Jerusalem, but wait for the gift my Father promised, which you have heard Me speak about. For John baptized with water, but in a few days you will be baptized with the Holy Spirit." (Acts 1:4-5) Just as Jesus promised during His ascension, the birth of the early church was born by the advent of the Holy Spirit. And missionary fields were opened through Paul, Silas and Barnabas as the Word of God spread to West Asia, Europe and the ends of the earth. The extension of mission work continues through believers today just as Jesus had commanded to His followers at the time.

The Synoptic Gospels

The Book of Matthew, Mark and Luke are called, 'The Synoptic Gospels' which means 'these gospels have the same view.' It is because of the content similarities in events, sequence, expressions

Chart 4 Framework of the New Testament

History Books	Letters	
	Pauline Letters (13 Books)	General Letters (9 Books)
Matthew, Mark, Luke, John, Acts	Romans, 1 & 2 Corinthians, Galatians, Ephesians, Philippians, Colossians, 1 & 2 Thessalonians, 1 & 2 Timothy, Titus, Philemon	Hebrews, James, 1 & 2 Peter, 1 & 2 & 3 John, Jude, Revelation

used with regard to the life and teachings of Jesus. We must note that the sequence of events in the book of John is different from The Synoptic Gospels.

Mark is the shortest gospel and is made up with 103 stories. Among those, 98 stories are also found in Matthew and more than 50 in Luke. It appears that among Mark's 661 verses, 606 verses are consistent with Matthew and 350 similar verses in Luke. The commonality of these three gospels is that they have the same sequence of events. Having said that, it is very difficult to piece together all the events in the four gospels and follow in chronological order. But I have made my own efforts to record Jesus' ministry selectively from the four gospels in chronological order in this book. Specifically following the sequence from the gospel of Matthew closely, since the book has made the most effort to record the teachings of Jesus in detail. In addition, I must ask my reader's understanding and excuse for the partiality in this section for not discussing all the events mentioned in the gospel. (I promise that I will take upon the task in filling these portions in the near future.)

. . .

"She will bear a Son; and you shall call His name Jesus, for He will save His people from their sins." Now all this took place to fulfill what was spoken by the Lord through the prophet: "BEHOLD, THE VIRGIN SHALL BE WITH CHILD AND SHALL BEAR A SON, AND THEY SHALL CALL HIS NAME IMMANUEL," which translated means, "GOD WITH US."

Matthew 1:21-23

JESUS COMES TO HIS OWN LAND

Matthew 1, Luke 1-3

If believers were to choose two events in the Bible that is hard to believe, it would probably be the virgin birth and the resurrection of Jesus. Mainly because such events cannot be understood with a cool-headed rationale and a logical thought process. Since the birth of Jesus is recorded only in Matthew and Luke, we will examine these two Gospels relating to the Virgin Mary being conceived by the Holy Spirit and the genealogy of Jesus.

Was Jesus Really Born of a Virgin?

Is it really true that Jesus was conceived by the Holy Spirit and born of the Virgin Mary? Can you believe this? In Luke 1, God sent Gabriel the Angel to prophesize about the birth by a virgin. First, he appeared to Zechariah, an old priest who happened to serve at the temple in Jerusalem and prayed requesting for an heir. "Do not be afraid, Zechariah; your prayer has been heard. Your wife Elizabeth will bear you a son, and you are to give him the name John." (Luke 1:13) "And he will go on before the Lord, in the spirit and power of Elijah…to make ready a people prepared for the Lord." (Luke 1:17)

These were shocking words for Zechariah. Being a priest he must have known better than anyone else of the words spoken by Malachi, the last prophet in the Old Testament. "See, I will send you the prophet Elijah before that great and dreadful day of the LORD comes." (Malachi 4:5) He must have been shocked to find out that such prophecy would be accomplished through his own son. When Zechariah did not believe these words, angel Gabriel told him, "And now you will be silent and not able to speak until the day this happens, because you did not believe my words, which will come true at their proper time." (Luke 1:20) Therefore, he became mute until the day his son was circumcised.

Six months later, God sent Gabriel to Mary who was living in Nazareth, a small farming town located Southeast of Lake Galilee, and said "Greetings, you who are highly favored! The Lord is with you." (Luke 1:28) He further prophesied, "You will be with child and give birth to a son, and you are to give him the name Jesus...The Lord God will give him the throne of his father David, and he will reign over the house of Jacob forever; his kingdom will never end." (Luke 1:31-33)

What a preposterous idea! How can a virgin conceive without ever having a relationship? Mary immediately countered, "How will this be, since I am a virgin?" (Luke 1:34) Then angel Gabriel clearly stated, "The Holy Spirit will come upon you, and the power of the Most High will overshadow you. So the Holy One to be born will be called the Son of God." (Luke 1:35) Therefore, the child was to be conceived through the Holy Spirit. "You will receive power when the Holy Spirit comes on you." (Acts 1:8) This means that when the power, authority, and the energy of the Holy Spirit manifest their presence in someone such an event can happen. What did Mary confess afterwards? (Luke 1:38) When the power of the Holy Spirit, i.e., God's mighty power, came upon the foundation of Mary's faith, a life was conceived. It is puzzling why it is so hard to believe in the virgin birth when we readily believe in God who "formed the man from the dust of the ground and breathed into his nostrils the breath of life" (Genesis 2:7) thus creating a "living being."

Why Did Jesus Have to be Born of a Virgin?

Through many prophets of the Old Testament, God clearly indicated the coming of the Messiah: "A shoot will come up from the stump of Jesse; from his roots a Branch will bear fruit." (Isaiah 11:1) This meant that the Messiah was to come as a descendant of David. However, it would have been a problem if this was the case. If the coming Messiah came as the descendant of David, who was a sinner, that would have meant the Messiah would come in sin and His purpose in the atonement for mankind's sin and the work of redemption could not have been fulfilled. This was the very crucial point and dilemma of the Messianic Birth.

It would have been very simple if there were no such prophecy in the Old Testament. God just needed to drop a sinless being from Heaven for the atonement for mankind and proclaim, "This man is the Messiah!" But He did not intend it that way. Instead, He promised to send the Messiah as a descendant of David which will make Jesus a sinner if physically born. Therefore, Jesus had to be born as a sinless person as well as a descendant of David at the same time. God resolved this dilemma by utilizing an outstanding aspect of the Jewish marriage customs.

The Jewish marriage customs had a distinctive feature unlike any other nation. The Jews usually arranged an engagement when the children were young by both parents agreeing to marriage. After their children underwent the 'adult ceremony' (bar mitzvah) at the age of thirteen, they were entitled to arrange for marriage by themselves. After coming to an agreement, they registered themselves to become lawful husband and wife. However, even if they became legally married they had to keep themselves chaste for one year. They would officially make a promise as husband and wife and then return to their respectful homes and live separately. After one year they would hold a wedding ceremony. And at the night of their wedding, the bridegroom would go to the bride's house to bring her, who in return, prepares a lamp to reveal to the bridegroom that she is indeed the bride. Threader: The parable of the Ten Virgins in Matthew 25 refers to this Jewish wedding customs.

Mary was conceived by the Holy Spirit between this interval of the legality of marriage and the wedding ceremony. Therefore, not having had physical relations with Joseph even though they were legally married, she was still a virgin. In such a way, God fulfilled the prophecy of Jesus to come into the world as a descendant of David and a branch from Jesse's roots as well as a sinless being through the birth of a virgin.

Mary's Song

Joseph heard the news of Mary's pregnancy while he was dutifully carrying out his virginity upon their marriage. He probably tossed and turned through sleepless nights pondering whether he should take Mary as his wife or not. The Bible states that since he was a righteous man he had in his mind to "divorce her quietly." (Matthew 1:19) What would have happened if the news leaked out? According to the Jewish law, Mary would have had to be stoned to death. So, Joseph thought that it would be better to quietly break off the relationship. This is when the angel appeared to Joseph in a dream and said, "Joseph, son of David, do not be afraid to take Mary home as your wife."(Matthew 1:20)

As a matter of fact, this was also a frightening event for Mary as well. Being engaged she was expected to keep chaste, but she became pregnant. This could not only ruin her family honor but also bring her condemnation of death by stoning. This was such a horrible predicament. Even though she received the prophetic message by Gabriel the angel, she must have been greatly troubled. Shortly after, she went to meet her relative, Elizabeth. She "hurried to a town in the hill country of Judea, where she entered Zechariah's home and greeted Elizabeth." (Luke 1:39-40) Mary went to see and confirm what the angel had said about Elizabeth who had become pregnant six months ago despite her old age knowing such an encounter would be of great comfort to her.

When Mary reached Elizabeth's home, she was greeted by Elizabeth, "But why am I so favored, that the mother of my Lord should come to me?" (Luke 1:43) As soon as Elizabeth saw Mary who was conceived by the Holy Spirit, she confessed to Mary that she is "the mother of my Lord." And continued to say, "The baby in my womb leaped for joy." (Luke 1:44) Mary then stayed with Elizabeth for about three months. "Mary stayed with Elizabeth for about three months and then returned home." (Luke 1:56) During this time they must have talked in length of the prophecies of the Gabriel the angel and the grace of God that was bestowed upon them and comforted each other. Although Mary's predicament was still not over she praised God during her stay at Elizabeth's home proclaiming, "My soul glorifies the Lord and my spirit rejoices in God my Savior, for He has been mindful of the humble state of His servant." (Luke 1:46-48) The content of the song Ave Maria came from these verses.

The Reason for the Discrepancy in Jesus' Genealogy_Matthew 1, Luke 3

Many people complain about the repetitiveness of the phrase "... was the father of..." in the first chapter of Matthew and find it difficult to understand its significance. However, after having finished studying the Old Testament you will not find it boring anymore as you read it again. "Abraham was father of Isaac; Isaac the father of Jacob" (Matthew 1:2) are all familiar names that we have learned already. We can only marvel at the fulfillment of God's promise as the familiar names of Old Testament make their appearance.

The problem is the difference in genealogy found in Matthew's "record of the genealogy of Jesus Christ the son of David, the son of Abraham" (Matthew 1:1) and Luke's that says, "Now Jesus Himself was about thirty years old when He began His ministry. He was the son, so it was thought, of Joseph, the son of Eli." (Luke 3:23) Matthew's genealogy starts from its ancestor and descends down, whereas Luke's starts from Jesus and traces up towards the beginning. Besides this technical difference, there is also a considerable difference in the names of the ancestors of Jesus. How can we trust in either genealogy when there is a complete different set of names between David and Joseph? Isn't this rather strange? With the Hellenistic thought process, one of them must be in error.

However, the Bible is compiled by the inspiration of God and is not a novel. Therefore, there must be a reason behind such difference. Why do you think God recorded two different ancestries of Jesus? In Matthew, the names of the Davidic kings that we learned about in 1 Kings appear as, "David was the father of Solomon, whose mother had been Uriah's wife, Solomon the father of Rehoboam, Rehoboam the father of Abijah, Abijah the father of Asa, Asa the father of Jehoshaphat." (Matthew 1:6-8) The monarchy ended with the Babylonian captivity and Joseph, the father of Jesus comes into scene after the 13th generation.

During the period of the Romans, the Jews were desperately longing for the Messiah who was prophesized through the prophets as a descendant of David and the ruler over the house of Judah forever. The Jews would have lost the purpose of their existence if it weren't for this intense longing for the Messiah. God says in the Gospel of Matthew that Jesus indeed came as the King of Israel whom they had been waiting for. The New Testament begins with the proclamation of its fulfillment by the birth of baby Jesus, which was promised in the Old Testament through Abraham (Genesis 12:1-3) and David (2 Samuel 7:8-16).

Luke, the author of the Gospel of Luke, was a Greek physician who came to believe in Jesus Christ through the Church of Antioch, one of the early Christian churches. In today's terms, he would be someone who is fluent in a global language such as English, exceptionally knowledgeable, adept at dealing with many different beliefs and ideologies and yet faithful to Jesus. The reason why God had Luke write one of the Gospels is because he wanted the Gospels to reach beyond the restoration of the state of Israel and transform the entire world to experience the Kingdom of God.

Luke was a Greek, a Gentile. The Jews regarded the Gentiles like dogs in those days. But Luke proclaims that even the Gentiles, like the Jews, will receive salvation through the presence of the Holy Spirit if one receives Jesus as their Savior. Therefore, the Messiah that manifests Himself in the Gospel of Luke is to atone for the entire human race. Luke testifies that Jesus came to the world as a human to sacrifice Himself on the cross and make atonement for our sins thus fully discharging His duty as a priest.

While Matthew uses the phrase "…was the father of…" and listed the genealogy from the first to the last, Luke chose to list the genealogy from the end and traced it back to the beginning. Luke uses the phrase "…the son of…" and follows the ancestry of Mary. Thus, Nathan comes before David. While Matthew follows the ancestry of Joseph, the legal father of Jesus, Luke apparently follows the ancestry of Mary who was conceived by the Holy Spirit and was, thus, the true blood lineage of Jesus. To emphasize the virgin birth by the power of the Holy Spirit, Luke uses the expression, "Being as was supposed the son of Joseph" (Luke 3:23) Hence, he does not use the lineage of Solomon who became king after David. Instead, he uses the lineage of Nathan, another son of David. While Matthew starts from Abraham, Luke writes his Gospel from the point of view that Jesus is the Savior and the One who makes atonement for the entire human race. Therefore, he depicts Jesus the Messiah as the descendant of Adam, the first created Son of God.

Luke points out in the latter part of Luke chapter 3 (Luke 3:23-38) that Jesus was the descendant of the first Adam and also came as the second Adam. And he introduces the genealogy of Jesus in between the first part of chapter 3 where Jesus received baptism from John the Baptist and chapter 4 where Jesus received temptation of the devil. He explains the background of why Jesus who came as the second Adam had to overcome the temptations of the devil, specifically of the trial items which the first Adam failed in the Garden of Eden.

It is known that Luke, who became a believer in the Church of Antioch, visited the Church of Jerusalem and remained there for quite a long period of time and learned from Mary, the mother of Jesus the details about the circumstances surrounding the birth of the Lord. So, Luke naturally focused on Mary being conceived by the Holy Spirit and thus, followed the lineage of Mary instead of that of Joseph.

From here we can see how God makes His revelation in part. If it were today, there would be a theological controversy regarding the difference in the genealogy of Jesus between the two gospels of Matthew and Luke. But there is no evidence that such controversy existed in the Bible. This is what "All scripture is God-breathed…" (2 Timothy 3:16) means that revelations are revealed in part as guided by the Holy Spirit.

Some people say that Jesus came from David's lineage of kings (as in Matthew), but others say that even though he was a descendant of David, he didn't have to be born from the lineage of kings (as in Luke). Nevertheless, they are not necessarily contradictory. Revelations in part come together to result in God's perfect will. Matthew emphasized Jesus as King of Israel from the lineage of David as prophesized in the Old Testament. On the other hand, Luke, a Gentile, went a step further and emphasized that Jesus was a descendant of Adam. Luke wanted to illuminate that not only was Jesus the light to the Jews, who regarded the Gentiles as dogs in lieu of Jesus being a descendent of Abraham, He also came as the light to the Gentiles.

Since all revelations are revealed partially if one keeps focusing on the difference in the two genealogies you may end up getting tested.

Knowledge Search 18

Four Women Appearing in the Genealogy of Jesus

In the first chapter of Matthew, there are four women in the genealogy of Jesus whose names are generally not mentioned in the Old Testament.

"Judah the father of Perez and Zerah, whose mother was Tamar" (Matthew 1:3)

"Salmon the father of Boaz, whose mother was Rahab, Boaz the father of Obed, whose mother was Ruth" (Matthew 1:5)

"David was the father of Solomon, whose mother had been Uriah's wife" (Matthew 1:6)

These four women were: a prostitute, a widow, or adulteresses, who were considered social outcasts or sinners. By recording these names in the genealogy of Jesus, it showed that Jesus was not a person born of noble birth. On the contrary, God showed that He would choose the lowly, the outcast, and the sinners, to use them in a mighty way.

When Jesus received baptism from John the Baptist, He mingled with sinners and got baptized with them (Luke 3:21). Also, when facing the last moment of His earthly life, He was among the thieves and died together with them. "But made himself nothing… he humbled himself and became obedient to death." (Philippians 2:7-8)

Let us not get caught up with just one aspect of the revelation, since all revelations, as inspired by the Holy Spirit, are done in part. This may also be a warning to those who swear by some of the so called 'prophets' of today. Even Apostle Paul suggested that prophecy must be confirmed by two or three prophets. (Biblical prophecy is for diagnosing our faith and gift; it is not a form of fortune telling, such as prophesying whether one's daughter will marry a tall person or marry a doctor.)

Childhood of Jesus_Luke 2

Although the Gospels recorded the birth and the public life of Jesus in detail, there is no record of how He lived and what kind of education He received until He turned 30 years of age. Throughout the entire four Gospels, only one event, that of Jesus' visit to Jerusalem when he was 12 years old for the Passover, is uniquely recorded (Luke 2:41-52). Joseph and Mary had taken the 12-year old Jesus to Jerusalem to attend the Feast of Passover where they lost Him. After three days of searching they found Him in the Temple courts.

Some people may think how careless Joseph and Mary were for them to lose their 12-year old child. But the reason why they lost him was because of the layout of the Temple. At that time there were separate courts within the Temple, one for the Gentiles, one for the Jewish men, and one for the Jewish women. But a 12-year old was allowed to move around between different courts because he was not an adult. Since he was able to move around from one court to another one of the parents probably thought that he was with the other parent when they lost him. They also had to deal with congestions and huge crowds who came to Jerusalem from all over the country to celebrate the Feast of Passover.

According to the Jewish customs, a boy received his education in the Torah (The Book of Law) at home until age 12 and then was able to begin his religious training at a local synagogue from the age of 13. Apparently it was at this juncture that the boy Jesus decided to remain at "His Father's house," the Temple, and discuss the Law among the scribes. Although as the Son of God, He had perfect knowledge of the Law. He chose to listen to their opinions attentively as well as give them His point of view. "But he made himself nothing, taking the very nature of a servant, being made in human likeness. And being found in appearance as a man, he humbled himself and became obedient to death." (Philippians 2:7-8)

Mary must have been a very gentle person. If we were the parents we would have gotten very angry and might have screamed at him if we found him after three days of searching. But Mary simply stated, "Your father and I have been anxiously searching for you." (Luke 2:48) He then replied, "Didn't you know I had to be in my Father's house?" (Luke 2:49) Thus, prior to attaining His adulthood he clarified to His parents that 'God the Father' took precedence over his earthly father. He further announced that His mission was to 'be about My Father's business' and therefore, He must stay at his Father's house.

What do you think the boy Jesus saw at the Temple? The Temple of the Old Testament period was a place full of foul smell of blood. This was due to the animal sacrifice that was carried out for the atonement of the sins of the Israelites. Seeing this, the boy Jesus must have understood His mission deep in His heart, as stated in, "He did not enter by means of the blood of goats and calves; but he entered the Most Holy Place once for all by his own blood, having obtained eternal redemption," (Hebrews 9:12) to make atonement for humanity at His "Father's house." It is written, "God raised him from the dead and seated him at his right hand in the heavenly realms, far above all rule and authority, power and dominion, and every title that can be given, not only in the present age but also in the one to come. And God placed all things under his feet and appointed him to be head over everything for the church." (Ephesians 1:20-22)

Thus, Jesus became the head of the Church after His resurrection. As the head of the Church, Jesus will stay in His Father's house forever. This is the reason behind His confession "I had to be in my Father's house." A confession such as this is truly an astounding confession.

Who is Jesus?

God the Son Who was Present before the Creation of the World

There are some Christians who mistakenly believe that Jesus was born about 2000 years ago in a manger in Bethlehem who did not exist before this birth. Perhaps, it is easy to think that way, as the story of the 'birth' of the baby Jesus is told in Matthew 1 following the prophesies of the coming of the Messiah in the Old Testament. It may sound as if God finally got Himself a long awaited son. But God proclaims in the Gospel of John that the Son who came to this world was with the Father in Heaven before the creation (John 1:1-2) and that they shared glory together before the world began (John 17:5).

God's Purposes for Sending His Son to the World

First, it is to manifest the love of God the Father, who is an invisible Spirit and the true form of love, for His people "When the time had fully come, God sent his Son···"(Galatians 4:4), so that people will see with their eyes and understand and believe Him. In the Old Testament, this was done only through hearing the words of God.

Second, it is to sacrifice His Son as the peace offering, so that people, who otherwise could not come into His presence because of their sins, may have the way to do so. (Leviticus 17:11)

Third, for those who believe, it is to make them the children of God and to give them privilege and all the blessings that come with it. (John 1:12)

Fourth, it is to abundantly pour His Holy Spirit into the hearts of the believers after Jesus died on the cross, resurrected, and sat beside the throne of God. (Romans 5:5)

Trinity of God

It has been explained earlier in the Old Testament portion that Jesus, who came to this world as the Word in flesh, is God in essence and the exact representation of His being. And the Holy Spirit, who opens up our hearts to receive God the Son, is also God in essence, and thus we call this the Trinity of God. There is only one God, yet He exists in three distinct yet co-equal persons. (Deuteronomy 6:4; Ephesians 4:5-6) And the Bible testifies, "In the beginning was the Word (Son), and the Word was with God (Father), and the Word was God. He was with God in the beginning." (John 1:1-2) "Have this attitude in yourselves which was also in Christ Jesus (Son), who, although He existed in the form of God, did not regard equality with God a thing to be grasped." (Philippians 2:5-6) Jesus Himself stated "I and the Father are one." (John 10:30) Upon His resurrection before ascending to His throne in heaven, Jesus told His disciples that the Holy Spirit will be poured onto them instead. "He will give you another Counselor to be with you forever··· He lives with you and will be in you." (John 14:16-17)

Moreover God carries on His distinctive role according to His Person in Trinity:

> But when the fullness of the time came, God sent forth His Son to this world. (Galatians 4:4);
> God the Son prays to His Father (John 17:1) and obeys him. (Philippians 2:8);
> The Holy Spirit will glorify the Son of God (John 16:14) and testifies about the Son. (Acts 1:8);
> The Son of God having received the Holy Spirit from Father will pour it to His believers. (Acts 2:33)

The presence of the Holy Spirit allows us to experience the presence of Jesus, the Son of God and the Father God. This is because they are one and the same God.

Jesus delivered the love of God of Trinity to humans to whom this love is intended. He took on the role of receiving the honor, praise and the glory from them. Therefore, the believers' object of worship is Jesus Christ and this is why they are called 'Christians' (people who belong to Christ).

Jesus, Immanuel God who is with us forever, presently sits beside the throne of God the Father and lives within us through the Holy Spirit. It is through Jesus that we have come to know God; through Him we have received forgiveness of our sins and have become children of God. Furthermore, it is because of Jesus that we are able to receive and enjoy all of God's blessings. And it is through the guidance of the Holy Spirit that we live a sanctified life and are transformed according to the image of our Lord.

This is the reason why we praise the glory of grace of Christ forever. Hallelujah!

JESUS BEING BAPTIZED

Matthew 3-4, Luke 3-4

Jesus underwent a preparation process before He started His ministry. First, Jesus received baptism from John the Baptist and then, led by the Spirit, fasted for forty days and overcame the temptations of the devil.

Baptized by John the Baptist_Matthew 3, Luke 3

As a young man, Jesus practiced carpentry with his father until one day, he abandoned his wood shavings and hammer and headed towards the Jordan River leaving Nazareth altogether. There Jesus was baptized by John the Baptist. For the Gentiles, the meaning of 'baptism' was to be born again as people of God. As for the Jews, it meant to be recognized as true Israelites by bringing them out of water which symbolized the pit.

What was the reason for John the Baptist to perform baptism to so many people? John the Baptist proclaimed that even Jews must repent their sins and be baptized to avoid the anger of the Lord. It meant that as God can raise up the descendants of Abraham out of stones, it was more important to repent their sins and receive baptism to be recognized as true Israelites rather than merely being born as Abraham's descendants. He proclaimed, "I baptize you with water for repentance but after me will come One who is more powerful than I, whose sandals I am not fit to carry. He will baptize you with the Holy Spirit and with fire" (Matthew 3:11) He also foretold the Israelites that as God had promised they would be born again as the people of the new covenant through the baptism of the Holy Spirit followed by the Messiah's redemption at the cross and resurrection.

God was promising to pour His Spirit into the hearts of people as it has been proclaimed through Jeremiah and Ezekiel: "The time is coming, declares the Lord, when I will make a new covenant with the house of Israel and with the house of Judah. It will not be like the covenant I made with their forefathers when I took them by the hand to lead them out of Egypt, because they broke My covenant, though I was a husband to them, declares the Lord. This is the covenant I will make with the house of Israel after that time, declares the Lord. I will put My law in their minds and write it on their hearts. I will be their God and they will be My people." (Jeremiah 31:31-33) and through Ezekiel, "I will give you a new heart and put a new spirit in you; I will remove from you your heart of stone and give you a heart of flesh." (Ezekiel 36:26)

There was no baptism ceremony in the Old Testament period, but through John the Baptist a new "repentance ceremony for forgiveness of the sins" was being conducted. Jesus also baptized with water during His ministry. For Christians, the meaning of baptism of the water is that we have been united with Jesus Christ in death. (Romans 6:3) Therefore, those who have received baptism after receiving Jesus must not commit sins with their body again. This is because baptism is a devout promise with Jesus that we will no longer commit sin again since we have been crucified and dead along with Jesus. A dead person cannot commit sin. "Do not offer the parts of your body to sin, as instruments of wickedness, but rather offer yourselves to God, as those who have been brought from death to life; and offer the parts of your body to him as instruments of righteousness." (Romans 6:13)

Why did Jesus receive baptism from John the Baptist? John the Baptist already knew that Jesus was the Messiah when He came to him to get baptized. So, he dissuaded Jesus by saying, "I need to be baptized by You but why are You coming to me?" (Matthew 3:14) Then,

Jesus replied, "Let it be so now; it is proper for us to do this to fulfill all righteousness." (Matthew 3:15) It meant that the will of God could not be accomplished without receiving baptism from John the Baptist. Jesus had to receive His baptism with water by John the Baptist in order to carry on God's promises that came through the Law of the Old Testament and the prophets.

When Jesus was baptized by John the Baptist, he saw "the Spirit of God descending like a dove and lighting on Him." (Matthew 3:16) Jesus was sealed with the Holy Spirit. "And a voice from heaven said, this is my Son, whom I love; with him I am well pleased." (Matthew 3:17) Threader: Without the presence of the Holy Spirit, we cannot hear God's voice. The Holy Spirit dwells among us when we pray. After receiving baptism and as Jesus prayed, the heaven opened and the Holy Spirit descended on Him in bodily form like a dove and a voice came from Heaven. (Luke 3:21-22) Upon Jesus' ascension, the Holy Spirit came upon each disciple's head like tongues of fire while they gathered at Mark's attic room "devoting themselves to prayer." (Acts 1:14)

Some theologians explain this as the "Inauguration of the Messiah." Jesus promulgates that He is the Son of God through the sealing of the Holy Spirit and the voice of God. By humbly kneeling and receiving baptism from John the Baptist, Jesus, the Son of God, showed true obedience to the Father's will and also showed that He came to serve and not to be served.

The two ceremonial orders of Baptism and Holy Communion are living guidelines for Christians today. By uniting with Jesus on the cross and in His resurrection from the dead, we have been freed from our sins. As a result of this, we are a 'new' spiritual being now and must love God and our neighbors to establish God's kingdom in this land.

The same voice was heard at the Mount of Transfiguration before Jesus took up His cross. "This is my Son, whom I love; with him I am well pleased. Listen to him." (Matthew 17:5) Before the morbid suffering on the cross, God transfigured Jesus with glory in front of His disciples confirming that Jesus was truly the Son of God.

Temptation in the Wilderness_Matthew 4, Luke 4

Jesus was led by the Spirit into the wilderness to be tempted by the devil. Some people ask, 'Why was it necessary for Jesus to be tempted by the devil before starting His ministry?' By winning over the temptation that the first Adam failed in the Garden of Eden, Jesus wanted His believers to be able to overcome temptations. The sin of Adam has been inherited to all mankind and this blood of sin is still running inside us today (Take note of the genealogy of Jesus). Jesus took upon the temptation in order to give us salvation as an inheritance.

Jesus replied to all three temptations with the Word of God, "It is written." Jesus used the Word of God from Deuteronomy 8 and others written in the Old Testament. Jesus conquered Satan's temptation with the shield of faith and the sword of the Spirit which is the Word of God. There is no time to pray when Satan tempts us. This is the reason why we need to study the Bible. Without putting the Bible inside our heart, we will never be able to conquer Satan's temptations. The Word of God must always live within our heart in order to defeat and cast out Satan's temptation before it builds a nest.

It is important to note that Jesus was led by the Spirit and that He fought the temptation in Spirit. The Spirit that came upon Jesus' head like a dove as soon as He came out of the water after being baptized was in the midst of His temptation in the wilderness and throughout His ministry.

The First Test: Temptation of Disbelief_Matthew 4:3-4

The first temptation that Jesus received was a temptation of disbelief — to make bread out of stone and eat it. It was a test related to self-reliance rather than relying upon God which basically was to deny God the Creator. It was the same temptation as "the cravings of sinful man" (1 John 2:16) and Satan's temptation to Eve to eat the fruit from the tree of the knowledge of good and evil. (Genesis 3:5)

This is also the same way we live today. We wake up early to study for an exam, open our business, or go to work, but we do not have time to pray or read the Bible at early dawn. These are all acts of self-reliance -- 'I make my own bread; I live according to my own ability.' Faith is when we live our lives following God's way and trusting in Him. The very first temptation that the devil throws at us is to 'eat and live with our own capability' which is the temptation of disbelief. This disbelief makes a person hard to believe that everything is provided by the grace of God. Jesus won over the temptation with the Word of God, "Man does not live on bread alone but on every word that comes from the mouth of the Lord." (Deuteronomy 8:3) The Word of God is the prime energy of all creation. "For the Word of God is living and active." (Hebrew 4:12) Not only is the creation created by the energy of the Word of God but also all existing beings in the world are held by the Word of God (Hebrew 1:3). By holding onto the Word of God, we live by the energy that comes from it and not by our own strength and ability.

The Second Test: Temptation of Personal Boastfulness_ Matthew 4:5-7

The second temptation is a temptation of 'showing off.' The serpent tempted Eve with this exact intention that when she saw the fruit of the tree it looked "delightful and desirable enough to gain wisdom." (Genesis 3:6) This is the "boastful pride of life." (1 John 2:16) The devil said, "If you are the Son of God throw yourself down. For it is written He will command his angels concerning you and they will lift you up in their hands so that you will not strike your foot against a stone." (Matthew 4:6) Satan was tempting Jesus that if He did what He was asked to do then everyone would recognize Him as the Messiah. Satan constantly tempts us daily by asking us not to deny ourselves and boasts us to reach up to the ends of the heaven by ourselves.

But Jesus performed miracles neither to receive applause nor personal recognition. Jesus, "being in very nature God, did not consider equality with God something to be grasped…" Jesus received the glory of resurrection by "humbling himself and becoming obedient to death." (Philippians 2:6-8) Jesus rejected the temptation by the Word, "Do not put the Lord your God to the test." (Matthew 4:7) Instead of being glorified and exalted through performing miracles, Jesus had to receive His glory by humbling Himself through the suffering of the cross.

The Third Temptation: Temptation of Earthly Glory_Matthew 4:8-11

Satan said, "I will give you all this if you will bow down and worship me." (Matthew 4:9) Satan was saying that all the visible things would be given such as a nice car, a nice house, etc. Many times people worship Satan for the sake of wealth, fame, fortune — all the visible things of the world. This is a test of lustful glory of the world. After listening to Satan, Eve found the tree of the good and evil "pleasing to the eye." (Genesis 3:6) It is a temptation of the "lust of the eyes." (1 John 2:16) The book of Hebrews says, "Faith is the assurance of things hoped for the conviction of things not seen." (Hebrews 11:1) All the worldly glories such a perfect house and a dream car will not last and eventually rot away. The faith grown from an imperishable seed (1 Peter 1:23) is to be sure of the unforeseen without any experimental verification. "All men are like grass, and all their glory is like the flowers of the field; the grass withers and the flowers fall, but the Word of the Lord stands forever. And this is the word that was preached to you." (1 Peter 1:24-25)

The Christian life desires for things that are invisible, not visible glory. "God is Spirit (invisible) and His worshipers must worship in Spirit and in truth." (John 4:24) This is the reason why Christians give worship captivated by the invisible Holy Spirit and the Word of God.

Jesus won over the temptation with the Word of God, "Away from Me, Satan! For it is written: 'Worship the Lord your God, and serve Him only." (Matthew 4:10)

Preaching at the Synagogue of Nazareth_Luke 4:16-30

After the temptations in the wilderness, Jesus headed towards a synagogue in His home town, Nazareth. Jesus visited His home town before officially starting His ministry. "He went to Nazareth, where he had been brought up, and on the Sabbath day he went into the synagogue, as was his custom. And he stood up to read." (Luke 4:16)

It was the day of Sabbath at the time. It was customary for someone other than a high priest to explain the Old Testament to the crowd in the synagogue on Sabbath. Jesus entered the synagogue and read a passage from Isaiah which was given from the synagogue ruler. The passage said, "The Spirit of the Sovereign Lord is on me, because the Lord has anointed me to preach good news to the poor. He has sent me to bind up the brokenhearted, to proclaim freedom for the captives and release from darkness for the prisoners, to proclaim the year of the Lord's favor and the day of vengeance of our God, to comfort all who mourn, and provide for those who grieve in Zion to bestow on them a crown of beauty instead of ashes, the oil of gladness instead of mourning, and a garment of praise instead of a spirit of despair. They will be called oaks of righteousness, a planting of the Lord for the display of his splendor." (Isaiah 61:1-3)

Anointing comes with the presence of the Holy Spirit. In other words, anointing means to be given a mission or calling. By the presence of the Spirit of God and the Holy Spirit, a mission is given to spread the good news to the poor. What is the good news? It is the Gospel - a praise filled with healing, freedom, release, comfort and joy. "The day of vengeance of our God" means "Jubilee." It is a day to release all the slaves. Jesus did not bother explaining or preaching further about this message. He only proclaimed that "Today this scripture is fulfilled in your hearing." (Luke 4:21) and said, "I am the Messiah who is in front of you that the Bible promised."

Jesus came as the Messiah to this earth to free people from captivity and oppression. People in captivity can be seen as the ones hurt by others, trapped by Satan's spirit, and by their own selves. It is just like autism or depression. People can not make the right decision out of their own freewill if their spirit is oppressed. They can not choose God voluntarily. They must receive freedom back so that they can choose God. Only then, they will be able to focus on others as well. Sin, hurt and resentment can be released only through the Holy Spirit, setting people free from captivity. The Bible can not be understood when it is interpreted literally. Why did Jesus have to be born through the Virgin Mary? Why did Jesus have to get baptized by John the Baptist? In order to answer all questions, one must look at it from the standpoint of the Holy Spirit.

With a distinct purpose from the beginning, Jesus took up the cross. And that is not the end. The Gospels are followed by the Book of Acts and is referred to as the 'Acts of the Holy Spirit.' We are living in the era of the Holy Spirit today, and the work of the Holy Spirit can not possibly take place without the event of the crucifixion of Jesus. Jesus' crucifixion is a warning signal for the beginning of the period of the Holy Spirit, and is not a message of: "Now that we believe in the cross there is nothing more to do for us." The way in which the Holy Spirit works unfolds throughout the entire New Testament - the four Gospels, the Book of Acts and the Letters.

When Jesus said, "I am the Messiah" the crowd responded, "How dare he speak such blasphemy?" The Jewish faith was completely an ideological faith. The Jews thought God was too holy and mighty for them to see, touch, or feel. They thought that God was so majestic and untouchable that if they saw Him with their own eyes they would die. This belief made it difficult for them to acknowledge that their

Messiah came as a human being. This is the limitation of Judaism. It is the first and last reason why they captured and killed Jesus.

After Jesus boldly revealed the purpose of His coming to the world as the Messiah in the synagogue of Nazareth, His ministry was fully carried out in the vicinity of Capernaum and Sea of Galilee.

. . .

Now when all the people were baptized, Jesus was also baptized, and while He was praying, heaven was opened, and the Holy Spirit descended upon Him in bodily form like a dove, and a voice came out of heaven, "You are My beloved Son, in You I am well-pleased."

Luke 3:21-22

ENJOY THE KINGDOM OF HEAVEN ON THIS EARTH; THE BEATITUDES

Matthew 4-10

We will now focus on the book of Matthew and take a close look at Jesus' life and ministry as if we were watching a film. Before His early ministry, Jesus worked alone in solitude.

EARLY MINISTRY OF JESUS

The Beginning of Ministry_Matthew 4:17

Jesus' first outcry was, "Repent, for the kingdom of Heaven is at hand." (Matthew 4:17) In fact, this was the outcry of John the Baptist in the wilderness. Upon receiving His baptism from John the Baptist, Jesus had taken over all the promises from the Old Testament and was saying, "The Kingdom of Heaven is here already." In other words, 'The Kingdom of Heaven' means 'His presence.' As a lyric in one of the hymns says, it is true that "in cottage or a mansion fair, where Jesus is, 'tis Heaven there." Jesus was actually saying, "Repent because I am the Heaven and already here beside you." Even though we are of flesh, because of His presence in our heart we have the spiritual blessings from Heaven and taking upon the image of Jesus, we can lead a sanctified life in His love. The Kingdom of Heaven on this earth starts in us.

Although the idea of heaven came naturally to the Jews, they

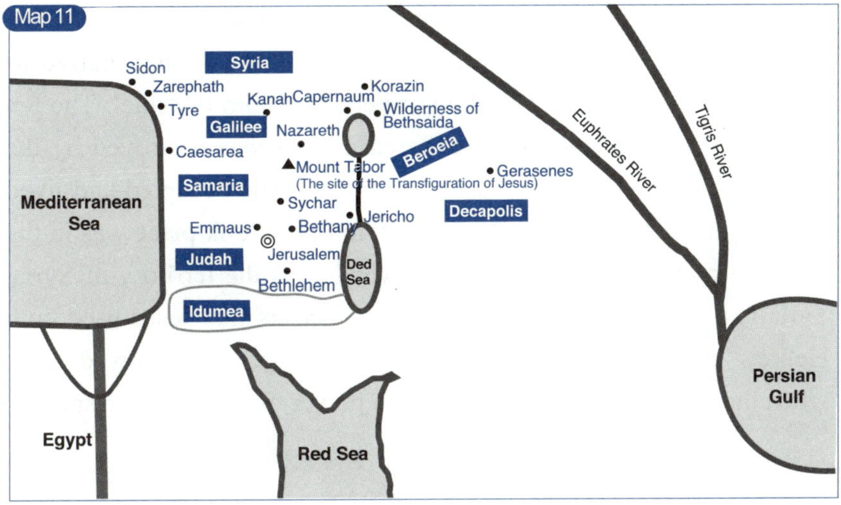

Jesus' early ministry locations Below the Sea of Galilee is Nazareth where Jesus lived. And below Nazareth is Mt. Tabor which the people of Israel regard as a 'spiritual mountain' even today. It is assumed that Mt. Tabor is Mount of Transfiguration.

didn't think of it as something to be seen or touched. But Jesus came to tell us that we could enjoy the kingdom of heaven on this earth! The kingdom of God that was kept veiled during the period of the Old Testament was clearly revealed. After calling the 12 disciples, Jesus painted a vivid picture of the heaven and God.

"Jesus went throughout Galilee, teaching in their synagogues, preaching the good news of the kingdom, and healing every disease and sickness among the people. News about him spread all over Syria, and people brought to him all who were ill with various diseases, those suffering severe pain, the demon-possessed, those having seizures, and the paralyzed, and he healed them." (Matthew 4:23-24) This is a short summary that shows the ministry of Jesus. Jesus, who preached about the kingdom of heaven and God, died on the cross and resurrected. The Holy Spirit came after His death and resurrection, and with that, the mystery of the kingdom of heaven was revealed, which is the Church today. The mission of the Church is "evangelism and teaching" (Nurturing) and "giving" (Matthew 2:23) which is what Jesus Himself carried out in the land of Galilee.

News about Jesus spread all over Syria. Jesus was a native of Nazareth which was part of the northern kingdom of Israel. The ten tribes of northern Israel had scattered after it was destroyed by the Assyrians. Since then, the Assyrians and Syrians occupied and lived in Nazareth. The main area that Jesus' ministry took place was in the northern part of the Sea of Galilee which was the territory of Syria. Syria is also referred to as Aram and it appears that Jesus used both Hebrew and Aramean. Tens of thousands of people followed Jesus when the news of His miracles and the power of His message spread.

Characteristics of the Early Ministry_Matthew 4:23, 9:35

"Jesus went through all the towns and villages, teaching in their synagogues, preaching the good news of the kingdom and healing every disease and sickness." (Matthew 9:35) One of Jesus' disciples, Matthew, arranged all the events occurred during Jesus' ministry in an orderly manner. Some of these events include the great Sermon on the Mount, the Beatitudes in Matthew 5-7, where Jesus delivered the gospel of the kingdom of heaven, taught His teachings in many synagogues and healing the sick as seen in Matthew 8-9.

One of the main characteristics of Jesus' early ministry was revealing Himself as the promised Messiah of the Old Testament to the people of Israel (Isaiah 61:1-3). He did this by preaching the gospel of the kingdom of heaven which had never been heard before, by healing, and by casting out evil spirits.

BLESSINGS IN THE SERMON ON THE MOUNT_Matthew 5-7

Jesus gave two powerful sermons during His ministry: Sermon on the Mount (the Beatitudes) and the Sermon on Mount of Olives (Matthew 24-25) given before His crucifixion concluding His ministry. The teachings of the Beatitudes are about how we can enjoy the kingdom of heaven on this earth. They reveal the heart of God the Father and how He wants us to live.

What Can We Do to Enjoy the Kingdom of Heaven on this Earth?

There is a small hill called Mt. Beatitude behind the village of Capernaum located northwest of the Sea of Galilee. It is a beautiful site looking down at the Sea of Galilee from this hill. We do not know exactly whether there was an original name for this hill, but it appears that the next following generation named it after Jesus gave His sermon about the blessings of the kingdom of heaven.

With the great sermon of the Beatitudes (Matthew 5-7), Jesus taught the people of Israel. He preached about the attitudes of citizens of the kingdom of heaven with concrete examples such as blessings, lifestyle of salt and light, teaching of the righteousness of God's kingdom, salvation and fasting; concept of wealth, and compassion for neighbors.

The main interest of the following crowds of Jesus at the time was more tuned in external things like miracles and healings. (Matthew 4:23-25) After realizing that people were following Him out of curiosity and for the purpose of healing their diseases, Jesus abruptly went up to the mountain and sat down and poured out the secret of the kingdom of heaven. He wanted to alert them that the kingdom of heaven has to be accomplished in them (inwardly) first. Jesus was trying to shift the focus of the flesh (healing) and visible things (various miracles) to invisible things (inward). Many people gather when a miracle is performed, yet it does not lead to salvation as it is by listening to the Word of God that people are saved.

Majority of people think that the Sermon on the Mount is some secret method to enter the kingdom of heaven. They ask questions like: "How to enter God's kingdom" "How God's kingdom will be established on this earth" assuming the message is about the 2nd coming of Jesus. The essence of the message of the Sermon on the Mount is not "how to enter the kingdom of heaven" after death but "how to enjoy the kingdom of heaven while living in this troubled world." That is why the Sermon on the Mount is referred to as the 'Constitution of the Kingdom of Heaven.' In a way, it is life-keeping guidelines for the citizens of the kingdom of heaven. In another words, it is the "Law of the Spirit."

"Therefore, there is now no condemnation for those who are in Christ Jesus, because through Christ Jesus the law of the Spirit of life set me free from the law of sin and death." (Romans 8:12) The reason why there is no condemnation and no judgment for Christians is because of Jesus who is in us. We must realize how important it is for us to be in Christ.

Those who abide by the Word and obey it are the ones in Christ, not the ones who simply believe in Christ. (John 14:21) Even though living in flesh, the ones who abide by the Word will not feel suppressed or tossed around by the law of sins and death since the law of life and Spirit has released them. Therefore, there is no condemnation. There are all kinds of turbulences that we experience in our lives but we are given the blessings of the kingdom of heaven to overcome them. We have the peace that the world can not give.

If someone strikes you on your right cheek, give him your other cheek; if someone asks you to join him to go one mile go the extra mile, and etc. are the teachings of the Sermon on the Mount — which probably is more difficult to do than keeping the Ten Commandments of the Old Testament. But be assured that ordinary people like us can live a sanctified life in the Holy Spirit. With the strength from above, all we need to do is to follow the image of Jesus who lived according to the Sermon on the Mount. This is the main key point of the Sermon.

Constitution of the Kingdom of Heaven; The Beatitudes_Matthew 5:1-12

The primary focus of the Beatitudes is on the internal transformation of the heart through the Messiah (the anointed one from the descendant of David) that the Jews so anxiously waited for. The focus is not on the political reform or the external blessings of material blessings. "The kingdom of God does not come with your careful observation, nor will people say, ''Here it is," or "There it is," because the kingdom of God is within you." (Luke 17:20-21) Jesus was proclaiming for the first time that the kingdom of heaven is felt within our heart through the Holy Spirit. It appears the disciples and the crowd could not comprehend its true meaning and were disappointed when they heard it.

The Beatitudes are not simply eight secret ways to receive blessings. It means that a person who passionately feels the love of Christ within his/her heart through the Holy Spirit will have these eight attitudes and as a result, not only will he/she enjoy the blessing (kingdom of heaven) but also great rewards will be reserved in the eternal heaven. With this in mind, some theologians insisted that rather than calling it as the 'Beatitudes' it would be more appropriate to refer them as 'Be-Attitudes.' At first glance, it appears like an enumeration of eight blessings but the only common ground is the experience of the heavenly peace.

The actual attitudes of the Beatitudes in our daily life are based on sacrifices and suffering for the love of others which the Bible expressed as entering through the "narrow gate." (Matthew 7:13) For this reason there are few who seek this path.

Out of the eight attitudes of the Beatitudes, let's say a believer does not desire to have such attitudes or reflects only one of them in their lifestyle. Then, that person is not a believer of Jesus. On the other hand, if a believer claims to have all eight attitudes, then that would be very startling for sure as well.

The Poor in Spirit → Kingdom of Heaven is Theirs

Even among the believers of Jesus, there are people under the "law of sin and death." (Romans 8:2) People living under the law of sin and death are totally different from those who live under the law of the Holy Spirit. The people living under the law of sin and death are rich in spirit. Why? Because they are filled with their own thoughts and plans.

One of my colleagues had all the plans laid out for him and said, "I'm going to work in such and such country this time, then go to another country and upon my return I'm going to become a certain director, then become a certain chief, then afterwards become an assistant foreign minister, and then become a vice foreign minister, and finally become a foreign minister."

I have yet to see anyone whose plans became a reality. Jesus said, "I am the Alpha and the Omega, the first and the last, the beginning and the end." (Revelation 22:13) We may start according to our plans but can never finish it as we had planned. There is only one who can plan the Alpha and finish with the Omega-it is God. And yet we are filled with our own thoughts and plans. This kind of people do not have the grace of God and only rely on self-ability and sufficiency. And then eventually they will experience a terrible breakdown and despair. Needless to say, the kingdom of heaven will become out of their reach and they will experience hell during the course of their life.

A person who lives under the law of the Spirit is just like a year old child. Would a child have his own thoughts or plans? Would a child have "things that was accomplished by me?" Instead, a child needs only to be in the bosom of the mother and leave everything to her. Therefore, there would be no worries or anxieties whatsoever. The reason why people suffer from sleepless nights is because of self-reliance. We want to do everything according to our own thoughts and plans, not realizing we are heading towards the wrong direction each time. This is the life under the law of sin and death. When we become poor in spirit by laying down all our thoughts, plans, and opinions, it is at that moment we experience the kingdom of heaven.

Peter is one of the Bible characters who represents someone poor in spirit. He had spent all day and night long without catching any fish in Galilee. (Luke 5:5) From the worldly standpoint, how frustrating it is if a person worked all day without profiting anything? How would a person feel if he invested everything he had for the success of his business but failed?

Right then, Jesus said, "Put out into deep water, and let down the nets for a catch." (Luke 5:4) Peter could have complained and said "God, I am a seasoned fisherman but what a disgrace" but instead he confessed to Jesus and obeyed by saying, "As an experienced fisherman I worked hard all day long but could not catch any fish. I can not do it on my own." When Peter had done so, he caught such a large number of fish that the nets began to break. (Luke 5:6) Poor in spirit is when you are able to go into the arms of God as the way you are. By confessing that you cannot do anything is when you experience the kingdom of heaven. 'For theirs is the kingdom of Heaven' is present tense and not future tense. It means the kingdom of heaven is experienced now and not in the future.

Those Who Mourn → Will be Comforted

People do not like pain. Secular people call a person blessed if the person does not have any sufferings. Naturally, we want to avoid sufferings and live a happy life in the world but our life consists of trials, despair or worries under the law of sin and death.

Over 90% of troubles that we experienced originated from our own sin and wrong choices. However, just as God refined Job like pure gold, there are instances where He gives us perseverance and suffering for the sake of disciplinary training, so that we may become a new person through the anointing of the Holy Spirit in order to give us a mission. So, suffering comes to us even though we believe in Jesus. Does anyone like suffering? No one does. But the citizens of the kingdom of heaven believe that suffering is the beginning of a blessing. There will be genuine comfort if we thank God when our ego and sinful nature break down through suffering.

People who rely on the Holy Spirit are able to be thankful that their egos are being shattered in the midst of their severe suffering and say, "Lord, I am nothing. There is nothing I can do through this suffering. The only thing I can do is look upon you, Lord." This type of person can experience God's true comfort. This is the blessing of the kingdom of heaven.

On the other hand, people who do not pray can not be comforted no matter how much they know the Bible. We see the truth of our sins when we pray through the guidance of the Holy Spirit. With our limited memory, how much can we repent our sins? Many sins vanish away in our consciousness. A person can only remember less than 5% of their sins. But the Holy Spirit makes us confess the sins that we have completely forgotten. Through prayer we begin to realize what terrible sinners we are, and that's when we repent wholeheartedly, spilling our guts out and mourn. When we mourn and repent our sins, the spirit of Satan is driven out and the comfort of the Holy Spirit fills our heart. At that moment, the Word of Jesus is accomplished for the first time. "Whoever believes in Me, as the Scripture has said, streams of living water will flow from within him." (John 7:38)

Do you experience any oppression caused by sin? When you mourn and break down through prayer guided by the Holy Spirit, God's comfort is there for you. If you empty your spirit, the Holy

Spirit will make you mourn. One who is poor in spirit will mourn.

The Meek → Will Inherit the Earth

Courage was a virtue that the Romans held in greatest regard. The only people who could occupy the land were those who had courage and strength or those who had the power and ability to exercise violence. If one uses the worldly courage and power to occupy the land there will always be victims of sorrow.

Jesus said not to be envious of those who have lots of land or wealth but instead to be humbled by the Spirit and serve our neighbors with meekness and humility. If we do so, God promises to give us His heavenly land as inheritance.

Among those who have received Jesus, there are some who attend church once a week on Sunday and worship, but then back in the world they live according to their greed and trample down their neighbors to fill their worldly needs. For this type of believers, there will be no heavenly land for inheritance. We commonly refer to them as "Shameful Salvation."

A meek person does not retaliate or make excuses but humbly takes it when criticized. It is another level of attitude of emptying ourselves.

Those who Hunger and Thirst for Righteousness → Will be Filled

What kind of people are considered rich in this world? It is people who make tons of money and great success. But citizens of God's kingdom are filled with God's spiritual food of life. Even though they do not have much money nor succeeded or are not successful in life, they enjoy sharing with others the blessings they've received from God. People who are compassionate in giving as much as they can to those who are less fortunate are the ones who hunger and thirst for righteousness. God promises to this type of believers that they will be filled and overflowed both on earth and in His kingdom. As stated in

Amos, "Let justice roll on like a river, righteousness like a never-failing stream" (Amos 5:24), God's righteousness flows from top to bottom like water. Among the believers, there are people who are driven by the law of death that they try to cut down the wages of their employees. Do you think they will be filled?

The Merciful → Will be Shown Mercy

The Beatitudes can be divided into two sections: First half of the 4 Beatitudes (blessings of those who empty themselves) and the second half of the 4 Beatitudes (voluntary attitudes of those who are filled). Christians who have emptied their spirit and filled it with the Holy Spirit are voluntarily merciful towards others and reveal their purity of the heart. Not only are they blessed with peace within themselves but also they share peace with people around them and gladly receive persecution for the sake of righteousness.

Normally, people despise the ones who have hurt them or have somehow damaged them. But Christians who experience the love of the Holy Spirit react differently. In a similar situation, they may momentarily hate the person who has harmed them but because the Holy Spirit gives a merciful heart they put aside the anger and pray for the person's weakness instead. The more people realize there are flaws and mistakes of their own, the more merciful they are towards others. Realizing their own flaws and shortcomings is a blessing to those who live under the laws of the Holy Spirit.

People who are led by the Holy Spirit will have a merciful heart and intercede for their pastors after discovering their faults within a church. But on the contrary, people who live according to the law will condemn, correct and drive the church into destruction.

What kind of people cause envy in the world? People who have achieved great success and wealth. But people who have no fortune or success but are merciful and give comfort to the less fortunate are truly the ones who are of the kingdom of heaven. This type of people will be blessed with the kingdom of heaven.

The Pure in Heart → Will See God

You 'will see God' means 'you will experience God in you' or 'feel the love of God in you.' When you pursue the glories of the world with all kinds of wicked heart and poisonous mind, you will eventually experience hell. We must not pursue the thoughts of the world but be led by the Holy Spirit to purify our heart with prayers and the Word of God which is life-giving water. Many times we say that we don't have time to listen to the Word of God or pray, because we are so busy with our studies or work. However, these are all excuses. Believers who have filled their hearts with the Holy Spirit by empting their spirit have cleaned up the worldly thoughts in their mind and purified themselves to enjoy the kingdom of heaven in the world and experience God. "Do not conform any longer to the pattern of this world, but be transformed by the renewing of your mind." (Romans 12:2) It is the attitude that is in accordance with our lifestyle.

The Peacemakers → Will be Called Sons of God

The world is far away from peace. The world accelerates people into competitions, fights and alienate them from one another. Believers who are of the world are the same with the worldly people. Whoever compete, fight, spread malicious gossips and alienate are not citizens of the kingdom of God and Jesus referred to them as Satan's children.

In order to live in peace with other people whether at home, work place or church, we must take a loss. Without doing so, we will not be able to live peacefully with our neighbors or colleagues. There will be peace when we have a mentality of "let me take a loss." Jesus said blessed are the peacemakers for they will be called sons of God. In spite of believing in Jesus, people tread down and compete with others with all their might to get ahead and occupy a higher position. It is for this reason that non-Christians pass remarks like, "It is those people that make me not want to go to church."

As explained earlier, believers who have filled their heart with the

Holy Spirit by emptying their spirit does not limit their blessing of peace to themselves but voluntarily create harmony in all their surroundings.

Those Who are Persecuted Because of Righteousness → For Theirs the Kingdom of Heaven

What does 'persecuted because of righteousness' mean? If you think these words have nothing to do with us assuming persecution days are over for Christians, that is a great misunderstanding. To be persecuted because of righteousness means to obtain faith to pay the price for God's kingdom. A believer who says, "I will pay the price to build God's world (kingdom) and to build a (His) church. It may be difficult but I will endure the pain." will surely possess the kingdom of heaven. "If anyone would come after me, he must deny himself and take up his cross and follow me." (Mark 8:34)

When believers' heart is filled with mercy, purity and peace even in the midst of persecutions, they can be assured that the kingdom of heaven is already in them.

Salt and Light

Jesus continued to preach about salt and light after the sermon of the Beatitudes. "You are the salt of the earth. But if the salt loses its saltiness, how can it be made salty again? It is no longer good for anything, except to be thrown out and trampled by men." (Matthew 5:13)

We Christians should also have a salty taste in us. "We have this treasure in jars of clay." (2 Corinthians 4:7) Being a vessel of His spirit, we must reflect on ourselves whether we are delivering the water of life to others through the Spirit of Jesus.

We can not possibly become salt unless we continuously wash off our sin and unclean thoughts through the Holy Spirit and fill our hearts with God's good virtues. There is nothing that is good except the "Spirit of God," so we need to fill our spirit with the Spirit of God through the Word of God and prayer. "The good man brings good things out of the good stored up in him." (Matthew 12:35) With the good inside us, we must become salt of the world to prevent our society from further decaying and bring a refreshing taste to the dull state of mind. In the days of the Roman Empire, salt was so precious that it was even given as a monthly wage for soldiers. A believer whose heart is filled with the good is very worthy and set apart from the world.

"You are the light of the world…. In the same way, let your light shine before men, that they may see your good deeds and praise your Father in Heaven." (Matthew 5:14-16) We are beings that were formed from the dust of the ground and became alive with the breath of life from God. How can we become the light? We become the light when the Word of God and Jesus, who came as light, come into our hearts. The phrase 'become light' is the same message given to Abraham by God, "you will be a blessing." (Genesis 12:2) With the light that came upon us, our role is to shine it upon the people of darkness so that they may receive it and come out of the darkness.

Shining a light to the darkness includes preaching the Word of God as well as doing good deeds. Not only should we intercede for others, but also be a participant of the answers to our own prayers. That is why we give offerings for missionary and charity work on top of our intercessory prayers. We can be a light in doing this.

We do not become a light merely by studying the Bible and by prayers. Without sacrificing or surrendering our flesh and ego, we cannot be a light for those who are suppressed and experiencing hardships. All these things cannot be done without the love of God through the Holy Spirit that works within us. (Philippians 3:8-9) Jesus referred to this light as 'good deeds.'

We can do good deeds for others when our ego is broken down. If we want to convey the light that has come upon us, we must surrender and sacrifice everything. It is only then the light in us will shine outwardly. Threader: It is just like Gideon and his 300 men's triumphal victory against the Midianites; the light swallowed up the darkness as they surrounded the enemy grounds and attacked by blowing the trumpets and smashing the pitchers with the torches inside them. In order to break the vessel, we must kneel before the cross on a daily basis.

Salt and light represent someone who is set apart from the world. The things of the world are dark and decay over time. As many enjoy and wander in the darkness, believers are set apart from this dark world. Jesus wanted His disciples to understand that they had great power and influence to change and light up the world even though they were weak in the society. Let us reflect for a moment and examine ourselves whether we are carrying out the role of the light and salt.

Jesus Came to Fulfill the Law

"Do not think that I have come to abolish the Law or the Prophets; I have not come to abolish them but to fulfill them." (Matthew 5:17) Jesus said He came to fulfill the Law. Some believers criticized one another and said, "Please do not be so legalistic. We are now living in the period of grace because of the cross of Jesus so why are you bringing up the old Law (Ten Commandments)?" But Jesus said unless the heaven and earth disappear, every letter in the Law will be fulfilled.

In fact, Jesus fulfilled the Law by completing the two paths mentioned in Deuteronomy; the paths of blessing and curse were lived out in His own life. Jesus had revealed the blessing of God through healing and various miracles and bore the curse of all mankind through taking upon the cross. Jesus said, "Come, follow Me and I will make you fishers of men." (Matthew 4:19) We feel that we can never obey the Law but Jesus said that we can do it if the Law of the Holy Spirit works within us.

"For I tell you, unless your righteousness surpasses that of the Pharisees and the teachers of the law, you will certainly not enter the kingdom of Heaven." (Matthew 5:20) This verse appears as if Jesus was going to give a more difficult command than the law that the

Pharisees and the teachers tried to follow. It is because the true law of God is exhibited, not through our outwardly deeds but our heart. The profound meaning of this message is that our inner self must be transformed in order to enjoy the blessings of His kingdom. (Philippians 3:9). The outwardly act is important as well but what God judges is the intention of our heart. The only difference between a murderer and us is that a murderer has been caught while we haven't. We must understand the love of God. He does not judge us through our actions - whether we have kept His command or not, but rather He looks at our hearts - whether we are putting our best efforts to obey His Word or not. That is why we must look upon Him.

The Law gives us an understanding of 'my' sin. The Law leads us to confess that we are incapable of keeping the Law and makes us kneel before God. Therefore, we must be careful not to apply the standards of the Law to others and scold them. Instead, meditate to understand the sins inside us so that we may repent and be alert with prayers at all times.

Do Not Murder

You have heard that it was said to the people long ago, 'Do not murder, and anyone who murders will be subject to judgment. But I tell you that anyone who is angry with his brother will be subject to judgment. Again, anyone who says to his brother, 'Raca' is answerable to the Sanhedrin. But anyone who says, 'You fool!' will be in danger of the fire of hell." (Matthew 5:21-22) Killing a person's body is murder according to the Ten Commandments of the Old Testament. Humans are spiritual beings, so the minute anger bursts out the spirit dies as well.

Calling someone a fool is a condescending act. It is quite easy to look down on a person who is inferior than ourselves. Even though the physical body remains as is, the spirit within the person receives a tremendous hurt. Jesus is telling us not to do this kind of act that kills the spirit.

Do Not Commit Adultery

"You have heard that it was said, 'Do not commit adultery.' But I tell you that anyone who looks at a woman lustfully has already committed adultery with her in his heart." (Matthew 5:27-28) After reading this verses, many people throw questions like, "With this kind of standard, would there be any man around who has not committed adultery?" Generally speaking, they are justified in asking this question. But you will be amazed that these lustful thoughts when looking at a woman will vanish if you read the Word of God, pray and let yourself be led by the Holy Spirit on a daily basis. Your interests will be shifted-which is the amazing work of the Holy Spirit.

Do Not Retaliate

"But if there is any further injury, then you shall appoint as a penalty life for life, eye for eye, tooth for tooth, hand for hand, foot for foot, burn for burn, wound for wound, bruise for bruise." (Exodus 21:23-25) In the Old Testament, it was commanded to punish a person who has harmed a neighbor. But Jesus said, "Whoever slaps you on your right cheek, turn the other to him also." (Matthew 5:39) Do not retaliate on someone who caused you harm. Instead, think of it as a "God given opportunity" and deny yourself completely. Then, there will be an exorbitant joy of victory. People with a worldly view will say, "How can anyone do this to you?" But a person who is captivated by the Holy Spirit will understand exactly what this passage means.

If Asked, Give

"And if someone wants to sue you and take your tunic, let him have your cloak as well. If someone forces you to go one mile, go with him two miles. Give to the one who asks you, and do not turn away from the one who wants to borrow from you." (Matthew 5:40-42) If someone asks to borrow something, lend it; if someone asks to give, give.

One day I found my two daughters arguing. One daughter was asking to borrow money and the other one was refusing. I scolded them fiercely with this verse at that time. A few years later, when my youngest daughter confessed to me that she felt my love through that incident, I was overjoyed.

This is a story about Missionary Yo Suk Kim who was serving Hansen's people in China when he met a robber. When the robber asked for money, Missionary Kim handed out the two bags of money from the sales of his farm produce. Then the robber said, "I've never seen anyone like you. You must be an extraordinary man so I am afraid of my future consequences." And gave them back - with additional money!

Love Your Enemy

"You have heard that it was said, 'Love your neighbor and hate your enemy.'

But I tell you: Love your enemies and pray for those who persecute you." (Matthew 5:43-44) Are you able to pray for a person who treats you badly? Jesus says this is possible with the power of the Holy Spirit. When I was in New York someone was determined to harass me and came all the way from Seoul. I remember holding on to this verse and praying for that person. I welcomed him warmly with the love of God. No one will ever know the unimaginable blessing I received from God at that time!

Do Not Break Any of These Commandments

"Anyone who breaks one of the least of these commandments and teaches others to do the same will be called least in the kingdom of heaven, but whoever practices and teaches these commands will be called great in the kingdom of heaven." (Matthew 5:19) This means not to omit any of the Commandments of God when you teach them. Just because you think some of them are difficult to keep. Also whoever practices and teaches the Commandments will be called great in the kingdom of heaven.

Do Not Be like the Hypocrites and Worry_ Matthew 6

Matthew chapter 6 is the so-called 'do nots' chapter, because majority of the message is about hypocrisy and worry.

Do Not be Like Hypocrites_Matthew 6:1-18

Jesus said 'not to be like hypocrite' when we pray and when we offer to help. He spoke two teachings regarding this topic.

First, do not be like hypocrites when we pray. (Matthew 6:5) Jesus said that the praying Pharisees on the street corners may appear godly on the outside, but inside them was like a whitewashed tomb. A person who has received Jesus needs to change their focus from self-centeredness to Jesus through the Word. Personal feelings, emotions and thoughts must gradually become Jesus' through prayers. A prayer is a personal relationship with God and also our way of responding to God's love. That is why we must not be self-conscious of the people around us when we pray. Jesus showed us how to pray to God by teaching us the Lord's Prayer (Matthew 6:9-13) and asked us not be like hypocrites and babble away. He also advised us that when fasting - do it discreetly and only reveal it to the Father instead of looking somber like hypocrites. Also, He asked us to refrain from storing treasures on earth but instead in heaven, since our heart will follow where the treasure is.

Second, give help in a discretionary manner. "When you give to the needy, do not let your left hand know what your right hand is doing." (Matthew 6:3) To give in a discretionary manner means to become more like the Lord and the Lord's instruments. As long as a person thinks the money they have earned is all 'due to their own efforts,' it would be impossible to share with others. The only time a heart opens for giving is when people realize that "everything has been provided by the grace of God"

Do Not Worry_Matthew 6:25-34

We worry about what to eat, drink or wear in our daily lives. But Jesus said, "Do not worry." (Matthew 6:34) "Look at the birds of the air; they do not sow or reap or store away in barns, and yet your heavenly Father feeds them. Are you not much more valuable than they?" (Matthew 6:26)

The core of this message is that we must believe in Father's love. Isn't it evident that our Father who takes care of all natures would surely look after His children? It is obvious that our Creator God will take care of His children's necessities in life when He actually created all things in the world through the energy of the Word. In case we might still worry about what to eat and wear while living in the world, God showed us the wilderness life of the Israelites in the Old Testament.

What is the root of all worries? It is the thoughts of the world. The worldly spirit gives worldly thoughts. "We have not received the spirit of the world but the Spirit who is from God, that we may understand what God has freely given us." (1 Corinthians 2:12) Without eliminating the worldly thoughts which are triggered by the spirit of Satan, it would be impossible to shake off anxieties, worries or fear.

Our worries and anxieties all disappear when the Holy Spirit destroys the worldly thoughts. That is why we are told to pray at all times by the guidance of the Holy Spirit. "And pray in the Spirit on all occasions with all kinds of prayers and requests. With this in mind, be alert and always keep on praying for all the saints." (Ephesians 6:18) Once you pray in Spirit, you will experience your worries fading away without you realizing it. Rather than struggling to resolve the worldly problems on our own, we need to hold on to God's promise. He promises that He will fill us with all the things we need to live in this world, if we seek His kingdom (God's presence) first and seek things for the sake of our neighbors (His righteousness). (Matthew 6:31-33)

Do Not Judge

The “Do not judge” phrase also appears in chapter 7. “Do not judge, or you too will be judged. For in the same way you judge others, you will be judged, and with the measure you use, it will be measured to you.” (Matthew 7:1-2)

With what standards do we judge others? It is with ‘my thoughts.’ It is good if I think it is right and bad if I think it is evil (in other words, eating from the tree of the good and evil). But the standards must be based on God’s Word (fruit of life), not ‘my thoughts.’ Whenever you have an urge to judge or condemn someone, I urge you to remember this message and zip up your lips. The easiest way of committing a sin for believers is by joining in the act of judging others. I am not an exception here, so that is why I find myself frequently repenting. When we eat the fruit from the tree of the good and evil our “eyes are brightened” and detect other peoples’ fault easily. We pick the speck in our brethren’s eye but fail to realize the plank-size sin within ourselves.

Promise for Prayer Response

A well-known promise of God responding to our prayers is found in Matthew chapter 7. “Ask, and it will be given to you; seek, and you will find; knock, and it will be opened to you. For everyone who asks receives, and he who seeks finds, and to him who knocks it will be opened.” (Matthew 7:7-8) This is God’s promise that whoever asks will surely receive, whoever seeks will surely find, and whoever knocks, the door will surely be opened.

It is God’s promise that He will meet us immediately if we ask for the presence of the Lord, who is already at our side, seek Him continuously, and knock on Him who is anxiously waiting inside the door. God promises that He will surely answer to those who pray to Him. But at the same time, it also means that those who do not ask will never be given, those who do not seek will never find Him, and those who do not knock He will not open the door. We can not meet Jesus if we do not pray and good things do not happen naturally. That is why we need to pray continuously.

Majority of us pray when there's a crisis or a problem but then it is too late. When your business goes bust, do you think that it can be recovered when you pray? If a person is diagnosed with cancer and then cry out and pray, "please, heal me"- it is too late.

It is important to build up an angel fortitude and prevent a disaster by praying ordinarily everyday. However, if a crisis has already occurred, be thankful even at that difficult moment and go forward to Jesus. He will wrap our lives around with peace (the peace of God that goes beyond our comprehension) which the world will never know and make us go through the tunnel of crisis in safety and ultimately resolves our problem at His appointed time. (Philippians 4:6-7)

Enter Through the Narrow Gate

Jesus tells (told) us to 'enter through the narrow gate.' "Enter through the narrow gate. For wide is the gate and broad is the road that leads to destruction, and many enter through it. But small is the gate and narrow the road that leads to life and only a few find it." (Matthew 7:13-14) The gate that leads to life is not very popular because it is narrow. But that is the way that leads to life. On the other hand, many people sought out the gate that leads to destruction because it is wide and broad. Many people gather because it is a lot of fun. There is a helping hand that leads to life and a helping hand that leads to destruction. Therefore, we need to discern well who the true leader is.

Threader: In the Old Testament, there were two paths, following the Law or idolatry. The two paths in Jesus' time in the New Testament, however, can be divided into the following: following the Spirit or the flesh (world). "For if you live according to the sinful nature, you will die; but if by the Spirit you put to death the misdeeds of the body, you will live." (Romans 8:13) Apostle Paul preaches about the two paths in his 13 letters: "Are you going to follow the flesh?" or "Are you going to receive the guidance of the Holy Spirit?" The main message of Pauline Letters is for us to live a life that is led by the Holy Spirit. When you are at a crossroads where you have to choose to follow what is visible or to follow the desire to follow the invisible Word of God, I would like to encourage you to choose the latter. I ask you to choose the path of the Spirit that leads to life.

Fruit Bearing Believers

This is the conclusion of the Sermon on the Mount. Jesus said that true and false believers can be sorted out by their fruit. "Watch out for false prophets. They come to you in sheep's clothing, but inwardly they are ferocious wolves." (Matthew 7:15)

Many people fall into the teachings of false prophets or heresies because of their logical interpretation of the Bible. People who lack biblical knowledge are intrigued by this formulated logical system created by heresies and false teachings. Many people follow false prophets because they are told that there is a wide gate that leads to heaven. Jesus said to be cautious of the false prophets, "How will you know the false prophets? Watch out what kind of fruit they bear." "You will know them by their fruits. Grapes are not gathered from thorn bushes nor figs from thistles, are they?" (Matthew 7:16)

"Not everyone who says to me, 'Lord, Lord,' will enter the kingdom of heaven but only he who does the will of my Father who is in Heaven." (Matthew 7:21) If this verse is true, are we saved through faith? Or are we saved by doing the will of God? For those who have faith, their action follows their faith. (Matthew 7:24) We must understand that a person is saved by the faith that leads to action, and not by the action itself. But the important thing is that Jesus will judge us by the fruits we bear. By examining our fruits, He will know whether we acted in the will of the Father or upon our self-interests.

Some may not agree to this. "Many will say to me on that day, 'Lord, Lord, did we not prophesy in your name; and in your name drive out demons and perform many miracles?" (Matthew 7:22) Jesus said, "And then I will declare to them, 'I never knew you. Depart from Me, who practice lawlessness!" (Matthew 7:23) The people Jesus mentions here used their spiritual gifts. It was easy for them to have an illusion that they were bearing fruits through their spiritual gifts such as spreading the Word of God, casting out demons, and prophesying in the name of Jesus Christ. People who have spiritual gifts need to be aware that there is a possibility of them being forsaken.

The conclusion of the Beatitudes is that Jesus will judge us by the fruits that we bear at the end of the time. Therefore, the key message is that we must bear the fruit of the Spirit. We must transform into the figure of God's love. The fruit of the Spirit is "love, joy, peace, patience, kindness, goodness, faithfulness, gentleness and self-control." (Galatians 5:22-23) Once our inner self is changed into the image of God, whatever we say, see, act with our body will be shown through our entire lifestyle. True believers who have transformed their inner self by fully receiving the love of Jesus will guide and lead other people to repent their sins to come before Jesus-ultimately changing them as well. They encourage them to bear the fruit of the Spirit. More than anything, we must be able to fulfill our own salvation with fear and trembling and also follow that up with a ministry that transforms others. Otherwise, we may end up like King Solomon who succeeded in saving others through his work but failed to save himself. The story is a loving reminder for us not to forget this message.

Spiritual Search 24

Gifts and Fruit of the Spirit

Spiritual Gifts

Apostle Paul spoke about spiritual gifts in 1 Corinthians chapters 12?14. There are various spiritual gifts (approximately 21 kinds): such as delivering the Word of God, interpretation of tongues and prophecy, healing and casting out evil spirits, and serving (elders responsible for administrative affairs on behalf of the church).

Spiritual gifts are a ministry calling from God. "This is why it says: "When he ascended on high, he led captives in his train and gave gifts to men." (Ephesians 4:8) This means that Jesus carried the cross down to the pits of hell and shone His light upon Satan and snatched away the keys of hell. And as He ascended to the side of the heavenly throne, He released the captives of Satan and shared the gifts of the Holy Spirit (receiving grace by doing the works of God) among them. Spiritual gifts are not given to utilize them on self but for the benefit of others. For instance, the gift of delivering the Word of God is to share God's message to many others and gifts of the interpretation of tongues and prophecy are to be used for encouraging and boasting the faith of fellow believers. A man of God always thinks first of the relationship with others. To be alone is what we refer to as Satan.

God has given spiritual gifts to us temporarily to help those who are in need until His 2nd coming. We must realize that the goal to achieve for believers in this world is to bear the fruit of the Spirit. The emphasis must be given on that receiving spiritual gifts are merely a process for us to bear the fruit of the Spirit and that it is partial and temporary. Therefore, it would be a big mistake to think that those who perform miracles, healing and deliver powerful messages have completed everything. At the 2nd coming of Christ at the end time, it won't be like a poor reflection in a mirror but instead tongues, prophecies, and knowledge will be entirely ceased. (1 Corinthians 13:9-12)

The Fruit of the Spirit

"But the fruit of the Spirit is love, joy, peace, patience, kindness, goodness, faithfulness, gentleness, self-control; against such things there is no law." (Galatians 5:22-23) Simply put, the fruit of the Spirit is love. It would be meaningless using any spiritual gifts without love. (1 Corinthians 13) Sanctification is the process for bearing the fruit of the Spirit. "Therefore, my dear friends, as you have always obeyed-not only in my presence, but now much more in my absence-continue to work out your salvation with fear and trembling, for it is God who works in you to will and to act according to his good purpose." (Philippians 2:12-13) The fruit of the Spirit is the image of Christ and agape love.

Filled with the Holy Spirit

To be filled with the Holy Spirit is a step prior to bearing the fruit of the Spirit. Jesus spoke to the disciples before His ascension, "Do not leave Jerusalem but wait for what the Father had promised." (Act 1:4) The Holy Spirit came just as He had promised. "All of them were filled with the Holy Spirit and began to speak in other tongues as the Spirit enabled them." (Acts 2:4)

Being filled with the Holy Spirit can be divided into two: "being filled with the Holy Spirit momentarily" and "living a life filled with the Holy Spirit." People were filled with the Holy Spirit when they were gathered in Mark's attic. They started speaking in tongues and a crowd pointed fingers at them. Then Peter, who was filled with the Holy Spirit, raised his voice and addressed the crowd boldly, "Fellow Jews and all of you who live in Jerusalem, let me explain this to you; listen carefully to what I say." (Acts 2:14) This incident was a moment of the fullness of the Holy Spirit which was temporary. Stephen was also filled with the Holy Spirit when he disputed with the people in front of the Sanhedrin in Jerusalem. "But they could not stand up against his wisdom or the Spirit by whom he spoke." (Acts 6:10)

We can find a description of living a life filled with the Holy Spirit in the book of Ephesians. "Do not get drunk on wine for that is dissipation, but be filled with the Spirit." (Ephesians 5:18) Just as we would forget ourselves completely when drunk with wine, we must get drunk with the Holy Spirit and surrender our lives to God. When we trust God with our lives not only momentarily but completely, the sanctification of our life happen.

In order to be filled with the Holy Spirit, we must trust and depend on God with total obedience. We must be able to deny and crucify ourselves daily and make a conscious decision to follow God. Jesus also prayed fervently his sweat became as great drops of blood at Gethsemane before His crucifixion, "Father, if you are willing, take this cup from me; yet not my will, but yours be done." (Luke 22:42) We must realize how difficult and tough it is to surrender ourselves to God. It is easier said than done.

The Holy Spirit of God came to accomplish this. When faith (the size of a mustard seed) grows within us, it shoots out branches, flowers blossom and finally it emits fragrance. A person filled with the Holy Spirit permeates with the fragrance of Christ. Fruit arrives when flowers fall off. In this same manner, people whose life exhibit the fullness of the Holy Spirit will bear the fruit-a resemblance of God's love and His image.

. . .

Jesus was going throughout all Galilee, teaching in their synagogues and proclaiming the gospel of the kingdom, and healing every kind of disease and every kind of sickness among the people. The news about Him spread throughout all Syria; and they brought to Him all who were ill, those suffering with various diseases and pains, demoniacs, epileptics, paralytics; and He healed them.

Matthew 4:23-24

JESUS HEALS THE SICK

Matthew 8-10

After the Lord's discourse on the Sermon on the Mount, He encountered many sick people as He came down the mountain. Matthew chapters 8-9 are the records of the events of Jesus' healing the sick.

MINISTRY OF HEALING

Do You Wish to be Healed?_Matthew 8-9

Healing of a Man with Leprosy

The first sick person Jesus encountered as He came down from the mountain was a leper. The leper said to Jesus, "Lord, if you are willing, you can make me clean." (Matthew 8:2) In the Old Testament, Naaman was cured of leprosy, but in reality leprosy was a difficult disease to be cured. Therefore, this leper's faith in Jesus' power to heal him was a tremendous one. He believed that Jesus was the Son of God. Jesus replied, "I am willing. Be cleansed!" (Matthew 8:3), and reached out His hand and touched this leper who was exuding pus from his wounds.

Lepers usually do not feel pain even when they suffer from a burn wound. Today, there are many who suffer from the spiritual leprosy, as they are oblivious to the pain of their own rotting flesh. And yet how proudly they speak of themselves! Evangelism is imparting the love of our Lord, who can heal this spiritual leprosy.

The Centurion's Great Faith

This time a centurion implored Jesus. "Lord, my servant is lying paralyzed at home, fearfully tormented." (Matthew 8:6) Jesus replied, 'I will come and heal him.' (Matthew 8:7) Then the centurion made his confession of faith, "Lord, I am not worthy for You to come under my roof, but just say the word, and my servant will be healed. For I also am a man under authority, with soldiers under me; and I say to this one, 'Go!' and he goes, and to another, 'Come!' and he comes, and to my slave, 'Do this!' and he does it." (Matthew 8:8-9) Upon hearing this, Jesus commended the faith of the centurion by saying, "Truly I say to you, I have not found such great faith with anyone in Israel." (Matthew 8:10) The centurion believed that Jesus was the King of God's Kingdom.

From this, we can recognize that the healing ministry of Jesus is established upon the basis of the faith of the ones who were healed. The centurion's confession of faith became the first example of salvation among the gentiles. Jesus then healed Peter's mother-in-law who was suffering from a fever and then drove out demons from two demon-possessed men as He was walking past a graveyard.

The Paralytic and His Friends

After crossing over a river on a boat to Capernaum, Jesus healed a paralytic. Although it is not recorded in Matthews, it is reported in other Gospels that the paralytic's friends let him down on a mat from the roof after they dug a hole in it. Jesus healed this paralytic man after He saw the faith of his friends who actually dug a hole in the roof to lower him down. This is the evidence of how Jesus hears our intercessory prayers on behalf of our neighbors. The reason why sickness is not healed is not because Jesus does not have the ability to heal, but because there is lack of faith on our part. Even if I do not have faith myself, I can be saved if I have faithful friends who intercede on my behalf.

As Jesus was healing the paralytic, He said, "Take courage, son;

your sins are forgiven." (Matthew 9:2) Then many who were listening grumbled among themselves, "This fellow blasphemes." (Matthew 9:3) Knowing this, Jesus said, "Why are you thinking evil in your hearts? Which is easier, to say, 'Your sins are forgiven,' or to say, 'Get up, and walk'? But so that you may know that the Son of Man has authority on earth to forgive sins." Then He said to the paralytic, "Get up, pick up your bed and go home."(Matthew 9:4-6) "The Son is the radiance of God's glory and the exact representation of his being, sustaining all things by his powerful word. After he had provided purification for sins, he sat down at the right hand of the Majesty in heaven." (Hebrews 1:3)

Obviously not all illnesses come about because of sin. For example, Job underwent a trial to be like pure gold. In other instances, bodily injury can come about by just trying too hard. However, in many instances we become sick because of our sins. Even though in the beginning God resolved chaos, humanity destroyed its bodily order by committing sin which resulted in the advent of diseases. For this reason, the forgiveness of sin brings forth healing of diseases.

For the Jews of this period who believed that only the invisible God has the authority to forgive sins, what Jesus said was a blasphemy. This event occurred during the initial phase of Jesus' ministry, and by this, He revealed Himself to be the Messiah in His own subtle manner. By no means was He trying to brag. Rather, Jesus took this as a first step in His march towards the cross. Thus began His journey towards the ultimate goal of His ministry - the cross.

Faith of the Hemorrhagic Woman

After seeing the faith of a hemorrhagic woman who wished to get well by just touching the edge of His cloak, Jesus said to her, "Daughter, take courage; your faith has made you well." (Matthew 9:22) The Book of Matthew emphasizes that Jesus observed the faith of the sick before His healing.

Faith of Two Blind Men

Jesus asked two blind men, "Do you believe that I am able to do this?" (Matthew 9:28) as they followed Him and called out, "Have mercy on us, Son of David." (Matthew 9:27) When they replied, "Yes, Lord" (Matthew 9:28), Jesus touched their eyes and said, "According to your faith it will be done for you." (Matthew 9:29) A person who confesses the faith that they will be healed will be healed accordingly. (Matthew 9:27-30)

New Covenant, New Faith

The disciples of John the Baptist came to Jesus and asked Him, "Why do we and the Pharisees fast but Your disciples do not fast?" (Matthew 9:14) To this Jesus pointed out that while He recognized the need for fasting, there were occasions that required fasting, and there were occasions that did not. While Jesus, the bridegroom, is with us, we ought to be joyous and take pleasure in His company but after He departs we shall then fast. "Jesus answered, "How can the guests of the bridegroom mourn while he is with them? The time will come when the bridegroom will be taken from them; then they will fast." (Matthew 9:15) The time we feel like Jesus is far away is when we need to fast. Fasting ought not to be done to achieve our personal goals; rather it ought to be done to seek the Lord's presence.

Jesus then said to those who have discarded the old ways and put on the clothes of new faith that He will give them the new covenant of blood (the new wine). "They pour new wine into new wineskins, and both are preserved." (Matthew 9:17) If we try to compromise our faith by maintaining our old habits we will be destroyed. We must transform ourselves into a whole new being. To believe in Jesus is to undergo a substantive transformation and change in character, rather than just doing good deeds. For this, we need the process of sanctification.

DISPATCHING OF THE DISCIPLES _ MATTHEW 10

Workers of the Harvest

As Jesus drew near to the end of the initial stage of His ministry, He dispatched His 12 disciples to the world. This was done to typify the Church ministry which was to begin after Jesus' ascension and the coming of the Holy Spirit. Jesus shed tears as he saw numerous sick people seeking relief during His ministry. The reason why He healed them was His compassion and love. "When he saw the crowds, he had compassion on them, because they were harassed and helpless, like sheep without a shepherd." (Matthew 9:36)

"Then he said to his disciples, 'The harvest is plentiful but the workers are few. Ask the Lord of the harvest, therefore, to send out workers into his harvest field." (Matthew 9:37-38) It was not just during the time of Jesus that the harvest was plentiful. It is plentiful even now. Many people thirst for the Word. They wait for salvation and healing. There are so many people in the world suffering from diseases and who wander aimlessly without knowing the Gospel.

Indeed the workers are few. Therefore, when we pray we ought not to pray for our own interests but ask for workers who can harvest the field. The fact that there are many who are in need of the Gospel is a blessing to all believers who are given the chance to harvest. Those who pray to God to send workers are actually praying "please make us as your workers." We may believe that we are going out to plant the seed, but Jesus says that He will give us the joy of harvesting. How thankful we ought to be!

● ● Calling of the 12 Disciples

One commonality found among the 12 disciples was that despite their various backgrounds, they belonged to the poor and marginalized rather than to the elites in the society. "Brothers, think of what you were when you were called. Not many of you were wise by human standards; not many were influential; not many were of noble birth. But God chose the foolish things of the world to shame the wise; God chose the weak things of the world to shame the strong. He chose the lowly things of this world and the despised things - and the things that are not - to nullify the things that are, so that no one may boast before him." (1 Corinthians 1:26-29)

The 12 disciples were very important for God's ministry of atonement. "Having been built on the foundation of the apostles and prophets, with Christ Jesus himself as the chief cornerstone. In him the whole building is joined together and rises to become a holy temple in the Lord." (Ephesians 2:20-21) Jesus promised the 12 disciples that they will sit on 12 thrones as judges beside Him when He sits on His glorious throne to judge the world. (Matthew 19:28) He also promised that at the 2nd coming of Christ, their names will be written on the 12 foundations for the walls of the city of New Jerusalem (Revelations 21:14), which was indeed a great blessing.

Authority Given

Until now Jesus carried on His ministry alone, but from this point on He gave His authority to His disciples and sent them out to the villages of Judea. Instead of just sending them out to preach, He gave them the power to reveal the presence of a living God. The disciples received the power to heal the sick, cast out demons, and raise the dead. Jesus also said, "I tell you the truth, anyone who has faith in me will do what I have been doing. He will do even greater things than these, because I am going to the Father." (John 14:12)

It has been promised that the power will be given to those who ask the Lord for the Holy Spirit to be used as His instruments. There is also lack of workers in comparison to the plentiful harvest. "I tell you, though he will not get up and give him the bread because he is his friend, yet because of the man's boldness he will get up and give him as much as he needs." (Luke 11:8) I urge you to believe God's promise that He will give the gift of the Holy Spirit to anyone who earnestly seeks to be a carrier of His love.

The power (spiritual gifts) is given to us because of the love of God. Therefore, when you desire a certain gift, do not pray vaguely about it, but pray, "As you said, Lord, the harvest is plentiful but the workers are few, and therefore, please anoint me with Your power and use me, a wretched sinner, as one of Your workers." "Follow the way of love and eagerly desire spiritual gifts." (1 Corinthians 14:1) Do not be afraid when the Lord calls you. If you believe that the Lord has prepared the gift for you to be sent out with, then His power will be revealed.

Mission Guidelines from Jesus

Jesus first limited the mission field of the 12 disciples to the lost sheep of Israel, and later expanded it to the Gentiles through Apostle Paul. The first mission work the disciples had to do was spreading the Gospel, and the second was healing the sick. I urge you to believe that those saints who go out and spread the Gospel in obedience are also given the power to heal the sick. Missionaries do not need to worry about financial problems. God has already promised that He will fill the necessary needs.

Preciousness of Life

As He sent out His disciples, not only did Jesus give them power but He also told them of the preciousness of life in preparation for the upcoming persecution. "Are not two sparrows sold for a penny? Yet not one of them will fall to the ground apart from the will of your Father." (Matthew 10:29) One assarion (in Greek) was the smallest copper coin at that time. God considers the life of a sparrow precious even if it is virtually worthless.

Therefore, how much more precious will God consider the lives of His disciples who march on to the world to show His love and who are called to become His workers of the harvest! No matter how difficult it is, even when faced with death in the mission field, people with the mission from God will never fall to the ground.

JESUS REVEALS HIMSELF AS THE MESSIAH

Matthew 11-15

Jesus' ministry between dispatching the disciples and crucifixion is what we refer to as the second half of His ministry. Jesus did not reveal Himself as the Messiah in the beginning, but in the latter part of His ministry He revealed Himself as the Messiah as He approached the cross. He ministered primarily in the vicinity of Lake Galilee in the first half of His ministry. In the second half, He traveled throughout Israel and then headed towards Jerusalem.

The Lord Came as the Humblest One_ Matthew 11

John the Baptist's Illusion

While John was held prisoner after accusing king's mistake, he sent his disciples to Jesus to ask a question. "Now when John, while imprisoned, heard of the works of Christ, he sent word by his disciples and said to Him, 'Are You the Expected one, or shall we look for someone else?' (Matthew 11:2-3)

Instead of responding with "I am the Messiah," "Jesus answered and said to them, "Go and report to John what you hear and see." (Matthew 11:4) What did they hear and see? They had witnessed the works of Jesus — casting out devils, healing the sick, the blind, leprosy, and bringing back life to the dead. These were exactly what the prophet Isaiah had prophesized at the Nazarene

Synagogue before Jesus started His ministry. By telling John's disciples how the prophets' prophesies have been fulfilled through His ministry, Jesus proved that He was the Messiah.

Jesus also testified that the prophesies were being fulfilled through John. "This is the one about whom it is written, Behold, I send My messenger ahead of you, who will prepare Your way before You." (Matthew 11:10) John was Elijah that was prophesized by Malachi. "Behold, I am going to send you Elijah the prophet before the coming of the great and terrible day of the Lord. He will restore the hearts of the fathers to their children and the hearts of the children to their fathers, so that I will not come and smite the land with a curse." (Malachi 4:5-6)

This is what Jesus said about John the Baptist; "Truly I say to you, among those born of women there has not arisen anyone greater than John the Baptist! Yet the one who is least in the kingdom of heaven is greater than he." (Mathew 11:11) How was he considered greater than anyone? According to the promise, not only was John the Baptist the only prophet who testified Jesus as the Messiah in His presence, but he also passed all of God's promises from the Old Testament to Jesus by baptizing Him. . Then, why did Jesus say the humblest person in heaven is more privileged than John? Though John the Baptist played a significant role in testifying the coming of Christ, he had died before experiencing the works of the Holy Spirit that was to come after the resurrection of Jesus. Jesus regarded him as the last prophet in the Old Testament. (Matthew 11:13-14)

John the Baptist clearly knew that Jesus was the Son of God and that He was the Messiah. "I myself have seen and have testified that this is the Son of God." (John 1:34) But he was unable to distinguish the first from the second coming of Christ. John was expecting the Messiah to come and judge this land with His power and glory. Rather, what John saw was Israel that remained under the Roman Empire, and John must have felt puzzled while in prison.

The message of John the Baptist was "Jesus is going to judge the

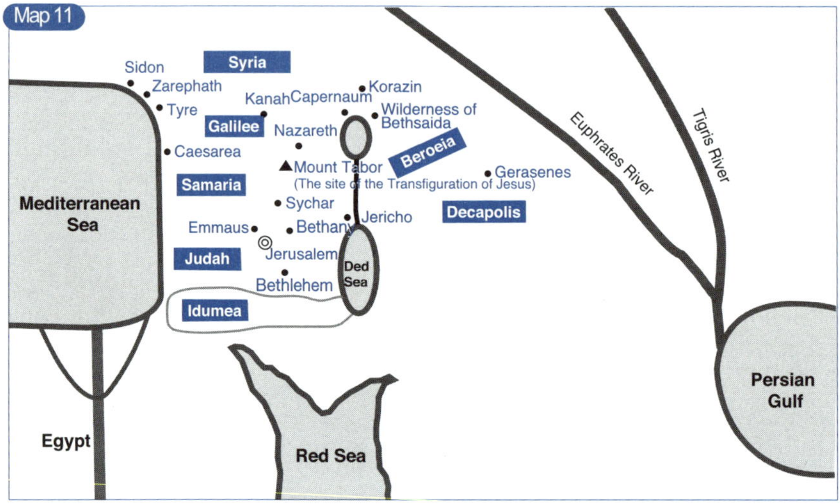

The second half of the life of Jesus Capernaum is located southwest of Lake Galilee and behind it is Chorazin. If one takes a boat from Capernaum towards east is the wilderness of Bethsaida.

living and the dead." "Repent, for the kingdom of heaven is at hand." (Matthew 3:2) "Indeed the ax is already laid at the root of the trees; so every tree that does not bear good fruit is cut down and thrown into the fire." (Luke 3:9) He assumed Christ to be the Savior and the Judge, but the reports of Jesus were different from his expectations. Jesus was hanging out with beggars, tax-collectors and prostitutes the so called outcasts and was starving along with them. So, John asked 'Are You the One?' in prison. (Matthew 11:3)

Christ came as the humblest of the humble in His first coming. He came in the humblest manner and revealed the invisible love of Father God. John the Baptist was unable to comprehend the concept of this love and thought that his prophecy of judgment was unfulfilled. He was left with no choice but to hear the words of "the one who is least in the kingdom of heaven."

Salvation Does Not Appear in Miracles

The last prophet, John the Baptist testified that Jesus was the

Messiah. Jesus also revealed to John the Baptist and His disciples that He was the Messiah. In Matthew 11, it is being evidenced that there are two categories. Matthew 11 talks about how there are those who receive the Messiah and those who do not, and there will be judgment and blessing accordingly.

Most of Jesus' miracles took place in a small area of the northern end of Lake Galilee, around Capernaum, Chorazin and Bethsaida. They created much excitement but many villages did not receive Him as the Messiah (fail to receive salvation). Towards the unrepenting villages, Jesus cursed, "Woe to you, Chorazin! Woe to you, Bethsaida! For if the miracles had occurred in Tyre and Sidon which occurred in you, they would have repented long ago in sackcloth and ashes. Nevertheless I say to you, it will be more tolerable for Tyre and Sidon in the Day of Judgment than for you. And you, Capernaum, will not be exalted to heaven, will you? You will descend to Hades; which occurred in you, it would have remained to this day." (Matthew 11:20-23) Chorazin was where Jesus fed the 5,000 people. The people there experienced the living miracles of God which was to change their lives and lead them to repentance. The whole purpose of these signs was to bring divine healing and release ordinary people who had been crippled by physical, psychological, social or spiritual disorders. Yet they failed to receive salvation.

If one goes on a biblical trip there is nothing left in this particular area. There is no trace of any villages of Bethsaida or Chorazin. Only a stone pillar remains in Capernaum which is assumed to be a temple that existed somewhere around A.D. 3-4. This was not even a temple where Jesus taught in, but in order to attract tourists the government of Israel has put up a sign on top of the pillar stating 'Jesus Town' and collects entrance fees. As Jesus had cursed, there is nothing left behind.

Salvation is not revealed through miracles. Salvation cannot be fulfilled through healings, casting out evil spirits, or raising the dead. Jesus was lamenting as He saw that the only way to provide salvation to mankind was through His suffering and shedding His blood on the cross as the Son of God.

Invitation to Eternal Rest_Matthew 11:28-30

Jesus thanked the Father for saving the foolish and the weak, not the wise and the strong, through the help of the Holy Spirit. And after His suffering, the blessing to those who had received Him as the Messiah was given, "Come to me, all you who labor and are overburdened. I will give you rest." (Matthew 11:28) Even though many Christians are comforted by this verse, in reality, they are actually leading a hard burdensome life without rest.

"Shoulder my yoke and learn from me, for I am gentle and humble in heart and you will find rest for your souls. For my yoke is easy and my burden is light." (Matthew 11:29-30) What is a yoke? It is a device for joining together a pair of draft animals (oxen, donkey or horses) so that they are restrained from moving separately. Normally a more trained animal would take charge of the inexperienced one. Through suffering and enduring together, the younger of the two eventually learns the skills from the experienced one over time.

"Shoulder My yoke and learn from Me." (Matthew 11:29) This means that we must put ourselves under the yoke of God, so that we can be trained to eat from the tree of life (the Word) rather than the tree of good and evil. We must learn to throw away our thoughts and judgments and live according to God's way. Putting on the yoke also means to obey the Word and restrain from doing things that we think are right. Those who enter His service with the help of the Holy Spirit will find eternal rest in Him.

Jesus the Lord of the Sabbath_Matthew 12

Sabbath Dispute

Matthew 12 is filled with scenes of trouble over the Sabbath caused by the religious leaders who were forcefully opposing Jesus.

Jesus was going through the grain fields on the Sabbath and His disciples became hungry so they began to pick the heads of the grain and ate them. (Matthew 12:1) The Pharisees saw this and passed remarks on how His disciples were breaking the Sabbath and the Commandment (Word of God). After the period of Israel's exile, the law of Sabbath was re-enforced. According to the law, one had to observe the Sabbath by doing nothing and staying at home to meditate on Jehovah God and by restricting one's talks only about God.

But Jesus stated that it was more important to cater to one's need (eating when hungry) than to observe the law in formality. "Have you not read what David did when he became hungry, he and his companions, how he entered the house of God and they ate the consecrated bread, which was not lawful for him to eat nor for those with him, but for the priests alone? Or have you not read in the Law, that on the Sabbath the priests in the temple break the Sabbath and are innocent?" (Matthew 12:3-5) This meant that the priests were breaking the Sabbath in order to give offerings to God.

On top of that, Jesus proclaimed an explosive statement, "For the Son of Man is Lord of Sabbath." (Matthew 12:8) In other words, He was saying that He was God. This statement was a divinity insult to the Pharisees. The Pharisees and the scribes were grinding their teeth "what kind of a madman is this guy?" From this point on, they started to scheme a plan to kill Jesus. Ultimately, their reason for crucifying Jesus was the crime of insulting the divinity.

Jesus also healed a man's withered hand who was suffering for a long time. Upon seeing this, the Pharisees went mad. "A man was there whose hand was withered. And they questioned Jesus, asking "Is it lawful to heal on the Sabbath?" (Matthew 12:10) Jesus responded. "What man is there among you who has a sheep, and if it falls into a pit on the Sabbath, will he not take hold of it and lift it out? How much more valuable then is a man than a sheep! So then, it is lawful to do good on the Sabbath." (Matthew 12: 11-13) The Sabbath existed for the purpose of treasuring precious lives.

Jesus commanded something impossible to the man with withered hands, "Put out your hands." The man obeyed by stretching out his hands and he was healed. When God commands us to do something, He also gives the ability for us to do so. Miracles can be experienced when we put our full trust in God and obey Him.

The knowledge of the Word of God (Bible) was so overwhelming for the Pharisees and the scribes that their heads were spinning. In today's term, they were Ph.D. holders in theology. They were consumed with knowledge and yet were unable to recognize the true Lord of Sabbath. The Bible says "The letters kills but the Spirit gives life." (2 Corinthians 3:6) The written letters, the Law, kills, but the Holy Spirit gives life to us. That is why God says, "For I delight in loyalty rather than sacrifice, and in the knowledge of God rather than burnt offerings." (Hosea 6:6)

This brings me back to my own personal experience I had with the strict Jewish observance of Sabbath. My family and I were in a condo in Florida on vacation. We were inside an elevator waiting to get off on the 43rd floor. Unfortunately, the elevator was stopping at each floor so at first we thought some kid had played a prank and pushed all the buttons in the building. It wasn't until later that we realized that the Sabbath for the Jew had begun in the evening of Friday. The elevators were programmed to stop automatically at each floor for the Jewish people, since they were prohibited from pushing the button on the Sabbath. We also found out that the owner of the condo was Jewish just as almost all major highly priced condos were owned by wealthy Jewish people in the area.

Dispute of Beelzebul

The Pharisees saw Jesus as a devil's agent (Baalzebub) after witnessing Jesus' healing of the demon-possessed man who was blind and mute. Despite the transparent goodness of Jesus' work, they stubbornly denied the work of God's Spirit. Threader: The plague of flies that Moses performed prior to the Exodus was also regarded as the work of Baalzebub. King Ahaziah of Northern Israel also died after consulting Baalzebub as predicted by Elijah.

Jesus tells them that it was the work of God's spirit. "But if I cast out demons by the Spirit of God, then the kingdom of God has come upon you." (Matthew 12:28) "Therefore I say to you, any sin and blasphemy shall be forgiven people, but blasphemy against the Spirit shall not be forgiven." (Matthew 12:31) Here, Jesus points out what great sin it is to deny the Holy Spirit that testifies about Him.

"Truly, truly, I say to you, the Son can do nothing of Himself, unless it is something He sees the Father doing; for whatever the Father does, these things the Son also does in like manner." (John 5:19) This verse indicates clearly the works of the Trinity God. Jesus claims that whatever He does is due to the power of the Father. It also means that the kingdom of God will have been established on earth by the power of the Holy Spirit.

Then, the scribes and Pharisees wanted to see Jesus perform a miracle-a sign that would bear out his claims. "Then some of the scribes and Pharisees said to Him, 'Teacher, we want to see a sign from You.' But He answered and said to them, 'An evil and adulterous generation craves for a sign; and yet no sign will be given to it but the sign of Jonah the prophet.' (Matthew 12:38-39) He would not perform for their benefit since He had actually performed many miracles already. What does He mean by the sign of Jonah the prophet? As we know, Jonah had sunk into the water (hell) and rose from the dead after 4 days. This symbolizes the cross. The Son of God and the Messiah's glory are completely covered until His resurrection from the dead. This is the incontrovertible proof that His message is true - that He is who He claims to be. Mark spends one-third of the book portraying Jesus as the suffering Son of Man.

Jesus continues to tell a story of the unclean spirit, as a warning, and the grave danger unrepenting people will face unless they take a further step of making a whole-hearted commitment. He is also making a point that the bond amongst those who respond to God is stronger even than family ties.

Parables of God's Kingdom_Matthew 13

There were many miracles that Jesus performed, but what's more precious than all of them is His kingdom stories.

The Parable of the Seed and the Soil

Jesus teaches in a parable that "The kingdom of heaven may be compared to a man who sowed good seed in his field." (Matthew 13:24)

First, there is a seed sown beside a road. This illustrates a person has heard the Word of God, but the person has neither understanding nor interest in finding out more about it. So the evil one (Satan) comes and snatches it away.

Second, there is a seed sown on the rocky places. This shows a person who hears the Word and receives grace but since the root is not firm whatever has been received dries out. This is one of the major problems among many believers. It is somewhat like the Pharisees. They receive the Word as some kind of a report (news) but it fails to sink down into the heart. That is why the emphasis is given on that we must acknowledge with our lips and confess (prayer) once we receive the Word. Without this process, the Word cannot sustain itself as the Spirit within us. "For with the heart a person believes, resulting in righteousness, and with the mouth he confesses, resulting in salvation." (Romans 10:10) All the process of receiving the Word, learning & studying is to sow it in our heart, so that the Word becomes the Spirit within us.

We are filled with worldly thoughts and all kinds of sins before receiving the Word. The seed of the kingdom that penetrates through the stone marble-like hearts of ours is what we refer to as 'receiving Jesus.' The reason why this seed is unable to grow is because it is

Knowledge Search 19

Why did Jesus Speak in Parables?

The disciples came and said to Jesus, "Why do You speak to them in parables?" (Matthew 13:10) He responded, "To you it has been granted to know the mysteries of the kingdom of heaven, but to them it has not been granted." (Matthew 13:11) "Therefore I speak to them in parables because while seeing they do not see, and while hearing they do not hear, nor do they understand." (Matthew 13:13) Here, He is speaking of people who have heard the Word and yet become even more hardened that they block their eyes & ears and refuse to open their hearts. Jesus also explains that parables can reveal many layers of His teaching to those who are ready to listen to Him.

Not everyone is interested in God's kingdom. Sunlight can melt butter but can harden the ground at the same time. A worm wiggles to find a place to hide when sunlight penetrates into the darkness it's hiding in. A person interested in hearing the Word and alert to it will understand God's kingdom correctly and be filled with joy. "For whoever has, to him more shall be given and he will have abundance; but whoever does not have, even what he has shall be taken away from him." (Matthew 13:12)

suppressed by the energy of the flesh. The more we vacuum out this fleshly energy within us, the wider the place the seed will spread out to. This is the parable of the mustard seed.

In order to get rid of the fleshly energy, we must pray for the Word to remain in Spirit. Prayers of lament and prayers guided by the Holy Spirit can break through the rocky hearts. Then, the seed will expand its growth and we will be able to feel the expansion of His kingdom in our hearts.

Third, there is a seed sown among the thorns. The seed has been sown but worries of the world and deceitfulness of wealth choke it up, making it unfruitful. Among many thoughts that continuously seep into us, the main thing that preoccupies us with is our worries and greediness of wealth which is not easy to wash away even through reading the Word on a daily basis.

Let's say somebody was running a store and his attending morning services brought much prosperity to his store business. Due to the great success, the store expanded and eventually a building was purchased, but the owner found no time left for bible studies or early morning prayers. Instead, more worries compounded for him 'I better get my act together otherwise the building is in jeopardy.' All the earnest prayers and passion for God's love were gradually being replaced with worldly worries and financial matters.

Such people like this store owner is called reminiscing believers. God gives worldly blessings to young adolescents who serve Him. Even if they start to forget their faith in their youth as they grow older, their success in the world continues. Forgetting the love of Christ and His grace, they start to think success is due to their worthiness. No matter how one reminds them of the religion they fail to return. They boast about the 'old days' how they were led by the Holy Spirit in a passionate way that they would get on an early train to help new churches on Sundays. They recall their faith of the past assuming that they have done enough and comfort themselves without repenting their lack of faith in the present. Their life bears no fruit and withers away. There are many believers who fall into this category today.

In spite of their belief in Jesus people who are bound by their circumstances identify themselves with their names on their name cards. "I am currently an Assistant Manager at such and such place. I am a President of so and so company. I am an elder at such and such church." They start to worry after finding an identity and positions in various places. Afraid that they might get fired the next day and afraid that their position or wealth would no longer exist, they say, "I am going through an unbelievable state right now··· Collection problems, drastic cut in customers and issues in delivery, etc." while confessing that they believe in Jesus. These believers are bound by Satan's spirit as they pursue fleshly pleasures and as they start to think, "Is there anything exciting around? I'm bored."

No matter how much grace a person has received, if that person doesn't pray it is not easy to overcome hardships in life. But those who pray will be able to rise above their current difficult circumstances and reality. "Be anxious for nothing, but in everything by prayer and supplication with thanksgiving let your requests be made known to God. And the peace of God, which surpasses all comprehension, will guard your hearts and your minds in Christ Jesus." (Philippians 4:6-7) 'Surpassing all comprehension' here can be interpreted as overcoming all knowledge including worldly knowledge and whatever we see with our own eyes. Even though our current situation may seem devastating, the peace of God will guard our hearts and minds.

"Lord, it is unbearable to handle this tough situation. It is difficult for me to accept it. But Lord! Please give me Your peace so that I might be able to rise above the reality that I know with my five senses." Pray like this with the help of the Holy Spirit. Pray just for an hour in tongue. The Holy Spirit will start to touch your heart and you will surely overcome the present situation.

Fourth, there is a seed sown on the good soil. This good seed bears fruit and brings forth some hundredfold, some sixty and some thirty. The seed is the same but the problem is the soil. Conclusively, this parable teaches us to tame our hearts with the Word and prayer. It is necessary for believers to go through the process of allowing the seed to grow, so that the soil may be changed (change of our inner self) and we prepare ourselves to go to His Kingdom on this earth. The parable of the leaven falls under the same theme as well. (Matthew 13:33)

The Parable of the Weeds

This parable is concerned with the mixture of the good and the bad in this life. A wicked man came and sowed weeds in someone's field, and went away. The servants asked the master whether they should gather the weeds along with the wheat that had sprouted. The master replied, "Allow both to grow together until the harvest." (Matthew 13:30) The reason for this is "while you are gathering up the weeds, you may uproot the wheat with them." (Matthew 13:29)

After the judgment of the flood, God promised Noah a rainbow, which is a reminder that evil ones will not be judged until the 2nd coming of the Messiah on His final judgment day. (Genesis 9:12-13) At times we complain to God why the wicked people are left in this world, but what God is concerned with is that He might harm the righteous while judging the bad. God does not want to hurt us (suffering) and this is the love of God.

God does not discriminate and showers His rain equally to the good and the bad. But, what about us? "I like this person but not that person so I'm not going to give water to him." Making a judgment on what is good and bad ourselves is something that can be seen as eating from the tree of good and evil and something that God forbids us from doing.

The Parable of the Mustard Seed

The kingdom of God forms quietly and unnoticed. It is God who sows. God's kingdom is like a small seed that at times gets eaten by birds, gets stomped on, wilts away from the glaring sun, or gets tangled in the thorns. It may often appear dead but it has life inside that it can come alive, symbolizing eternity.

Once a mustard seed is sown, it grows into a seedling and eventually a big tree with many branches where birds come to nest. The tree grows and bears fruit but it can never eat its own fruit. The fruit is for others. This message of this parable is for us to expand the growth of God's kingdom in our hearts so that others may rest in Jesus' peace, love and grace. Those who have received salvation through Jesus (salvation of justification) must teal good soil (process of sanctification), so that the fruit of the kingdom of heaven will be born.

The Parable of the Hidden Treasure

"The kingdom of heaven is like a treasure hidden in the field, which a man found and hid again; and from joy over it he goes and sells all that he has and buys that field. Again, the kingdom of heaven is like a merchant seeking fine pearls, and upon finding one pearl of great value, he went and sold all that he had and bought it." (Matthew 13:44-46) The kingdom of heaven is like a businessman. A businessman would easily pay any amount for the most valuable pearl in the world. Such pearl is the kingdom of God. Those who have discovered the kingdom will forego any kind of pleasures in the world - bars, games, internet, golf, even the pursuit of wealth and success, reputation, status and flush them all down like a waste and confess, "There is only Lord Jesus."

What kind of person sells everything to purchase one treasure that was found? This person can be seen in believers who, after finding the truth and selling everything that they own, takes off to a mission field leaving everything behind. This parable also shows us the love of Christ who gave everything up for our sin and salvation.

Miracles of Jesus_Matthew 14-15

Food for Five Thousand

King Herod heard about the miraculous powers of Jesus and was afraid that John the Baptist had risen from the dead (whom he had beheaded). Upon hearing this, Jesus withdrew to a secluded place momentarily because it was not the time of crucifixion yet.

A huge crowd followed and gathered around Him. Jesus felt compassion for them and started to heal the sick. As they listened to the words of Jesus, day had turned to evening. While the supernatural power of Jesus was at work, a realistic problem of food surfaced before them. The disciples proposed that the crowd should take care of their own food for themselves but Jesus said, "They do not need to go away; you give them something to eat!"

"I am the bread of life; he who comes to Me will not hunger, and he who believes in Me will never thirst." (John 6:35) Jesus spent the whole day healing people who were suffering from illness. In spite of His own fatigue, Jesus had a merciful heart and decided to feed them. Threader: Just as God had fed the Israelites with manna in the wilderness after their exodus, Jesus healed them and fed loaves of bread in Chorazin. There were about 5,000 men so in actuality we are to assume that about 15,000 people were fed.

Frequently, people debate whether Jesus actually fed them or not, but He did. "But seek first His kingdom and His righteousness, and all these things will be added to you." (Matthew 6:33) As indicated in this verse, in order to reveal Father's love to the people who were seeking His kingdom, Jesus 'added all things.'

Threader: Jesus fed five thousand people with the five loaves and two fish offered by a young boy. (Matthew 14:19-21) If we also offer what we have to Jesus, like this young boy, whatever amount or how little it may be, to share with others, a miracle of feeding 1000s or 10,000s will happen. Just as the widow of Zarephath, offering our last resort to share with others will bring forth the same kind of blessings that she experienced. (1 Kings 17:14-16) Have no doubt what a small amount of offering can do because as long as the hand of the Lord is with it a remarkable number will be multiplied to save others. You will be full both spiritually and physically.

People marveled at the miracles of Jesus and said, "This is truly the Prophet who is to come into the world." (John 6:14) Anxiety would keep them awake throughout all night since they wanted Jesus to be made king right away. When Jesus commanded, "Lazarus, come forth" (John 11:43) and raised Lazarus who was dead for four days, just imagine how people must have reacted. But strangely, they were not as marveled as they were at the miracle of feeding the five thousand. Through all the miracles of Jesus, the people benefited the most from the feeding of the five thousand which clearly indicates that the bottom line for human interest lies on 'resolving of food issues.'

Worldly people are flattered when they receive recognition for their achievements. What happens next is 'falling from heaven.' (Isaiah 14:12) Jesus did not do what the crowd wanted Him to. "So Jesus, perceiving that they were intending to come and take Him by force to make Him king, withdrew again to the mountain by Himself alone." (John 6:15) Jesus headed towards the mountain to pray and knelt in front of the Father to and humbled himself. He returned all the highest glory and praise to God the Father by denying Himself. For Jesus, the glory of the Son of God was to be revealed not through the applause of people but through the suffering on the cross.

Walks on the Water

After the miracle of feeding the five thousand, the excited disciples left for Capernaum on a boat where they were struck by a strong wind. At that moment Jesus was walking on the water drawing near to the boat. Truly if this wasn't the Son of God, it is a totally impossible thing to do. Why did Jesus walk on the water? He wanted His disciples to know with assurance that He was the Messiah. Even though they saw all the supernatural acts being performed, Jesus had to prepare them for His death on the cross and resurrection. Ultimately He had to die on the cross and resurrect.

The disciples were trembling with fear in the midst of the strong wind and Jesus quieted the water by walking on it. Let us also be comforted that the love and grace of Jesus will quiet the waves of our turmoil of life. How wonderful it is to have such hope!

The Lord sends off His disciples (believers) out to the strong wind where there is nothing to lean or depend on. A person will sink in the water just like Peter if one looks at the surrounding circumstances (strong wind). One can overcome it when the focus is towards the Lord who has the authority to quiet the waters.

The Lord Looks at the Heart of Man_Matthew 15

After feeding the five thousand people, Jesus got on a boat and went to Capernaum. The land of Canaan was a sand-blowing desert where not only people's feet but their hands got dirtied as well, so it was a tradition for them to wash their hands before eating. Hearing a rumor that the members of Jesus were not washing their hands before eating, the Pharisees and scribes from Jerusalem started to dispute them. Jesus then spoke. "Do you not understand that everything that goes into the mouth passes into the stomach, and is eliminated? But the things that proceed out of the mouth come from the heart, and those defile the man." (Matthew 15:17-18)

Animals act on their basic instincts, no bad intentions can be found in them. In comparison, human hearts are very deceitful. Things that come out of human heart make things dirty. "The heart is more deceitful than all else and is desperately sick; who can understand it?" (Jeremiah 17:9) Words that come out of a person's mouth may be kind but the heart where the spirit comes out from may be evil and vice versa.

Threader: When Jesus came to Caesarea Philippi, He foretold His death to the disciples. "From that time Jesus began to show His disciples that He must go to Jerusalem and suffer many things from the elders and chief priests and scribes, and be killed, and be raised up on the third day." (Matthew 16:21) Then Peter blurted out, "God forbid it, Lord! This shall never happen to You." (Matthew 16:22) Jesus then said, "Get behind Me, Satan! You are a stumbling block to Me; for you are not setting your mind on God's interests, but man's." (Matthew 16:23) These may be harsh words, but we know that they are supposed to be coming from the Spirit, meaning 'repent.'

Whatever we say the most important thing is our motives. We have no ability to distinguish between what is good and bad. Therefore, we must accumulate the good. In order to build the good (God's spirit) (Matthew 12:35) in us, we must not only receive the Word in our heart and keep it in us but also pray at all times to drive out the energy of the flesh. Praying in tongues is a valuable tool to accumulate the good in us.

A Canaanite Woman's Faith

Jesus was primarily working in the vicinity of Lake Galilee but during the latter part of His ministry He extended further to the region of Sidon which is Lebanon today. There He met Canaanite (Syrophoenician) woman pleading and requesting His mercy on her demon-possessed daughter. But Jesus answered, "I was sent only to the lost sheep of the house of Israel." (Matthew 15:24) In other words, He refused to heal a foreigner. The woman humbled herself and pleaded even further. "But she came and began to bow down before Him, saying, "Lord, help me!" And He answered and said, "It is not good to take the children's bread and throw it to the dogs." (Matthew 15:25-27)

Threader: As Jesus' Sermon on the Mount (the Beatitudes), we have learned that it is also a murderous act if we display anger, mock or pass insults to others. Jesus came to save the so-called rejected people since He was fully acquainted with sufferings Himself. (Isaiah 53:3) But then, why did Jesus respond harshly and refused to help this woman? Knowing that the woman had such tenacious faith, He wanted to reveal her faith in front of everyone. His intention was to make her faith as a role model to others. When seeing such faith, Jesus would have not refused this request and healed her daughter's illness.

At the time, the people of Judah regarded the people (Canaanites) of the northern part of Samaria as dogs.

Threader: As mentioned in the Old Testament, the 10 tribes had scattered and Samaria which was the capital of Northern Israel was occupied by foreigners after the fall of Northern Israel. These people constantly interfered with the Jews upon their return from the exile while rebuilding the temple and the walls of Jerusalem. From that point on, Jews and Samarians became enemies.

"Yes, Lord; but even the dogs feed on the crumbs which fall from their masters' table." (Matthew 15:27) The woman did not deter her attitude towards Jesus who said condescending words to her. She was quick to seize the opportunity and she lowered herself (self denial) to the level of a dog that was awaiting its master's mercy. Jesus praised her as a woman of great faith.

The woman's attitude coincides with the teachings of Jesus at the Mount. "Whoever slaps you on your right cheek, turn the other to him also." (Matthew 5:39) Many people say, "How is that possible? If someone slaps my right cheek I feel like slapping back both cheeks of the person 10 times!" With this Canaanite woman, Jesus wanted to show to them that there was such a person who would do just the opposite.

Four Thousand Fed

Jesus had not eaten for four days as He was healing the sick and preaching at the same time. It appears that Jesus must have wept with compassion in His heart upon looking at the sight of a man walking away after being healed. They had waited without food for their turn to be healed. "And Jesus called His disciples to Him and said, 'I feel compassion for the people because they have remained with Me now three days and have nothing to eat; and I do not want to send them away hungry, for they might faint on the way.'" (Matthew 15:32) Jesus asked the disciples, "How many loaves do you have?" (Matthew 15:34) This time He fed four thousand people.

Jesus' loving mercy and compassionate heart towards the sick people made Him perform many more miracles. Let us rely on this love of Jesus and bless others as we offer what we have, even if it's something small, to the Lord. Then, we will experience a similar miracle of feeding the five thousand.

. . .

"Come to Me, all who are weary and heavy-laden, and I will give you rest. "Take My yoke upon you and learn from Me, for I am gentle and humble in heart, and YOU WILL FIND REST FOR YOUR SOULS. "For My yoke is easy and My burden is light."

Matthew 11:28-30

JESUS FORETELLS HIS SUFFERINGS

Matthew 16-20

The disciples were now excited of worldly glories assuming that they would have influential positions after witnessing the miracles of Jesus. But at this moment, Jesus proclaimed of His suffering on the cross to the disciples. This wasn't the king of glory or the Messiah they had in mind. Jesus was to receive eternal glory after His crucifixion and resurrection.

The Pharisees and Sadducees Demanding a Sign

If chapter 12 is the disputes of the Pharisees and the scribes (people mastered in the Law and tradition), chapter 16 is where the Pharisees and the Sadducees, the ultra conservatives, joined in putting Jesus to the test - demanding a sign once more. They probably were requesting a miracle seen in the days of Elijah where a fire was sent from heaven to destroy the Roman army. In other words, their hostility prevented them from recognizing the works of Jesus healing the demon-possessed, blind, crippled, and leprosy. These were exactly what Isaiah said (Isaiah 61:1-3)

Jesus warned that the evil and adulterous generation seeks after a sign except the sign of Jonah. And Jesus began to prepare his disciples for the suffering that lied ahead. He was trying to make them understand that salvation is received not through a sign but through the redemption of the cross.

After 3 years of ministry in the area of Galilee, Jesus moved to

Jerusalem and gave warnings of His sufferings to the disciples. He was preparing the hearts of His disciples.

Foretells the First Suffering and the Birth of Church_Matthew 16

After completing His work in Galilee, Jesus headed toward Jerusalem in order to carry the cross. When Jesus came into the town of Caesarea Philippi which was the first stopover above Lake Galilee, He gathered His disciples and asked, "Who do people say that the Son of Man is?" (Matthew 16:13) They replied, "Some say John the Baptist; and others, Elijah; but still others, Jeremiah, or one of the prophets." (Matthew 16:14)

At the time, people thought Jesus was John the Baptist who had come alive after King Herod had killed him or Elijah in Malachi. "Behold, I am going to send you Elijah the prophet before the coming of the great and terrible day of the Lord." (Malachi 4:5) Then Jesus asked, "Who do you say that I am?" (Matthew 16:15) "You are the Christ the Son of the living God." (Matthew 16:16) answered Simon Peter.

And Jesus said to him, "Blessed are you, Simon Barjona, because flesh and blood did not reveal this to you, but my Father who is in heaven. I also say to you that you are Peter, and upon this rock I will build My church; and the gates of Hades will not overpower it." (Matthew 16:17-18)

The remarkable secret of heaven - 'church' is being proclaimed for the first time to the disciples. Even though the actual birth of church occurred after the crucifixion, Jesus was promising in advance that the Church will be raised on Peter's head after he confessed his faith. Jesus gave an amazing blessing to Peter. "I will give you the keys of the kingdom of heaven; and whatever you bind on earth shall have been bound in heaven, and whatever you loose on earth shall have been loosed in heaven." (Matthew 16:19)

Upon dying on the cross, Jesus went down to hell, overpowered the authority of hell, resurrected and ascended to heaven to the throne next to God the Father. He personally went down to hell and snatched away the keys of hell from Satan and rose to heaven. Jesus had taken away the authority of Satan to trap people in hell and gave the keys of the kingdom of heaven to Peter (believers). (Matthew 16:19)

Now Peter was excited upon hearing Jesus' promise that the Church was to be raised on his foundation of faith (confession). By right he should be, because he was regarded as the best disciple and in addition, the key to the kingdom of heaven was promised to him. Threader: In Catholicism, Peter was raised as the first Pope and they say that no one can enter the kingdom of heaven without passing through him. If you visit Saint Peter's square in Rome, a statue of St. Peter holding the key to the kingdom of heaven in his hand can be seen.

As Peter's head was still boastful, Jesus foretold His death to the disciples for the first time in His ministry. He told them that He must go to Jerusalem, suffer many things and be killed and be raised up. Jesus repeated the same message in three different intervals. For the Church to be born on this earth, He must first suffer, die on the cross and resurrect. He clearly taught them that the glory of the first coming of Christ would be revealed after His suffering on the cross.

But unfortunately, His disciples did not understand the truth. They were engrossed with thoughts of their own; they would get high positions once Jesus became the kingship of David, the land of Judah would be independent from Rome, and the country would be headed for prosperity. The 12 disciples were just like the crowds of presidential campaign workers and they obviously had no idea what Jesus was saying.

Quickly Peter rebukes Jesus, "Short while ago, you were talking as if something great was going to happen. And now, what do you mean that you're going to die? Lord! That will never happen to you." The rock becomes an obstacle, and a God's spokesman turns into a devil's advocate. Jesus scolds him, “Get behind Me, Satan! You are a stumbling block to Me; for you are not setting your mind on God’s interests but man’s.” (Matthew 16:23) Historically, what kind of a person would go back and forth between heaven and hell in a matter of minutes?

What does ‘man’s interest’ mean? It relates to ‘self-interest.’ If Jesus dies, the fact that “I” left everything behind in order to follow Him, what will happen to ‘me’ were Peter’s thoughts. Satan prevents you from thinking about God’s work and makes you focus on yourself instead. Then, what is ‘God’s work?’ Contrary to the Jews wish that Jesus would become an enthroned king, He had to suffer tremendously and shed blood to His death. By the death of Jesus, the Church for all mankind’s salvation was to be born. Even though Jesus promised Peter the birth of the Church, it comes with a price. There must be bloodsheds and a death. This is what Jesus told them.

Then Jesus told the disciples that the most important condition of discipleship was self denial. (Matthew 16:24) Jesus taught them that the most valuable principle needed for becoming like Christ is not to seek self gain but to sacrifice for others.

Foretells the Second Suffering_Matthew 17

The Transfiguration

Not understanding the secret of the Church, the disciples were sad. So, in order to show them that He was the true Messiah, Jesus showed the glory of God in advance through transfiguration. Some biblical scholars refer to the place of transfiguration as Mt. Hermon (behind Lake Galilee) and some as Mt. Tabor (southwest of Lake Galilee), but it does not really matter which mountain it was.

It is written that when Jesus went up to the mountain, He transfigured before them; His face shone like the sun and His garments became white as light. This shows that our Lord covered His glorious appearance and made Himself appear as an ordinary man.

Then simultaneously, Moses and Elijah appeared and started talking with Him. Moses symbolizes the Law whereas Elijah represents all prophets - the Law - who prophesized the coming Messiah (entire Bible Old & New Testament). By showing Moses and Elijah beside Him, Jesus was hoping His disciples would realize that He was Christ and the Son of the living God. Moses participated in God's glory after death whereas Elijah had risen to heaven without facing death. Jesus was also trying to comfort and give joy to His disciples by revealing Moses and Elijah. (1 Thessalonians 4:13-14)

How did Peter react to this? "Lord, it is good for us to be here; if You wish, "I will make three tabernacles here, one for You, one for Moses and one for Elijah." (Matthew 17:4) What he meant was 'let's just build a picturesque house in this green pasture and live happily ever after - just the three of us.' This is just like Christians who limit their prayers only for himself and his family. Peter treated Jesus to be equal as Moses and Elijah. But Jesus is above all laws and prophets.

God overshadowed the scene with a cloud and said, "This is My beloved Son, with whom I am well-pleased; listen to Him!" (Matthew 17:5) In other words, He was telling them to listen carefully to what the Lord had to say. This was the same voice as the one heard when Jesus was being baptized in the Jordan River. Jesus was being revealed as the Son of God in front of their eyes and ears, as prophesized by the prophets. Peter confessed that he had heard the voice directly twice. (2 Peter 1:17-18) Jesus then revealed that the coming Elijah was John the Baptist and urged them not to tell anyone about the transfiguration until His resurrection.

After the incident of the transfiguration, previews of the 2nd suffering are spoken by Jesus in Galilee. This meant that the glorious transfiguration will only occur after the suffering of the cross. "The Son of Man is going to be delivered into the hands of men; and they will kill Him, and He will be raised on the third day." (Matthew 17:22-23) Upon hearing this, the disciples were deeply grieved. Since they had assumed Jesus would become Israel's king and recover the glory of King David, there was no point in following Him any longer now that they found out that He was going to die. In spite of hearing about the suffering of the cross twice, the disciples did not comprehend what it meant.

Healing of the Epileptic Man

After coming down from the mountain of transfiguration, the disciples were unsuccessful in curing an epileptic man, so they privately asked Jesus, "Why could we not drive it out?" (Matthew 17:19) Jesus replied, "Because of the littleness of your faith; for truly I say to you, if you have faith the size of a mustard seed, you will say to this mountain, 'Move from here to there,' and it will move; and nothing will be impossible to you." (Matthew 17:20) In another gospel, it is written as "This kind cannot come out by anything but prayer." (Mark 9:29) This means that a person with faith of a mustard seed is a person who prays, and without prayer the work of the Holy Spirit cannot take place. The "power from on high" comes upon us when we pray. (Luke 24:49)

Tribute to Temple Tax

When they came to Capernaum, the Pharisees disputed against Jesus that He was not paying proper temple taxes. Jesus then asked Peter from whom he thought the kings of the earth collected taxes from, their sons or from strangers, making him realize that their sons are exempt. To avoid any unnecessary misunderstanding from the Jews, Jesus told Peter to pay taxes with the shekel found in the mouth of the first fish caught. Just imagine how surprised Peter must have been upon witnessing the works of the Creator Jesus!

Become Like Children

Jesus spoke about His death twice but the disciples forgot all about it. Instead they were excited that in a matter of time the power of government would be shifted to their favor. They were also excited because they received the promise of the key to His kingdom, and on top of that, the fact that Jesus was the Messiah was assured through Moses and Elijah. The disciples interpreted 'kingdom' according to their knowledge and were only interested in the ranking in the kingdom. The other disciples probably have felt jealous towards Peter - after all, it appeared that Jesus was giving more attention to him. They threw a question at Jesus. "Who is the greatest in the kingdom of heaven?" (Matthew 18:1)

The greatest one is no one other than Jesus Himself. Rather than scolding them for asking such an obvious question, He compared Himself as a child and told a parable that only those who become like a child will enter the kingdom of heaven. "Whoever then humbles himself as this child, he is the greatest in the kingdom of heaven." (Matthew 18:4) We must admit that it is not easy to humble ourselves to the degree of being like a child in our lives. We find many arrogant people not only in the world but also in many churches. Especially for those with a high position or a special gift, it is easier to be proud.

I like to share an incident that happened years ago when I attended a seminar as a visiting lecturer at KOSTA (Korean Overseas Student Training Association) in Chicago. Apparently all attending lecturers wore black t-shirts and volunteer workers wore red t-shirts. The volunteer workers included not only students but also high ranking officials, ministers, and missionaries. A young volunteer approached me acting as if he knew me. He said that he was a professor and attended this event not as a lecturer but as a volunteer, so that he could serve the students. He appeared to be at least 10 years younger than myself but spoke to me in a very casual manner. He probably assumed that I was around his age. Frankly, when he spoke to me in that manner, I was a bit upset thinking that I was at least 10 years older than him. Few days later, God opened my heart during my early morning prayers. 'You deliver the Holy Spirit with your lips, but this man has humbled himself through the guidance of the Holy Spirit to serve the students and lecturers without getting enough sleep. Who is greater? Who is higher?' I wept bitterly and repented that day. Putting ourselves on a pedestal and delivering the Word of God is meaningless. It is more important to apply and act upon the Word in our daily lives. That young man could have easily attended as a professor and wore a black shirt but instead he humbled himself like a child to serve. This type of person will get the highest rank in God's kingdom.

Blessing of a Disabled Person

Jesus says if one hand causes you to sin, cut off that hand, and if a foot causes you to stumble, cut off that foot, and if an eye causes you to stumble, pluck it out, since it is better to enter His kingdom as a cripple than not make it at all. (Matthew 5:29-30) We sin so much with our healthy bodies! So those who are crippled or disabled must never be discouraged.

In my opinion one of the harsh words that are frequently expressed in Korea is "What bad luck it is if you see a blind person in the morning." Having heard this while growing up, I actually thought it was true. I was afraid in meeting anyone who was blind so I would take longer routes at times. But through the works of the Holy Spirit, I felt compassionate towards the blind and ended up offering half of my savings to the church for the blind. Actually I had a close call of losing my sight completely when I was young. During my councilor days at the embassy in Geneva, I experienced a sudden loss of control of my eyeballs which made it impossible for me to look at a person face-to-face. Needless to say, I was devastated to the point where I wanted to end my life right there and then. But with God's grace I was cured. I took His healing as a voice of God that when I have my sight I must return the glory to God completely.

Jesus also says that whoever causes brethrens to stumble through words or actions would be better to have a heavy millstone hung around their necks and be drowned in the sea. (Matthew 18:6) There are so many disabled people around us who deliver testimonies and sing praises to God while going through their hardships. On the other hand, a lot of us with healthy physical bodies, try to expand our flesh through playing golf or running on treadmills. As a result our own flesh becomes a stumbling block in lifting ourselves to the third heaven to meet God. "You know that when you were pagans, you were led astray to the mute idols, however you were led." (1 Corinthians 12:2) "It is the Spirit who gives life; the flesh profits nothing; the words that I have spoken to you are spirit and are life." (John 6:63) We must remember these words.

Even if we cut off our right hand after sinning, our left hand can still commit sin. What if we cut off our left hand as well? We can still sin with our heart. Sin is deeply rooted in us. It is only Jesus who can cut us off from sin entirely. With the help of the Holy Spirit, we must put our efforts in changing our inner self like Christ through the Word and prayer.

The Power of Disciplinary Prayer

Jesus says, "If your brother sins" then first settle it privately between one another. (Matthew 18:15) Then, every fact must be confirmed through two or three witnesses and if he refuses to listen even to the church, we need to cut off the relationship. The importance of unity between brothers is being emphasized here. Brotherly relationships must cover each other's flaws and it is written that God will answer prayers when two are gathered to pray; "Again I say to you, that if two of you agree on earth about anything that they may ask, it shall be done for them by My Father who is in heaven. For where two or three have gathered together in My name, I am there in their midst." (Matthew 18:19-20)

"How could one chase a thousand, and two put ten thousand to flight, unless their Rock had sold them, and the Lord had given them up?" (Deuteronomy 32:30) This is the same interpretation of the promise in the Old Testament that with the help of God, if one person can chase one thousand two can chase double the number. After talking about the Father's precious love in finding that one lost sheep out of ninety nine, Jesus tells of how the Father will be overjoyed in pouring His love on those who have gathered to pray.

The Importance of Forgiveness

Peter asks Jesus, "Lord, how often shall my brother sin against me and I forgive him? Up to seven times?" (Matthew 18:21) Remembering the blessings given by God to Cain, "Whoever kills Cain, vengeance will be taken on him sevenfold." (Genesis 4:15) Peter mentions 'seven times.' At the time, the rabbis taught them to forgive up to three times. To this, Jesus responds, "Not only seven times but up to seventy times seven." (Matthew 18:22) This means to forgive unconditionally. But let's face it. It is not easy to forgive a person in our daily lives.

There was an incident when I was in New Zealand. One young man was caught for a rape. He deeply repented on his action. His act was undeniably a sin that could not be washed away but I called the family of the victim asking them to forgive the man.

"I will never forgive the man who raped my daughter. Do not call me again." The parents refused coldly. The Minister of Justice of that country who was an unbeliever of God had pardoned the man but the family who claimed themselves as devout Christians refused to forgive. But I persisted and continued to persuade them.

"Deacon, you know the Lord's Prayer, don't you? If you believe in the Lord's Prayer, how can you say that? The prayer says "Please forgive our sins as we forgive other people's sin." How can you not forgive the one who have sinned against you and ask the Lord to forgive yours?

"I still cannot forgive."

I didn't give up and continued to call them and prayed for them. Finally, the parents' hearts were opened and they forgave the man.

Jesus then told a parable about a slave who was forgiven of 10,000 talent debt ($1 million) and yet treated cruelly a man who owed him only 100 denarii (approx. $1000). If we fail to forgive God will also do the same to you. (Matthew 18:35)

God does not work where there is hatred. What use is it if you have hatred in your heart and go to church, pray and memorize the Word? Our God does not accept that kind of service. God who is Light exists where there is true repentance, forgiveness and love.

Marriage, Divorce, Singlehood_Matthew 19:3-12

In order to carry the cross, Jesus departed from Galilee and came into the northern region of Judea past Jordan. He healed the large crowd who had followed Him there. Some Pharisees came to Jesus to test Him and threw a question whether it was lawful for a man to divorce his wife or not. "When a man takes a wife and marries her, and it happens that she finds no favor in his eyes because he has found some indecency in her, and he writes her a certificate of divorce and puts it in her hand sends her out from his house." (Deuteronomy 24:1) At the time there were some disagreements about divorce. Some allowed it only for unfaithfulness in marriage while others for anything that displeased the husband. Apparently, the majority favored the latter.

They asked Jesus this question expecting that this would put Him in the spot. Instead of directly answering their question, Jesus diverted their attention by going back to God's purpose for man and woman at the very beginning. Teaching them once a couple becomes one in flesh no man can separate that relationship. (Matthew 19:6) That is how God meant it to be. Jesus reminded them that Moses, dealing with situations that fell far short of the ideal, placed a restriction on divorce, and that adultery was the only legitimate reason.

In other words, indifferences, lack of love, abuse and insults cannot be reasons for a divorce. (1 Corinthians 7:10-14) These standards seem too high for many yet Jesus says anyone who is unable to control their physical needs may select marriage but those who are able may remain single. "For there are eunuchs who were born that way from their mother's womb; and there are eunuchs who were made by eunuchs by men; and there are also eunuchs who made themselves eunuchs for the sake of the kingdom of heaven. He who is able to accept this, let him accept it." (Matthew 19:12) With high divorce rates nowadays, one must listen and obey the Word of God. We can have a successful marriage if Jesus helps us to focus (love) on one person.

The Story of the Rich Young Man_Matthew 19

One rich young man came to Jesus and asked, "Teacher, what good thing shall I do that I may obtain eternal life?" (Matthew 19:16) And Jesus responded that he should keep the commandments. The young man asked, "Which ones?" And Jesus said, "You shall not commit murder; you shall not commit adultery; you shall not steal; you shall not bear false witness; honor your father and mother; and you shall love your neighbor as yourself." (Matthew 19:18-19) The young man claimed he had kept all the commandments and asked what was lacking. (Matthew 19:20) Jesus said to him, "If you wish to be complete, go and sell your possessions and give to the poor and you will have treasure in heaven; and come, follow Me." (Matthew 19:21)

Jesus pinpoints the root of this man's trouble. His commandment-keeping is not done wholeheartedly. His possessions mean too much to him and because of it he fails to love God and his neighbor without any reservation. It is better to possess nothing than to love things more than God.

The young man was unable to obey and went away grieving. Then

Jesus said to His disciples, "Truly I say to you, it is hard for a rich man to enter the kingdom of heaven. Again I say to you, it is easier for a camel to go through the eye of a needle than for a rich man to enter the kingdom of God." (Matthew 19:23-24) The disciples probably thought, "Of course, the rich are difficult to enter the kingdom of heaven. It is people like us who will enter His kingdom - the poor and those who left everything behind to follow Him." But this is not what Jesus meant. "And looking at them Jesus said, 'With people this is impossible, but with God all things are possible." (Matthew 19:26) Only God can make things possible. It is through the Holy Spirit that will make us choose the narrow gate. Just as the teachings of the Beatitudes it is a positive statement that "even the rich man who is difficult to enter the kingdom of heaven will enter His kingdom as long as God is with him."

In addition, Jesus also promised His disciples that there will be rewards for them at the 2nd coming of Christ. "Truly I say to you, that you who have followed Me, in the regeneration when the Son of Man will sit on His glorious throne, you also shall sit upon twelve thrones, judging the twelve tribes of Israel." (Matthew 19:28) The apostles have a special place in the new kingdom. To those who have served Him while putting all the worldly riches and honor behind, a blessing was promised that they would sit next to His throne and judge the world together. Apostle Paul focused on this reward and was able to endure the sufferings before his eyes.

Foretells the Third Suffering_Matthew 20

The First and the Last

Jesus talks in a parable of a laborer's pay structure in the vineyard and mentions the last would be first and the first last. An owner went out early in the morning to hire laborers to work in his vineyard and agreed on one day's wage of one denarius (a Roman silver coin). Then, the owner brought laborers at noon and again one hour before sunset which was when all the laborers were paid for the day's work. When it was time to pay their wages for the day, everyone was paid the same amount of denarius — whether they started working early in the morning or at noon or late afternoon. The laborers who were brought early in the morning complained to the owner claiming that it was unfair. The owner responded, saying;

"Friend, I am doing you no wrong; did you not agree with me for a denarius? Take what is yours and go, but I wish to give to this last man the same as to you. Is it not lawful for me to do what I wish with what is my own? Or is your eye envious because I am generous? So the last shall be first, and the first last." (Matthew 20:13-16)

Most likely, the workers who started late must have felt grateful towards the owner after receiving the same wages as the ones who started early in the morning and would probably work even harder the next day. We frequently see similar situations at churches where a newcomer (beginner) who has realized God's love is more passionate and earnest before God than a long time believer. Who would long for God's grace and receive blessing? The laborer who came in the early evening and received one denarius would certainly be overwhelmed and would work much harder. The formula of God's reward works totally differently from the world's methods.

Jesus Talks of the Cross

Jesus' third foretelling of His suffering continues. Finally, He talks of the cross. "Behold, we are going up to Jerusalem; and the Son of Man will be delivered to the chief priests and scribes, and they will condemn Him to death, and will hand Him over to the Gentiles to mock and scourge and crucify Him and on the third day He will be raised up." (Matthew 20:18-19)

Surprisingly enough, the disciple's reactions were totally indifferent when Jesus was referring to His death along with criminals on the cross and that He would rise on the third day. They had misunderstood what Jesus had spoken earlier. “Truly I say to you, that you who have followed Me, in the regeneration when the Son of Man will sit on His glorious throne, you also shall sit upon twelve thrones, judging the twelve tribes of Israel.” (Matthew 19:28) They interpreted that they would be given high ranking governmental positions, so when Jesus spoke of His death the third time, the disciples were still not ready to grasp the meaning of what he shared with them. Death on the cross had to take place prior to “the Son of Man to sit on His glorious throne” but the disciples were wrapped in wishful thoughts of becoming high ranking officers.

The mother of James and John (Zebedee) was quite wealthy at the time and had treated Jesus frequently. So she could have easily thought ‘since I have treated Him (Jesus) well my two sons most likely will be given reputable positions when He becomes king.’ In the midst of the disciples, she boldly made a request to Jesus, “Command that in Your kingdom these two sons of mine may sit one on Your right and one on Your left.” (Matthew 20:21) In today’s term, she was requesting that her two sons be given positions of a Prime Minister and a Secretary of State each. Jesus did not scold her but instead asked her a question.

“You do not know what you are asking. Are you able to drink the cup that I am about to drink?” (Matthew 20:22)

What does ‘My cup’ mean? Later Jesus prayed in the garden of Gethsemane, “My Father, if it is possible, let this cup pass from Me; yet not as I will but as You will.” (Matthew 26:39) The disciples responded that they could drink the cup since they did not know the meaning of it.

The promise of blessing was fulfilled by Jesus who came to fulfill the Law during His three year ministry. He came to release the suppressed; heal the sick; free those who were in captivity, and on top of that, He had to fulfill the promise of the curse. The promise of the Law of the Old Testament included both the blessing and the curse. (Deuteronomy 11) “Are you able to drink the cup that I am about to drink?" (Matthew 20:22) This question was raised because of the promise that those who have abandoned the Word of God, in the midst of their sins, had to be judged.

At that moment, James and John answered, "We are able." (Matthew 20:22) And in line with their response, James was the first of the loyal apostles to meet a violent death and to become the first martyr beheaded by King Herod. During the time of persecution, Apostle John's exile on Patmos (a small Greek island off the west coast of Turkey) probably entailed hard labor in the island's quarries and there he wrote the book of John, Revelation as well as 1, 2 & 3 John before his death as a martyr. Just as they had spoken of their commitment they drank the cup of suffering for the sake of God's kingdom.

Upon hearing the conversation, the ten disciples misunderstood and became indignant towards these two brothers assuming they had received some sort of a special treatment from Jesus. Then Jesus told them that the authority inside the church is not for the one to be served but for the one who serves others. (Matthew 20:26-28)

Bartimaeus the Blind

Two blind men appear in the last portion of Matthew 20. Bartimaeus who was both blind and a beggar cried out to Jesus who was passing by him to leave Jericho, "Lord, have mercy on us, Son of David." (Matthew 20:30) The crowd sternly told them to be quiet but as they were told they cried out even louder. (Matthew 20:31) This is exactly what strong will power and determination is all about. For the sake of receiving mercy and love of Jesus, and to meet the Messiah one must cry out, "Lord, have mercy on us. Help us." That's when Jesus asks "Do you wish to be healed?" Our Lord is compassionate and most pleased when we trust in Him and confess our need for Him. He then quickly responds to us.

Blessing of a Church and the Position of a Believer

Church is the Hope of the World

The hidden secret of heaven revealed through the blood of Christ and resurrection on this earth is the Church. The Church is the only alternative hope that can overcome the lewdness of the corrupted world.

Jesus is the head of the Church who sits on the right side of God in Spirit. As we know, God and Jesus are both invisible spirits. A church is formed with believers who are like clay pots filled with the Spirit of God and are gathered together to deliver the gospel to the unbelievers or to save the poor.

"In whom the whole building, being fitted together, is growing into a holy temple in the Lord." (Ephesians 2:21) It is the Church as the head of Christ who must approach unbelievers in the world and deliver the message of God. We humans have no choice but to stand with our feet on the ground as we go out to the world, and the Spirit of God must be within us in order for us to spread the good news. The Church has been formed by God so that the blessings of heaven and God's invisible love may be shared and spread throughout the world by the believers.

By shedding blood on the cross, Jesus resurrected and defeated death and snatched away the key of hell from Satan and brought it up to the throne of heaven. That is why we are told, "Do not fear those who kill the body but are unable to kill the soul; but rather fear Him who is able to destroy both soul and body in hell." (Matthew 10:28)

Jesus will hand over the key of His kingdom to the believers who confess like Peter, "You are the Christ, the Son of the living God." (Matthew 16:16) "I will give you the keys of the kingdom of heaven; and whatever you bind on earth shall have been bound in heaven, and whatever you loose on earth shall have been loosed in heaven." (Matthew 16:19) Keys used in the Roman period were types that you turn. Whatever gets tightened on earth will be the same in heaven and whatever is loosened on earth will have the same effect in heaven. What this means is that the key of the kingdom of heaven is in the hands of the believers who are on this earth.

This is what we have received - the freedom of choice. If one opens the door of heavenly blessings and amazing treasure on earth everything will be poured upon us; but if it is locked on earth we will not receive anything from heaven in return. The fact that we are holding the key to the kingdom of heaven is an amazing blessing. It is clearly revealed that it is strictly upon our own freedom of choice whether to live in heaven or in living hell.

A Sanctified Life is the Goal of a Believer

We as believers have been predestined by God before creation and when we are called upon is when we become true believers. The Bible tells us that when Jesus ascended into heaven He raised the saints and lifted them up to His side of the throne. "And raised us up with Him and seated us with Him in the heavenly places in Christ Jesus." (Ephesians 2:6) We are in Christ so we are together with Him sitting next to the throne.

Under any circumstances, believers should not focus on going to heaven after death since we have been called upon to do God's work together with Him on this earth. Jesus said "My Father is working until now and I Myself am working" (John 5:17) during His ministry. Just as the Father is working without sleep or rest, Jesus is also working endlessly next to the throne upon His resurrection.

The position of a believer is the seat next to the throne of God but since we are physically on earth it is easy to drift away to the visible & fleshly things of the world. On the other hand, believers who are connected with the Spirit are constantly being lifted up by the guidance of the Holy Spirit. By following Jesus, not only should we feel Him inside us but we must put our continuous efforts to become like Him as well. In order to achieve this, prayer is essential. Those who have knowledge but don't pray cannot go up next to the throne. The Word of God is not the goal. Our goal is to feel God's love and become one in Him through prayers.

One of the reasons why many problems surface in today's churches is due to their interest only in evangelism and the Word that has been drastically simplified. "If you believe in Jesus you will be saved and will go to heaven. Everything has been fulfilled on the cross by Jesus so there is nothing we need to do." This kind of teachings will only make believers of the flesh. Instead, what needs to happens is once people come to church they must be given a distinct goal of sanctification that through the love of Christ they may eventually change into blameless and holy believers. As believers of God, we must carry out respective positions or gifts and confirm the present address of the kingdom of heaven.

We have no way of knowing how many talents of gifts we have received — whether it's one, two or five talents. But we need to partake in the work for the kingdom of heaven as we carry out our duties as teachers, deacons, elderess or elders of the Church. Kingdom of heaven is not a boring place. 'As Father is working so am I.' Just as Jesus says, it is a place where you serve joyfully. "Why do I have to do this at the church? Why do I need to work in the first place and besides I'm tired." Complaints like these belong to people who do not know the kingdom of heaven.

Church is the Source of All Blessings

"A church is His body, the fullness of Him who fills all in all." (Ephesians 1:23) The church is the source of all blessings. All creation is filled by our resurrected Lord and the church is the place filled with the Holy Spirit of Jesus. Therefore, no one can receive blessings outside the Church. The head of the Church is Christ. The Church is more than just a gathering of people, for the true Church is formed with Christ as the head. Christ as the head of the Church connects each joint of every believer and forms a temple. It is Christ who raises the Church; it is Christ who leads the Church; and it is Christ who gives blessings to each believer in the Church.

Believers are like electric wires. As we know, electric wires becomes tainted, crooked and rot as they wear off. But as long as they are connected, electricity and energy stream across them. This concept applies to believers as well. All the joints of believers are connected and as long as they remain in the Church and the head of church, who is Christ, will gather the Church into one with the energy of love. The role of a believer is to remain as a connector. Do you think the wire needs to be smart? A church that has many intellectuals does not necessarily make it successful. Some churches boast, "We have many doctors and lawyers which makes us a top ranking church." They might also say, "We have a hard time connecting with people because we're too smart." This is a problem. Being smart and intellectual can easily become an obstacle for a church congregation to stay united.

Even if the connection isn't all that great, patience and endurance will bring Christ's love that will eventually flow through different members of congregation and bring warmth to our hearts. The only person that can bring electricity into the Church is God so for that reason we must stay put no matter how inconvenient it may be at times. Let us refrain from being attention seekers inside in our churches. We do not want to leave our church - the source of blessing just because someone looked down on us, didn't treat us right or whatever upset situation there might have been.

BE ALERT FOR THE 2nd COMING OF CHRIST; TEACHINGS ON THE MOUNT OF OLIVES

Matthew 21-25

This is the last portion of Jesus' ministry. On Monday Jesus cleansed the Temple. The following Tuesday in the Temple He urged the Pharisees, scribes and elders to repent and spoke in various parables indicating that the gospel would first be received by the Gentiles. Then He left the Temple and went up to the Mount of Olives and spoke for the last time of His 2nd coming in front of His disciples. He proclaimed that there is an end to this world and that day will be the glorious day of His second coming. This is the work of Jesus before His death that was to follow four days later.

THE LAST WEEK OF JESUS' LIFE

The Triumphal Entry into Jerusalem

_ Matthew 21, Monday

Enters Riding a Donkey

It was not a grand entrance on a coach or horse but a donkey when Jesus entered the city of Jerusalem. He was revealing that He came to serve and not to be served. Threader: The reason why judges or their children rode in donkeys during the period of the Judges in the Old Testament was to show that they were leaders but as for Jesus, in order to show His humility and meekness He rode a donkey not a war-horse.

As He enters the city, the crowds going ahead of Him were shouting, "Hosanna to the Son of David; Blessed is He who comes in the name of the Lord; Hosanna in the highest!" (Matthew 21:9) But unfortunately, they were awaiting a Messiah that will recover David's kingdom and free them from the Roman colony. Their expectation of the Messiah and the cross of Jesus were worlds apart. At this point, Jesus no longer hid Himself as the Messiah and accepted the shouts from the crowds. Jesus already knew of the schemes and plots of the Pharisees and the scribes to kill Him that He wasn't afraid of them at all. He was taking steps towards His distinct goal - the cross.

Temple Purge

Having entered the city in triumph as the Messiah, Jesus showed His authority in the temple through dramatically overturning the money-changers' tables, which was a major demonstration against the commerce and big business that had taken over God's house of prayer. (Matthew 21:12-13) At the time, people had to pay temple taxes before entering. During a festival season, the Jews traveled to the temple in Jerusalem from all over the place and had to convert their currencies at the money changers to pay the annual Temple taxes.

Prayer is for us to confess our love for God and is a channel to receive His love. We become one in Spirit and experience His presence when we pray. Also, a temple is a place where we are filled with His complete love through the help of the Holy Spirit. A church is where you communicate and pray to the invisible God. Even today, Jesus will also throw people out of a church who attend strictly to make money or to receive material blessings.

Jesus clearly treated the people harshly who conducted evil doings in the temple but at the same time He also healed the blind and lame; let children sing and run around in the temple. This was pleasing to Jesus yet the high priests and the scribes were deeply annoyed at

Jesus' actions.

The Curse of the Fig Tree

Early morning Jesus was returning to the city of Jerusalem and became hungry. Seeing a lone fig tree He thought He would find a fruit but found nothing except leaves. The fig which bears no fruit is good for nothing but destruction. Upon seeing this, Jesus curses "no longer shall there ever be any fruit." This curse is actually a warning to believers who are spiritually barren at the end time who appear sanctified just like the leaves on the fig tree. Jesus uses the incident for a lesson on the power of faith. All things we ask in prayer, in faith, we will receive.

Parable of Two Sons

Jesus' authority is questioned by the chief priests and elders which is natural in the light of what has happened. Jesus makes no direct answer but it is clear that He and John the Baptist derive their authority from the same source. Then, He speaks in a parable of the two sons - asking them which of the two did the will of his father.

The first son didn't go to work in the vineyard as he promised while the second son ended up going when he initially refused to do so. "Which of the two did the will of his father? They said, "The first." Jesus said to them, "Truly I say to you that the tax collectors and prostitutes will get into the kingdom of God before you." (Matthew 21:31) The second son represents the tax collectors and prostitutes who were mocked by the Jews and who rejected God in the beginning but later repented and followed Him. The first son represents the high priests and elders. Jesus was rebuking the religious leaders through this parable.

Parable of the Wicked Vine-Growers

The parable of the vine-growers aggravated the chief priests. One landowner planted a vineyard and rented it out to vine-growers and went on a journey. At harvest time the owner sent his servants to the vine-growers to collect his produce but the vine-growers killed them instead out of greed for profit. The owner had no choice but to send his son but even his son was killed.

"Afterward he sent his son to them, saying "They will respect my son." But when the vine-growers saw the son, they said among themselves, "This is the heir; come, let us kill him and seize his inheritance." They took him and threw him out of the vineyard and killed him. Therefore the owner of the vineyard comes, what will he do to those vine-growers?" (Matthew 21:37-40)

People answered, "He will bring those wretches to a wretched end, and will rent out the vineyard to other vine-growers who will pay him the proceeds at the proper season." (Matthew 21:41)

Who are these vine-growers? They are the Pharisees, high priests and scribes. Jesus was challenging them and igniting Himself to be crucified. The men to whom God has entrusted spiritual leadership have abused the prophets and were about to kill Him. Even though they rejected the Messiah Jesus revealed that the stone which the builders rejected had become the chief corner stone. (Psalms 118:22)

We believers must choose either to humbly surrender our inner self to God or to receive judgment at the end time. The choice is ours. "And he who falls on this stone will be broken to pieces; but on whomever it fails, it will scatter him like dust." (Matthew 21:44)

Recently some liberalists that Jesus died on the cross out of bad luck. But clearly, out of obedience to the plan of God the Father, Jesus moved His steps one by one towards His distinct goal - the cross. There was a clear purpose in His redemptive offering to save all mankind on Mt. Moriah (Jerusalem) where Abraham had offered his only son Isaac.

Parable of the Wedding Feast

There was a king who prepared a wedding feast and invited guests. The first invitations went out. No one came even after the second invitations were sent out. Everyone had excuses and refused to come. "Sorry I'm busy and cannot attend. I have a business to attend to." "I cannot attend because I'm totally occupied with my farming."

Not only did they refuse the invitation but they also killed the king's servants who were delivering the message. The enraged king sent out his army and destroyed the murderers. He then commanded his servants to bring anyone from the streets and marketplaces and whoever they came across. (Third invitation) The day will come when God no longer invites those who repeatedly refuse Him. The invitation will go to others. This parable indicates that the gospel will go to the Gentiles instead since the people of Israel had rejected it.

Among the invitees there was "a man who was not dressed in wedding clothes." (Matthew 22:11) Obviously the man had no time to prepare himself since everyone was invited randomly from the streets. "But the king said to the servants, 'Bind him hand and foot, and throw him into the outer darkness; in that place there will be weeping and gnashing of teeth.' (Matthew 22:13) Isn't it strange to pass such a fearful judgment when in fact everyone was randomly invited?

During those days, it was Jewish customs where the host prepared wedding garments for the attending guests. "I will rejoice greatly in the Lord, my soul will exult in my God; For He has clothed me with garments of salvation, He has wrapped me with a robe of righteous, as a bridegroom decks himself with a garland, and as a bride adorns herself with her jewels." (Isaiah 61:10)

It meant that this man had not worn the wedding garment that was already prepared by the owner. They were given white garments (clothes of salvation) by the blood of Jesus and yet they were not thankful to the owner. This is a warning to believers. Those who wear their own clothes (self righteousness), instead of wearing the garment the owner had prepared, will be thrown out of the wedding feast. This man is like those who do not have the right attitude in sharing the joy of God and yet go to church but have no interest in the Word and never pray. Those who come must come on God's terms. "For I testify about them that they have a zeal for God, but not in accordance with knowledge. For not knowing about God's righteousness and seeking to establish their own, they did not subject themselves to the righteousness of God." (Romans 10:2-3) We must remember that many are invited to the wedding feast but few are chosen (those who will be called by name at the sound of the trumpet). (Matthew 22:14)

Tribute to Caesar

The Pharisees were plotting how they might trap Jesus so they asked, 'Do we need to pay taxes to Caesar?' And Jesus replied, "Render to Caesar the things that are Caesar's; and to God the things that are God's." (Matthew 22:21) Although all creation in the world belongs to God, here Jesus is telling us to obey and follow the rules of the present government in power. It also means that all human beings are created in the image of God so we must give ourselves to God.

The Kingdom of Heaven is Different from Earth

According to the law at the time a brother was to marry his brother's wife if his brother deceased since the wife of the deceased was forbidden to remarry outside the family. And if there was a child born between them, the name of his dead brother was to be assumed. Whatever was accumulated over the years was regarded as the dead brother's inheritance as well. (Deuteronomy 25:5-10) Sadducees are known to be secularist people and non-believers in resurrection. Since Jesus was emphasizing on resurrection they raised a question. "Now there were seven brothers with us; and the first married and died, and having no children left his wife to his brother; so also the second, and the third, down to the seventh. Last of all, the woman died. In the resurrection, therefore, whose wife of the seven will she be? For they all had married her." (Matthew 22:25-28)

Jesus provided them with an unexpected answer. "In the resurrection they neither marry nor are given in marriage, but are like angels in heaven." (Matthew 22:30)

What an amazing answer! It means that there are no family relationships in heaven. There are no children or parents because everyone is the children of Jesus; children of God. Resurrection is not an extension of this world but an opening of the eternal world which we cannot possibly fathom.

Then, why did God give us family on this earth? A family is our fundamental community where we deny self, sacrifice, and love according to the image of God and His loving Spirit. If God did not give us family the world could have fallen into an enormous confusion. Self serving and self pursuit would have destroyed mankind. Born in flesh, we have the tendency of focusing on 'self' and if left alone we would have become like animals-fighting. If there was no loving relationship the 'self' cannot be denied. But in God's kingdom such family is not necessary.

I was disappointed when I heard a statement from an elderess who had become a widow. Her only wish was to meet her husband in His kingdom who died 10 years ago. In God's kingdom there is no such family as on this earth and everyone becomes brothers and sisters in Christ-who is love itself. So, do not be too saddened because of your deceased loved ones.

The Agonizing Teachings of Jesus_ Matthew 22-23

The Greatest Commandment

This time a Pharisees who happened to be a lawyer asked a question realizing that the Sadducees were silenced. "Teacher, which is the great commandment in the Law?" (Matthew 22:36) Jesus responded, "You shall love the Lord your God with all your heart, soul and mind. This is the great and foremost commandment. The second is like it, 'You shall love your neighbor as yourself.' On these two commandments depend the whole Law and the Prophets." (Matthew 22:37-40)

We cannot love our neighbor without the love of God. It is only when we love God first that we will be able to love others. Those who love God must reveal their neighborly love; but for instance if one loves a neighbor strictly out of their own then that person is actually raising the so-called 'self-righteousness.'

Who is Christ?

Jesus asked the Pharisees who they thought Christ was and their response was "The son of David." He then pointed out that it was not possible for Christ to be the descendant of David. (Matthew 22:42-45) Ever since that day no one dared to question Jesus anymore. Our Lord is also asking us today, "Who do you think Christ is?"

The Pharisees Cursed_Matthew 23

Jesus launches scathing attack on the religious leaders - the Pharisees and curses them.

"You serpents, you brood of vipers, how will you escape the sentence of hell?" (Matthew 23:33)

Many of us are startled by this part when we read the Bible. The Pharisees are known to be religious and law abiding people. They actually memorized the entire Old Testament and taught people on a daily basis. They were knowledgeable rabbis and bible teachers in today's term. Threader: The opposing party to liberalism during the Hasmon Dynasty was the Pharisees.

But Jesus called them "Brood of vipers; Hypocrites! You are like whitewashed tombs." By 'whitewashed tombs' He meant that they appeared righteous outwardly but inwardly they were full of hypocrisy and lawlessness. Actually this does not apply only to the

Pharisees but to believers today. There are many who have tremendous knowledge of the Bible and teach people and yet they personally fail to live according to what they have taught.

Jesus makes specific charges against the Pharisees, each introduced with the same words: 'Woe to you~' (a regretful 'alas' not a pronouncement of doom). "Woe to you, scribes and Pharisees, hypocrites, because you shut off the kingdom of heaven from people; for you do not enter in yourselves, nor do you allow those who are entering to go in." (Matthew 23:13) Those who teach the Word so well but fail to live what they teach, not only prevent themselves but others from entering the kingdom of heaven as well. That is why Jesus has urged us to be alert in prayer so that we may live according to His Word.

Lament over Jerusalem

"Jerusalem, Jerusalem, who kills the prophets and stones those who are sent to her! How often I wanted to gather your children together, the way a hen gathers her chicks under her wings, and you were unwilling. Behold, your house is being left to you desolate!" (Matthew 23:37-38)

Jesus predicted the destruction of the city and wept. (Luke 19:41) The reason why Jesus scolded the Jews harshly was not because He disliked them but because He wanted to prevent judgment against them. Our Lord is merciful and sheds tears for us even when we sin.

TEACHINGS ON THE MOUNT OF OLIVES_ Matthew 24-25

The Destruction of Jerusalem and the 2nd Coming_Matthew 24

Before carrying the cross, Jesus taught His disciples on Mt. Olives near Jerusalem - which is referred to as the 'Teachings of Mt. Olives.' The two major sermons given by Jesus are the Beatitudes and the teachings of Mt. Olives. And the content of these two sermons are totally different. The subject in the teaching of Mt. Olives are the end times and Jesus' 2nd Coming.

The End Times_the 2nd Coming of Christ

The disciples' admiration for the great Temple buildings lead to Jesus' astonishing prediction of its utter destruction. "Do you not see all these things? Truly I say to you, not one stone here will be left upon another, which will not be torn down." (Matthew 24:2)

Further questions about the end times were followed by the disciples. Jesus answered saying when the physical world ends it will be totally unexpected (Matthew 24:9) and that would be the time of His return. It will be a glorious and joyful day for those elected believers of salvation (Matthew 24:31) but for unbelievers it will be a day of judgment filled with regret and outcries. (Matthew 24:30)

Jesus reassured His disciples with forthcoming glory and gave them hope since He knew that they would be shocked and discouraged upon His death which was quickly approaching. "But when the Son of Man comes in His glory, and all the angels with Him, then He will sit on His glorious throne." (Matthew 25:31) "For just as the lightning comes from the east and flashes even to the west, so will the coming of the Son of Man be." (Matthew 24:27) "Then they will see the Son of Man coming in a cloud with power and great glory." (Luke 21:27) "For whoever is ashamed of Me and My words in this adulterous and sinful generation, the Son of Man will also be ashamed of him when He comes in the glory of His Father with the holy angels." (Mark 8:38) The time of His 2nd coming was not clear because He spoke of His return and the fall of Jerusalem (A.D. 70) simultaneously. He probably did so on purpose because He didn't want them to be too alarmed by the upcoming drastic events. "But woe to those who are pregnant and to those who are nursing babies in those days! But pray that your flight will not be in the winter or on a Sabbath." (Matthew 24:19-20)

There will be many wars and natural disasters, persecutions, anti-Christs, and false Messiahs at end time. But let us not be misled because these are not the signs of the end times but only a warning that end times are approaching. "You will be hearing of wars and rumors of wars. See that you are not frightened, for those things must take place, but that is not yet the end." (Matthew 24:6) Even today, there are many signs throughout the world but as for the timing of 'that day'-the great day of judgment - God alone knows. "But of that day and hour no one knows, not even the angels of heaven, nor the Son, but the Father alone." (Matthew 24:36) In spite of Jesus' distinctively spoken words, there are still many ludicrous people who are trying to calculate the end times. "The 2nd coming of Christ is in such and such year and such month and day." For sure there are all such nonsense and useless doings.

No one knows the exact date of the 2nd coming of Christ but through the parable of the fig tree, Jesus says, one can assume when it approaches through the signs. "Now learn the parable from the fig tree: when its branch has already become tender and puts forth its leaves, you know that summer is near." (Matthew 24:32) Researchers of the book of Revelation apply the parable of the fig tree as Israel's disappearance for 2,000 years, its recovery as an independent country in 1949 and interpret that Jesus' return is near. But the detailed signs of His return must be sought out in the verse, "This gospel of the kingdom shall be preached in the whole world as a testimony to all the nations, and then end will come." (Matthew 24:14) When the number of the non-evangelized tribes (countries) decreases it means that the 2nd coming of Christ is approaching and when the gospel reaches to the ends of the earth it will be the end of times.

This also means that if we believers are alert in prayer and at the forefront in evangelism to all ends of the world we could actually accelerate the 2nd coming of Christ. In a way, God is waiting for His children to hasten His coming by being alert and ready at all times.

Threader: The conclusion of the New Testament which is the book of Revelation, Apostle John said, "He who testifies to these things says, "Yes, I am coming quickly." Amen. Come, Lord Jesus." (Revelation 22:20) As believers, we must keep the Lord's command to spread the gospel to the ends of the earth so that our Lord may come quickly.

Therefore Be Alert_Matthew 24:40-44

Jesus talks about what will happen upon His second coming. Of the two women who were grinding at the mill one will be taken and one will be left behind. Obviously, the story relates to believers and not to unbelievers since it is natural for unbelievers to be left behind.

In spite of their belief in Jesus, those who are taken up are focused in Spirit and the ones left behind are focused in flesh. Earlier we had mentioned about a man who was invited to the wedding feast but did not wear proper wedding garment. Churchgoers who attend services but have no interest in prayer or the Word to fully sanctify themselves and who are caught up in worldly desires are referred to as people in the flesh. All the chasing after the glory of the world leaves them with no time for bible studies or daybreak prayers. Not only does Jesus cast those people out but also says, "In that place there will be weeping and gnashing of teeth." (Matthew 24:51) Those who are of the flesh will surely not be taken up.

Then, what will happen to the ones in the flesh? Will they be sent to hell? In John, it clearly states that they will not go to hell. "Truly truly I say to you, he who hears My word, and believes Him who sent Me, has eternal life and does not come into judgment, but has passed out of death into life." (John 5:24) But scholars who study the book of Revelation have a different view. They claim that those who are in the flesh will not be judged upon the 1st coming of Christ but instead will go through 7 years of serious tribulation and will be saved at the time of the coming of Christ on earth. This could raise a theological issue for discussion but as an ordinary churchgoer I support this view. I believe that there will be a distinct different treatment between a spiritual and a fleshly believer. Our Lord says, “Therefore be on the alert for you do not know which day your Lord is coming... For this reason you must be ready; for the Son of Man is coming at an hour when you do think He will.” (Matthew 24:42-44)

The Life of a Believer Who Prepares the 2nd Coming_Matthew 24:45-25:46

Since Jesus’ return will be unexpected, He teaches His followers how they must be alert and lead their lives in preparation through the four parables.

Parable of a Faithful and Sensible Servant_Matthew 24:45-50

“Who then is the faithful and sensible slave whom his master put in charge of his household to give them their food at the proper time? Blessed is that slave whom his master finds so doing when he comes. Truly I say to you that he will put him in charge of all his possessions.” (Matthew 24:45-47)

Followers of Jesus must receive the Word of God diligently and meditate on it and share it with people who the master has left us with. This does not only apply to pastors but also to Sunday school teachers, group leaders and all church members. All church members must either learn or teach in order to receive God’s acknowledgement as a faithful and sensible servant.

Parable of Ten Virgins_Matthew 25:1-13

In Israel, there is a tradition that after one year from the engagement date the husband-to-be picks up his bride at night. So, prudent virgins who had oil in their lamps were able to greet their bridegrooms while those who did not, were not able to join the wedding feast. Jesus tells the story of the wise and foolish girls and makes the point that one day time will run out.

A similar situation will arise when we receive Jesus (the Holy Spirit). In the beginning, the lamp will be lit since there is a bit of oil in it but since not knowing when the bridegroom will come, the lamp cannot sustain its light with the oil first received. Oil must continuously be poured in. Since the oil comes from the Holy Spirit, it is an individual thing and cannot be borrowed from someone else. One must receive it directly from the Holy Spirit. Anointment of the oil means the presence of the Holy Spirit and the work of the Holy Spirit. The anointing of the Holy Spirit becomes a calling, and this calling can be seen its gifts and positions.

Then, what can we do to receive the anointing of the Holy Spirit? The Holy Spirit is poured upon a person who prays. "But keep on the alert at all times, praying that you may have strength to escape all these things that are about to take place, and to stand before the Son of Man." (Luke 21:36) There are many people in the church who are quite gutsy. In front of people, they pray fervently but neglect to have a private relationship with God. They are passionate in attending bible classes but do not pray. It is because prayer is difficult.

Jesus clearly indicated that oil cannot be borrowed from someone else. The foolish virgins who did not prepare oil were not able to enter the wedding feast and also experienced "weeping and gnashing of teeth." (Matthew 25:30) This is a fearful warning that spiritual believers will be differentiated from fleshly believers. Jesus' followers must always be ready and alert.

Parable of the Talents_Matthew 25:14-30

The master gave his servants one, two, and five talents. Each man was entrusted with a capital sum in line with his business ability and was expected to use it sufficiently. Finally the day arrived for the master to settle accounts with them. He extended praises to the one who had profited and scolded who was not. As believers of God, we have all received talents. What is talent? Majority of us think of it as a special gift from God - such as a person who is gifted in delivering the Word of God, a person who can heal, or a person who can cast out evil spirits. We know there are 21 different types of gifts of the Holy Spirit. Through various gifts, God wants us to serve in all different areas of the Church and neighbors. We must utilize all the talents received from God whether it is only one talent or five talents.

Occasionally there are some churchgoers who only attend church services and then disappear. This type of people are the same as the servant who hid the one talent that he had received. God scolds this type of person who knowingly refuses to serve, work or do anything in the church. We must constantly reflect on ourselves and on what we have done for Jesus with all the bible knowledge, time, money and abilities. Breaking the Ten Commandments is a sin but not utilizing talents received from God is also a great sin. Jesus sees this as being wicked and lazy. "You wicked, lazy slave··· in that place there will be weeping and gnashing of teeth." (Matthew 25:26-30) Jesus wants us to use our talents so that we may bear fruit. Those who diligently utilize their received talents will be rewarded heftily and receive praise in God's kingdom.

Separation of the Sheep and the Goats_Matthew 25:31-46

At judgment, Jesus will separate the sheep and the goats and put the sheep on the right and the goats on the left. To the sheep on the right, He says, "Come, you who are blessed of My Father, inherit the kingdom prepared for you from the foundation of the world.. Then the righteous will answer Him, 'Lord, when did we see You hungry, and feed You or thirsty, and give You something to drink?'" (Matthew 25:34-37) The believers on the right claim that they have not done anything for the Lord. How does Jesus respond to them? "Truly I say to you, to the extent that you did it to one of these brothers of Mine, event the least of them, you did it to Me." (Matthew 25:40)

Who are the least of all? Is it our relatives, children, friend or acquaintances? No. If any of our family members or anyone we know were left stranded in the street we would immediately pick them up in our car. We would ignorantly pass by without stopping if we didn't know the person. Someone who volunteers to help even though the person has no relation is the one who has shown the love of God.

The goats on the left failed to do what they should have done. However, they think they have done quite well in front of God. They loved God, studied the Bible and even prayed. By right, a person who prays and knows the Word is able to share their love to the least people but this is not all true to many others. "For I was hungry and you gave Me nothing to eat; I was thirsty and you gave Me nothing to drink; I was a stranger, naked and you did not clothe Me; sick and in prison and you did not visit Me." (Matthew 25:42-43)

To be able to have compassion and show love to total strangers is only possible with the heart of Jesus. It is imperative to share our love of Christ with our neighbors who are less fortunate than ourselves. Jesus clearly said during His teachings on the Mount of Olives: "Believers, listen carefully. Know that by the way you treat and comfort strangers who are in need it is as if you are giving the same treatment towards Me."

The teachings on the Mount of Olives carry the same message as the sermon of the Beatitudes in that they both talk about how not only is it a sin when we break the commandments of the Old Testament but also the true sin is when we show no interest (no interest in the 2nd coming of Christ, the Holy Spirit that prepares us, prayer or the Word of God, acknowledge the gift received, and no interest in our neighbors) in God's kingdom and His people. How people use what is given them in this life will determine their future destiny. We are being told that His 2nd coming is approaching quickly so therefore we must be alert and prepare at all times.

The Four Progressive Steps into Maturity of Faith

With an emphasis on being alert and preparedness, the four parables of the "faithful and sensible servant" 'ten virgins' 'talents' and 'separation of the goat and sheep' explain the progressive steps for the maturing of our faith.

Jesus has first called us and we have received salvation through our belief in the gospel. This level is what we refer to as the 'level of justification.' At this level, if we truly receive Jesus the Lord gives us the heart to desire for the Word. So we study the Word and try to get to know God by getting deeper into the Word. Prayer is not easy in the beginning but as we get closer to the Word, God gives us the heart to pray and gradually allows us to pray more frequently through the knowledge of the Word.

The Holy Spirit is poured upon those who are diligent and passionate in prayer. The spiritual gifts of the Holy Spirit (talents) are also given. In churches, various positions are given for instance, deacons, elders or eldress, etc. We must realize that positions at churches or special gifts are given for us to serve others and not for own benefit. In that regard, people who have been given such roles or gifts go through training by sharing and serving others. Realistically, we are all used to the worldly concepts of give and take so it is not easy for us to serve others. But then again, we must realize that special gifts or positions have been given to us absolutely free without any efforts on our part. Don't be deceived by the idea that we are a great Christian since we are simply sharing with others what we received for free.

In the past, I thought of myself as someone special since I had received the gift of delivering and teaching the Word of God. But now I think nothing of it since I realized that it is part of the process of growing. What level do we have to arrive? It is the level of being filled with the Holy Spirit. People at this level have the aroma of Jesus. This is what the fruit of the Holy Spirit is all about. And this is what we need to achieve by bearing fruit of the Holy Spirit. "The fruit of the Spirit is love, joy, peace, patience, kindness, goodness, faithfulness, gentleness, self-control; against such things there is no law." (Galatians 5:22-23) We must become like Jesus by bearing the fruit of the Holy Spirit.

Special gifts are given free but the fruit cannot bear itself. We have to grow in order to bear fruit. Those who deliver the Word of God, heal and do works of power are referred to as servants of power but these are only temporary effects. Though they may believe Jesus, deliver powerful messages, pray fervently and carry out special gifts of the Holy Spirit, it is of no use if they fail to bear fruit.

There was a minister who grew up in a den of beggars since he had lost his parents when young. Apparently the leader of the pack asked him to steal but he said that he would beg and bring something back rather than to steal. He was beaten up badly and thrown out in the street. He was in such a bad condition that he couldn't stand up and laid on the cold asphalt road. The next morning, he could hear the morning footsteps of people going to work since it was near a train station. In the midst of all the thousands of people that passed by, surely there must have been a deacon who fervently prayed at church or even a evangelical speaker who heals people that must have seen him but nobody bothered to look at him or offered help. It was a sad reality to think that people who were believers of Jesus had walked by without offering any help. Later when he finally woke up it was a group of beggar kids near the station who applauded.

There is a difference between love that is shown to others (symbolized as sheep) and powerful gifts a person might have in delivering the Word, praying or singing passionate praises. The level of the fullness of the Holy Spirit appears in a person through his/her character through the mind of Jesus (thought), the merciful heart of Jesus (emotion), the actions of Jesus (righteous) and the image of Jesus. This is the level to which we must all grow to.

In order to bear fruit, a willful commitment and training are necessary to become like Jesus. Of course it is God who helps us to bear fruit but as a believer we must choose Jesus continuously so that the Holy Spirit can help us to achieve it.

With the Word (faithful servant) and prayer (parable of the ten virgins) a gift (parable of the talents) is given but the road lies ahead for us is to bear fruit (neighborly love, parable of the sheep and goat). Never be boastful thinking, "I'm an elder," "I'm a preacher/deliverer," "I'm a healer" but instead strive to become like Jesus on a daily basis by denying the 'self' and seeking the help of the Lord.

The Biggest Problem Today For Christians

The gospel is about experience. The presence of God must be experienced in our hearts through the gospel but modern Christianity has somewhat replaced this with ceremonies and doctrines. Some Protestants think, "Maybe I should go to a Catholic church?" It is because Catholics have ceremonies that may appear 'holy.' Majority of people's heart have the longing desire to experience the presence of God. But since God is Spirit and invisible they seek for outward ceremonies. In order to satisfy the needs to experience the presence of God, many churches have placed ceremonies that appear holy.

Faith is our life and changes in life. The word 'faith' is only mentioned a couple of times in the Old Testament but is used frequently all throughout the New Testament. What is the reason for it? It is because the life story of Abraham and the people who met God and how their lives changed are all recorded in the Old Testament. The way in which their lives has changed after meeting God are shown through their stories and they tell us about their faith. Jacob who met God in Bethel, Joseph and David who trusted in God after their sufferings are clear examples of how their lives were changed. Faith was shown through their lives.

Today Christianity has put aside the necessity to change how we live our lives by focusing on faith and doctrines. Many churches and denominations are putting efforts in the systemization of truth instead of changes in lifestyle. There are many bible studies and programs in all churches. There are even people who say, "The gospel seems so easy that it is hard to believe." But actually, how easy it is to believe in Jesus wholeheartedly? Many churches are obsessed with the Word but fail to deny the 'self' within us in our daily lives. One may proclaim the Word of God powerfully but fail to meet the Master of the Word inwardly. Many understand God intellectually, which is what the Pharisees were.

The Pharisees in the Bible were not scolded by Jesus — "you brood of vipers; hypocrites" because they were evil or strange in their actions. They were stuck in the Word and had interests only in the doctrines and ceremonies and that is why Jesus cursed them. "But woe to you, scribes and Pharisees, hypocrites, because you shut off the kingdom of heaven from people; for you do not enter in yourselves, nor do you allow those who are entering to go in." (Matthew 23:13)

Isn't this quite shocking? Without the help of the Holy Spirit, one cannot experience God who is the Master of the Word. But many churches or denominations do not even utter or mention the Holy Spirit. They claim they have been hurt by the wrongful movement of the Holy Spirit in the past. People who think like this are voluntarily admitting themselves as the Pharisees. Without talking about the Holy Spirit, how is it possible to know the blood of Christ can actually forgive our sins? How did the blood of Christ save our sins? Our Christ who shed His blood has come into our heart through the Holy Spirit and with His presence our sins are forgiven. The comfort of the Holy Spirit captures the heart giving peace to our soul that cannot be expressed in words. This is the process in which the blood of Jesus forgives our sin.

JESUS WHO CONQUERED DEATH

The Four Gospels

We have looked at the life and ministry of Jesus focusing on the book of Matthew up until now. From this point on, the story of the cross will be talked about compiling different accounts from the four Gospels. Two days prior to Jesus carrying the cross is Wednesday in our calendar week. This day Mary prepared for the death of Jesus by breaking an alabaster vial of perfume. At the last supper with His disciples, Jesus gave His last farewell sermon to them.

MARCH OF THE CROSS OF JESUS

Mary's Precious Alabaster of Ointment
_ Wednesday

Jesus was in Bethany in the home of a leper when Martha's younger sister Mary visited and poured perfume on Jesus. In Matthew and Mark, it states that Mary poured the perfume on the head of Jesus (Matthew 26:7; Mark 14:3) but in Luke and John it says that the perfume was poured on His feet (Luke 7:38; John 12:3). Let us realize that it is not important where the perfume was poured but what's more important is that she had poured the whole flask of precious and expensive perfumed oil on Jesus showing a lavish, extravagant gesture of affection. The room was filled with sweet aroma.

But the disciples criticized her of the waste. "But the disciples were indignant when they saw this and said, "Why this waste? For this perfume might have been sold for a high price and the money given to the poor." (Matthew 26:8-9) In Mark and John it reveals the worth of the expensive perfume as "three hundred denarius" (Mark 14:5; John 23:5). At the time a working man earned one denarius/'silver coin' a day which meant that the perfumed oil was worth nearly a year's wages. This required tremendous savings for the woman and it was a great deal of money. The disciples thought the woman was out of her mind to pour such expensive oil on Jesus. This must have conflicted the disciples since Jesus had taught them to help the poor and now He was actually enjoying the expensive oil.

A few days before this, when Jesus spoke of His death and resurrection for the third time in Jericho, the disciples were excited only over the forthcoming prospects. They were preoccupied with the thoughts of their high positions on the day when Jesus enters Jerusalem as the Messiah, so they obviously could not understand Mary's action.

Jesus defends Mary, "Let her alone so that she may keep it for the day of My burial.' (John 12:7) 'Truly I say to you, wherever this gospel is preached in the world, what this woman has done will also be spoken of in memory of her." (Matthew 26:13)

Just as the disciples were thinking, was Jesus enjoying the expensive perfume contrary to His teaching?

Whenever Jesus came to Jerusalem He visited Mary's home in the village of Bethany across the Mount of Olives to rest. Martha being the eldest was always preparing food while Mary was sitting at Jesus' feet to listen to Him. It was pretty much the same scene the day when Mary broke the vial of the alabaster oil. The only difference was that the heart of Jesus was filled with distress. Jesus was a young 33 year old man who came into the world in flesh - 100 percent human - feeling the same hunger, fatigue and emotions as us and was thinking of His own death. Just imagine how He must have felt!

I was 47 years old when I was diagnosed with 4th degree of stomach cancer in Beijing, China. Even though I was past the midpoint of the life cycle my heart was filled with grief that was uncontrollable at the time. I sat on a park bench and thought, "Is this all that is to it? Is my life ending?" I felt numb and the sense of loss was tremendous. At this state, what thoughts would there possibly be? Ears become deaf to any kind of comforting words at this point.

Jesus grimly accepted His death. He must have endured a huge conflict between His own flesh and the love of Father God. The seriousness of the conflict is shown through His prayer at the garden of Gethsemane.

Mary was the only person who understood and felt compassionate towards the forthcoming death of Jesus. She was the one who sat on the feet of Jesus and listened carefully and understood the heart of Jesus. That is why she thought, "What can I do to comfort Him?" She decided to pour the expensive perfumed oil to anoint His body to commemorate His forthcoming burial. Jesus must have shed tears of joy and gratitude in His heart by Mary's action. This applies to us today as well. Our Lord remembers those who understand His heart and offer our most valuables to Him (time, heart, material things, etc.).

The Last Supper_Thursday

Washing of the Feet

Jesus wanted to eat the Passover meal together with His disciples and had the last supper with them which happened to fall on the evening before the festival of the Passover. As Jesus prepared to lay down His life for the world the old Passover was transformed into the Lord's Supper as the Lamb of God. Jesus then washed the disciples' feet before the supper.

"He got up from supper" (John 13:4) —>threw aside His heavenly throne

"laid aside His garments" (John 13:4) —>put aside His heavenly glory

"Taking a towel, He girded Himself" (John 13:4)—>took servant position (prepared to work)

"So when He had washed their feet, and taken His garments and reclined at the table again" (John 13:12) —> sat next to the heavenly throne after washing our sins away

Jesus showed in action, not in a parable, to His disciples who were arguing over who was the greatest. The Master willingly made Himself their servant being the role-model for His followers that the greatest one is the one who serves. With death approaching at a relatively young age of 33, Jesus denied His own grievous heart and loved His disciples to the end.

Years later Peter teaches about humility to the believers and encourages them to learn from Jesus' action as He washed the feet of His disciples. "You younger men, likewise, be subject to your elders; and all of you, clothe yourselves with humility toward one another for God is opposed to the proud, but gives grace to the humble." (1 Peter 5:5) Envisioning Jesus who girded a towel around His waist and bent down to wash the feet of the disciples we must also "bend down in humility" to serve others.

The Holy Communion

Next Jesus said, "He who eats My flesh and drinks My blood abides in Me and I in him." (John 6:56) and conducted the Holy Communion ceremony.

By receiving the communion the believer becomes one with God which is a symbolic ceremony. One of the reasons why we conduct communion ceremonies every major festival period is to commemorate Jesus' crucifixion and resurrection to share in the benefits of Jesus' sacrifice. It is not only to remember what he did but also to partake in the suffering of Jesus on the cross as we take the bread recalling the torture of His body and as we take the drink the blood-shed on the valley of Calvary for us.

Many people refuse to partake in the death on the cross while preferring to partake in the resurrection. Jesus has expressed that one must carry their own cross and follow Him but majority of people do not want to do this. For this reason it is difficult to reach to the level of being filled with the Holy Spirit. Those who really want to become 'one' with God must definitely partake in the cross. Those who really believe and love Jesus must be ready to pay the price of taking a loss (sacrifice for others) for the righteousness of God's kingdom. A true believer is someone who constantly thinks of Jesus (mind), trusts and is joyful at heart (emotion) and acts for the sake of Jesus (righteous). Trust in God and act for Him.(sacrificing yourself; giving up the things you've enjoyed and letting go of your most treasured things).

Jesus' Farewell Message_John 13-16

At the last supper, Jesus gave His final teaching with four themes in mind.

First, the new covenant was given.

When the disciples asked, "Which is the great commandment in the Law?" (Matthew 22:36) Jesus answered "You shall love your Lord God with all your heart, soul and mind. And love your neighbor as yourself." (Matthew 22:37-39) But at the last supper, Jesus gave a new command. "Love one another just as I have loved you." (John 15:12) Here Jesus stresses that the foundation of Christian commitment is to love each other. The two commandments combined together is 'to love one another.' "The whole Law is fulfilled in one word, "You shall love your neighbor as yourself.'" (Galatians 5:14) Followers of Christ are expected to carry out good deeds with the heart of Jesus in order to show love towards those who might be their enemies. Those who love Jesus can love one another but it does not necessarily mean that they love Jesus.

However, there are problems that arise when loving one another. The reality of today's religious communities and salvation entities are, in fact, far from being perfect. They think of themselves as especially loving but end up quarreling and taking sides with a number of different leaders and splinter groups. Their actions show that they have not understood the basic Christian attitude of love and it's because they love with their own efforts. It makes no sense when people hate one another when they claim they love Jesus. Hatred in churches is out of the question. "By this everyone will know that you are My disciples if you love on another." (John 13:35) Followers of Christ must not hate but love one another. We must not forget that God Himself is love and is the source and measure of all love. As Christians, our attitude and actions are everything and we must strive to become God's love partner as His love is complete.

Second, He is leaving to prepare a place.

Realizing that it was the last supper with Jesus Peter quickly cleared his head and asked, "Where are You going?" (John 13:36) Jesus answered, "You know the way where I am going." (John 14:4)

Shortly after Jesus' reassurance, it left Thomas even more confused so he asked, "Lord, we do not know where You are going, how do we know the way?" (John 14:5) Jesus said, "I am the way, and the truth and the life; no one comes to the Father but through Me." (John 14:6) Things that were to take place are all part of God's plan — crucifixion, blood on the cross are the ways leading to the Father.

By this time the disciples should have understood what was going on but Philip wanted to see God not realizing that he had already seen him, in Jesus. "Philip said to Him, 'Lord, show us the Father and it is enough for us.' (John 14:8) "Do you not believe that I am in the Father and the Father is in Me? The words that I say to you I do not speak on My own initiative, but the Father abiding in Me does His works." (John 14:10)

Soon Jesus was to return to the Father and it was something to be glad about. "In My Father's house are many dwelling places; if it were not so, I would have told you; for I go to prepare a place for you. If I go and prepare a place for you, I will come again and receive you to Myself, that where I am, there you may be also." (John 14:2-3) He was making a way to come to God which was a great promise of hope given to the disciples. His return to God would bring new power in action, new certainty in prayer. "He who believe in Me, the works that I do, he will do also; and greater works than these he will do; because I go to the Father." (John 14:12)

Third, He is leaving so that His followers will have a Helper. (John 14:16-17)The Holy Spirit will come to be with them always and everywhere and teach and counsel and bring to mind all that Jesus has said. "It is to your advantage that I go away; for if I do not go away the Helper will not come to you; but if I go, I will send Him to you." (John 16:7) "But when He, the Spirit of truth, comes He will guide you into all the truth; for He will not speak on His own initiative, but whatever He hears, He will speak; and He will disclose to you what is to come." (John 16:13)

Fourth, Jesus tells the parable of the vine and its branch.

"Abide in Me, and I in you. As the branch cannot bear fruit of itself unless it abides in the vine, so neither can you unless you abide in Me." (John 15:4) By sending the Helper Jesus promises His presence in us. Through Jesus' obedience to the will of God the Father from the beginning of creation and the work of salvation through the cross, the presence of the Holy Spirit is fulfilled by the grace of Father God and His Son.

In order to abide in Him, one must obey His word. If we disobey, not only the Holy Spirit does not work but the Lord will spit you out from His presence as well. "So because you are lukewarm, and neither hot nor cold, I will spit you out of My mouth." (Revelation 3:16) Those who obey will bear many fruits since Jesus is with them.

After speaking His last sermon at the last supper, Jesus and his disciples left for the garden of Gethsemane. As they headed to the Mount of Olives, Jesus told Peter of his denial - that he will deny

Him three times before a rooster crows.

Prayer at the Garden of Gethsemane

Jesus took His most beloved disciples, Peter, James and John to a special place, the olive-orchard of Gethsemane on the Mount of Olives to pray. But before He started to pray, Jesus requested His disciples to pray for Him. "He said to them, 'My soul is deeply grieved, to the point of death; remain here and keep watch with Me.'" (Matthew 26:38) This was the first time that Jesus spoke in this way. During the period of His ministry, it was Jesus who prayed for people, healed, cured people, and gave comfort to those in need but never once did He mention of His own pain.

But this time it was different. The prospect of His suffering filled Jesus with horror. In spite of being asked to prayer three times, His disciples ended up falling asleep. Probably they must also have been grieved with sorrow, which made it difficult for them to pray. In any event they failed in prayer. The disciples had followed Jesus for 3 years and listened and learned of all the heavenly secrets of the Word but they failed in praying.

The result of this was that every one of them ran away when Jesus got arrested. The love for Jesus was in their heart since they heard the Word and understood it in their head. Failing to pray results in a blockage of energy and power from above which are needed to act on what you know. So, fear overtakes the knowledge and you find yourself having no choice but to run away. Threader: As promised, the gift of the Holy Spirit was released after Jesus' resurrection. In the upper room of Mark, they gathered "all with one mind continuously devoting themselves to prayer" (Acts 1:14) and received the Holy Spirit after a few days. Upon receiving the "power from above" (Luke 24:49) they were ultimately changed into 'apostles' (calling) and spent their lives testifying Jesus to the ends of the earth.

Jesus prayed fervently until his sweat turned into blood. "And He went a little beyond them and fell on His face and prayed, saying

'My Father, if it is possible, let this cup pass from Me; yet not as I will but as You will." (Matthew 26:39) As a young man of 33 years of age, He confessed his pain of accepting the path of suffering to follow His Father's will.

Why did Jesus say, "My soul is deeply grieved to the point of death.' (Matthew 26:38) and 'My God, My God, why have You forsaken Me?" (Matthew 27:46) From the beginning to eternity He had shared the love of Father and now He had to leave Him for four days. He was momentarily being thrown away. Jesus knew that He had to completely detach Himself from the love of the Father and go down to hell in order to save mankind. The pain of leaving His Father's love was agonizing yet He had no choice but to pray fervently until his sweat became like drops of blood. (Luke 22:44)

Let us understand correctly that the remarks of Jesus do not signify failure. He had already gone through preliminary training and was prepared to give Himself up at the incident of Mary's precious ointment and the last supper. He humbled Himself to the level of a servant by washing the disciples' feet and teaching them the importance of service by His example. But ultimately, He won through His prayer in Gethsemane, for Jesus accepted the path of suffering as His Father's will. "All things are possible for You; remove this cup from Me; yet not what I will, but what You will." (Mark 14:36) Basically Jesus went through an internal battle between His own fleshly desire and His Father's plan. What does 'my will' mean? It means eating the fruit of the good and evil. Jesus chose not to eat from the good and evil and surrendered to His Father's will. He chose the tree of life instead. Right before His suffering on the cross, Jesus was battling in prayer to overcome 'His thoughts' and ultimately succeeded in total obedience to the Word of the Father.

Through the prayers of Gethsemane, Jesus overcame Himself completely and was able to say, "may it not be My will but Father's will." (Mark 14:36) and carry the cross. He could overcome the actual suffering that was about to take place because of the victory of His prayer in Gethsemane. Those who succeed in prayer also succeed in their livelihood as well. In one of the scenes of the Passion of Christ, Jesus confessed to the Father 'My heart is ready' right before the whipping lashes began before the courthouse of Pilate. This scene should be a challenge to us how powerful prayer could be!

Arrested and Crucified_Friday

As Jesus finished His prayer in Gethsemane, Judah came accompanied by Roman soldiers and a large crowd to arrest Him. Then Peter drew his sword and cut off the ear of the high priest's servant but the power of the 'sword of the world' that he tried to use failed to protect Jesus. Instead Peter received a scolding from Jesus. "All those who take up the sword shall perish by the sword." (Matthew 26:52) Peter was able to show his courage with the sword but failed miserably in praying for Jesus - not even for an hour. Threader: This reveals to us how difficult it was to pray before the will of Father (until the coming of the Holy Spirit). The anointing of the Holy Spirit came upon Peter as well as the 120 people who gathered to pray in Mark's attic. And from that point on, Peter was transformed into a powerful preacher with the sword of the Holy Spirit (sermon) and saved 3,000 people. (Acts 2)

After seizing Jesus, they handed Him over to the Sanhedrin Council which was the Supreme Court in Jerusalem. The council members consisted of people from influential families, elders, lawyers, Pharisees and Sadducees. And they had a wide range of powers in civil and religious matters. "When it was day, the Council of elders of the people assembled and led Him away to their council chamber." (Luke 22:66) And they asked, "Are You the Son of God?" (Luke 22:70) Jesus responded, "Yes, I am." The trial makes it clear they condemned Jesus to death for His claim to be the Son of God. There were no defense witnesses whatsoever and with this simple question and answer, a death sentence was pronounced immediately. Of all sins blasphemy was a capital charge under Jewish law. They believed in the invisible God intellectually and through the Law. They failed to understand the will of God the Father who showed His love and Word through His flesh. So they concluded to kill Jesus for blasphemy.

As prophesized by Isaiah about 700 years ago, Jesus was rejected and went through suffering (Isaiah 53-the suffering servant). Under the Roman rule, the Jews did not have power to carry out the death sentence. So Jesus had to appear before the Roman governor (Pontius Pilate) with a charge which would merit the death sentence under the Roman law.

Trial of Pilate: Political Trial

Jesus received a death sentence in the political trial. Actually the death sentence should not have been pronounced till the day following the trial but it was conducted very swiftly. For the Jewish Sabbath ran from sunset to sunset and since crucifixion could not be conducted during the Sabbath, they had to quickly resolve this case before sunset on Friday. Jesus was arrested on Thursday night and received His trial at dawn on Friday and was crucified in the morning the same day.

The Roman governor, Pilate knew that Jesus was innocent. "For he knew that because of envy they had handed Him over." (Matthew 27:18) Since it was a custom to release a prisoner at the time of feast, Pilate wanted to release Jesus and asked the people, 'Whom do you want me to release for you?' The crowd responded, 'Barabbas' (which means 'son of father') who was a convicted murderer. They chose the son of the world instead of the true Son of God the Father. This scene gives us an outlook on how people will react and give ovation to the 'anti-Christ' at the 2nd coming of our Lord. The people shouted, "His blood shall be on us and on our children!" (Matthew 27:25) Basically they brought their own tremendous calamity upon themselves as well as their descendants after the crucifixion and the resurrection of Jesus.

Before the crucifixion, Jesus was despised, scourged, spat at and suffered unbearable beatings just as Isaiah had prophesized. (Isaiah 53) But He silently endured them all. Jesus being our role model lets us refrain from shouting out loud when we argue or when confronted with conflicts with one another and avoid passing any threatening remarks.

The Crucifixion

In today's term, Jesus was on the cross from 9 am until 3 pm in the afternoon-approximately 6 hours. Dying on the cross is a prolonged torture and its cause of death is known to be of suffocation and not of blood loss. The main weight of the upper body cannot be sustained with the hands and feet nailed down so eventually the respiratory tract is blocked when the body falls downwards. Basic instincts for the crucified are to put strength on the feet to pull the body up but since both feet are nailed down - the pain is just a horrifying torture. Jesus suffered on the cross all day and died due to respiratory blockage. There are absolutely no miracles in His redemptive cross. He suffered and endured an agonizing death to the very end.

The crowds that were watching must have felt uneasy for they lifted a stick with a piece of cloth saturated with wine drink mixed with gall towards Jesus' mouth for Him to drink. But Jesus refused even that. He was unwilling to paralyze His body and chose to endure the agonizing pain. His denial of Himself was completed through the suffering of the redemptive cross. As prophesized about 1000 years ago through the psalms of David, Jesus poured Himself out like water. "I am poured out like water and all my bones are out of joint; My heart is like wax; it is melted within me." (Psalm 22:14) Jesus was pouring 'Himself' out like water because the 'self' was the channel of Satan. Our sins are forgiven by the blood of Christ. "And according to the Law, one may almost say, all things are cleansed with blood, and without shedding of blood there is no forgiveness." (Hebrews 9:22)

According to the Bible, when Jesus was on the cross the curtain that separated the Temple and the Most Holy Place was completely ripped apart from the top to the bottom. The Most Holy Place was where the Ark was kept and once a year only the high priest entered into it with the blood of lamb. The way to enter God's kingdom was opened through the blood of Jesus making the boundaries of heaven and earth completely open. He had pioneered the way to the Father's presence for all who place their trust in Him. "And not through blood of goats and calves, but through His own blood, He entered the holy place once for all, having obtained eternal redemption." (Hebrews 9:12) Threader: Through the blood of Christ, a way for the Holy Spirit to enter the hearts of believers had opened and through Pentecost, is the Church was born.

DEFEAT OVER DEATH

Lord, Resurrected

God the Father so loved His Son who obeyed to His death raised Him among the dead. "Which He brought about in Christ, when He raised Him from the dead and seated Him at his right hand in the heavenly places, far above all rule and authority and power and dominion, and every name that is name, not only in this age but also in the one to come. And He put all things in subjection under His feet, and gave Him as head over all things to the church." (Ephesians 1:20-22)

As He predicted three times to the disciples during His ministry,

Jesus received suffering of the cross and resurrected on the third day. "Now on the first day of the week, Mary Magdalene came early to the tomb while it was still dark and saw the stone already taken away from the tomb." (John 20:1) The sorrow turns to awe and joy as the women hear the angel's message. "An angel of the Lord descended from heaven and rolled away the stone and sat upon it··· The angel said to the women, "He is not here, for He has risen, just as He said." (Matthew 28:2-6)

There are so many graves around the Temple in Jerusalem as well as the Mount of Olives but the gravesite of Jesus is nowhere to be found. It is because resurrected Jesus had returned to the glory sitting next to the heavenly throne. Think of it this way. The cross is an act of payment for our sins whereas resurrection symbolizes a receipt for that complete payment. God the Father had received His Son's death for our sins and our salvation. After His resurrection, Jesus spent 40 days on earth and appeared eight times to many people.

Appeared to Mary and His Disciples & Many Others

First, Jesus appeared to Mary Magdalene who broke the valuable alabaster jar of perfume for Him. She was the first to be at the tomb after the Sabbath bringing spices and perfumes to anoint His body but she didn't recognize Him. Jesus called out to her. "Jesus said to her, "Mary!" She turned and said to Him in Hebrew, Rabboni! (means Teacher)." (John 20:16)

Here's a question: If I were to arise from the dead, who would be the first person that I would be most anxious to meet? Wouldn't it be the person who loved me the most?

Second, Jesus appeared among His 10 disciples but Thomas was not with them at the time. (John 20:19-20)

Third, Thomas was a suspicious realist so when he was together with the other disciples Jesus appeared in front of them and had Thomas touch His crucifixion scars. (John 20:26-29)

Fourth, Jesus appeared in front of Peter. (Luke 24:34)

Fifth, Jesus appeared to the two disciples going to Emmaus and walked with them explaining about Moses and the prophets and who the Bible was referring to. (Luke 24:13-35)

Sixth, Jesus not only appeared to His disciples but also appeared to more than 500 people near the mountain next to Lake Galilee preaching about the kingdom of heaven. (1 Corinthians 15:6)

Seventh, Jesus appeared in front of His seven disciples at Lake Galilee. (John 21)

Eighth, Jesus appeared in front of His brother, James.

When Jesus died, the disciples not only lost a much loved friend and a teacher but the focus of all their hopes. They had heard Jesus' last sermon of His coming death but also of His resurrection at the Last Supper. But even after meeting the risen Jesus they doubted whether it was real Jesus or a ghost. (Matthew 28:16-17) The '12 disciples' (people who have learned of Him) were not changed into 'apostles' (those who receive a calling) yet. The actual resurrection of Jesus did not transform the disciples to apostles. But as promised, upon His ascension He released the gift of the Holy Spirit (Pentecost) to His followers in Jerusalem and they became apostles from this point on.

Recovery of Peter

Chapter 21 in John tells us the moving story of how Jesus came to His disciples (this is His 8th time appearing after His resurrection.) as they were fishing. Peter was still mourning even after witnessing the risen Jesus and returned to his old fisherman job in the Lake of Galilee. Along with seven disciples, Peter spent all night on the boat but caught nothing.

Then at dawn break, Jesus appeared and specifically said to Peter who had denied him three-times, "Simon, son of John, do you love Me more than these?' He said to Him, 'Yes, Lord; You know that I love You. Jesus said him, 'Tend my lambs." (John 21:15)

Peter now realized his own destiny and set the record straight by admitting his weakness - 'You know that I love You.' He humbled himself in front of Jesus. He also realized that human's love for another person is limited to the love of a man (Phileo) and cannot reach the love of God (Agape). It was more of a personal confession that as a human being one becomes an egoist when one's life is threatened and denies the truth for the sake of his own life. On the other hand, it is also a confession of "You know that I am much loved by You." Previously, Peter was boastful that he loved Jesus the most but now he confessed that it was him who was loved the most by Jesus. Those who feel the love of God in their life are the ones who love Him. Peter was now a new man. Despondency, mourning, fears are replaced by indescribable joy.

Jesus gave Peter a chance to cancel out his three-fold denial by asking Him the same question three times, 'Do you love Me?' Then He said, "Tend My sheep." (John 21:17) and restored Peter as a leader giving him the task of caring for His people. The words spoken by Jesus were now being confirmed. "I also say to you that you are Peter, and upon this rock I will build My church." (Matthew 16:18) Those who have received God's love and those who love Him in return become the rock of faith. Those with this confession can tend the sheep and the Church was to be born upon this foundation. Jesus had loved Peter deeply in spite of his flaws.

The Ascension

After gathering the disciples together to pray Jesus commanded them not to leave Jerusalem and wait for what the Father had promised, the Holy Spirit, and returned to heaven by ascending from the earth. (Acts 1:4-5)

Jesus had sprinkled His own blood at the heavenly altar once and for all and fulfilled the work of redemption. "And not through the blood of goats and calves, but through His own blood, He entered the holy place once for all, having obtained eternal redemption." (Hebrews 9:12) Jesus had returned to His place of privilege and power, seated at the right hand of the Father and waiting for the Father's timing for Him to return to earth in glory. He has taken our humanity into heaven and lives to share the concerns of His people and to make intercession for us. By completing His work, the promised Holy Spirit is released to us as His gift. And now through the guidance of the Holy Spirit, the road leading to the seat next to the throne has been opened for us.

Jesus who shed His redemptive blood and resurrected is now seated next to the throne of Father and loves us this moment. Threader: Throughout the Old Testament period, the life of the Israelites was greatly influenced by the state of the king's faith and they experienced all kinds of judgments by the Gentiles whom God used as His tool. The Israelites must have felt unstable and been full of worries like, 'Now that the good king Hezekiah who walked in the ways of God is dead, what will become of us if an evil king takes over?' Alternately, when King Manasseh who walked in evil ways against God died, they must have let out a big sigh, 'Whew! We're now okay.' And they were equally anxious whether the next king would follow God's ways or not. Now, we no longer need to feel uneasy or anxious in this world, since Jesus who defeated death sits next to the heavenly throne and keeps us under His wings and provides everything for us. Each day our soul is set alive and is recreated into a new being. Our mind, soul and heart are looked after by Him. This actual fact encourages Christian believers here and now to enter into the benefits of Christ's eternal peace.

The Meaning of 'Church'

Jesus demolished the boundaries of heaven and earth through His death. This is the work of the redemptive cross. Through the redemptive cross and resurrection, Jesus had put all things of heaven (invisible) and earth (visible) under His feet and became the head to the Church.

The Church "is His body, the fullness of Him who fills all in all." (Ephesians 1:23) Only the Church unites the heaven and earth in Christ. "Summing up of all things in Christ, things in the heavens and things on the earth in Him." (Ephesians 1:10) Only in the Church, heaven and earth become one and there is glory and joy in both heaven and earth. Offering the earthly power, authority, materials to the Church also brings glory and joy in heaven.

As Christians, our dissatisfaction in the world can turn into satisfaction through the Church where God fulfills everything. It is at the Church where God fills us with the blessings that cannot be received elsewhere other than in the Church. One cannot expect good things to happen after leaving the Church. We must learn the lesson from Abraham when he left the Promised Land and went to Egypt was where he almost lost his wife. The importance of the Church must be learnt from this incident.

BRIDE OF JESUS: BIRTH OF THE CHURCH

The Book of Acts 1-11

The birth of the Church on the Day of Pentecost was fulfilled as promised by Jesus. Persecution of the new born church by some Jewish elements drove the apostles with the direction of the Holy Spirit to Samaria and other regions. Eventually this became an international, world-wide church movement through the national frontiers of Israel.

THE BIRTH OF THE FIRST CHURCH _ Acts 2

Empowerment of the Holy Spirit

"Gathering them together, He commanded them not to leave Jerusalem, but to wait for what the Father had promised, 'Which,' He said, 'you heard from me; for John baptized with water, but you will be baptized with the Holy Spirit not many days from now.' (Acts 1:4-5)

On the 10th day of praying, the Holy Spirit came upon the disciples and hundreds of people who had gathered in the upper room of Mark's place. "And suddenly there came from heaven a noise like a violent rushing wind, and it filled the whole house where they were sitting. And there appeared to them tongues as of fire distributing themselves and they rested on each one of them." (Acts

2:2-3) Tongues of flame came upon all the gathered people as a result of the empowerment of the Holy Spirit. It was an evident sign that the presence of the Holy Spirit had come to earth.

The Holy Spirit came upon with the movement (energy) that appeared as a gush of strong wind and tongues of fire. The impact of this is like a burning fire within our heart. The Holy Spirit can clearly be felt with five senses of our human body. It proves that God is alive and works within our hearts. (Hebrews 4:12)

Many Jewish people had gathered from all over the place to observe the Passover in Jerusalem at the time. Just imagine how loud it must have been when 120 people all prayed in tongue simultaneously in the upper room which happened to be located in the center of the city of Jerusalem. 3,000 Jews and converts from widely scattered countries came to the upper room. Now, to their astonishment, each heard their own mother tongue (Parthians (Iran), Babylon (Iraq), even Rome and Greece) being spoken by these 120 people.

The people assumed that they were 'drunk' and Peter who filled with the Holy Spirit addressed them. (Acts 2:14-36) Threader: 'Consumed with the Holy Spirit' here has a meaning of 'arrival' of the Holy Spirit. Let us not be mistaken that just because we experienced the Holy Spirit once it does not mean that we are living the life filled with the Holy Spirit.

"It will come about your this that I will pour out My Spirit on all mankind; and your sons and daughters will prophesy, your old men will dream dreams, your young men will see visions." (Joel 2:28) Peter delivers a moving message that the prophecy of Joel has now been fulfilled and then testifies of Jesus. "Men of Israel, listen to these words: Jesus the Nazarene, a man attested to you by God with miracles and wonders and signs which God performed through Him in your midst, just as you yourselves know this Man, delivered over by the predetermined plan and foreknowledge of God, you nailed to a cross by the hands of godless men and put Him to death. But God raised Him up again, putting an end to the agony of death, since it was impossible for Him to be held in its power." (Acts 2:22-24) "He looked ahead and spoke of the resurrection of the Christ, that He was neither abandoned to Hades, nor did His flesh suffer decay. This Jesus God raised up again, to which we are all witnesses. Therefore, having been exalted to the right hand of God, and having received from the Father the promise of the Holy Spirit, He has poured forth this which you both see and hear." (Acts 2:31-33)

Upon Peter's speech the people responded, "Brethren, what shall we do?" (Acts 2:37) This meant that their hearts were pierced and they received God's grace. The baptism of 3,000 people followed, and this is the birth of the first church, a new joyous community. Actually the first church started off as a big sized church as opposed to a small founding church. Peter witnessed the promise of Jesus being fulfilled. "I say to you that you are Peter, and upon this rock I will build My church." (Matthew 16:18) Tears of joy must have rolled down on the face of Peter! A similar incident happened to me when I was in Geneva, Switzerland. At the time, along with four other family members we had invited a pastor from Seoul, Korea and conducted our first service in the spring of 1992 (Founded the Korean Church of Geneva). I recall feeling overwhelmed with joy and shedding uncontrollable tears of joy.

Efforts on Teaching, Fellowship and Prayer

Continually devoting themselves to the apostles' teaching, fellowship, breaking of bread and prayer were the characteristics of the first church. (Acts 2:42) Apostles' teaching meant bible studies, breaking of bread meant sharing meals together, and fellowship meant 'everyone (us) in Christ.' Due to the strong sense of community, there was readiness to share money and possessions, which meant that the concept of wealth had disappeared. "All those who had believed were together and had all things in common." (Acts 2:44)

Following the gift of God's Spirit at Pentecost, the members of the first church not only studied the Bible and conducted fellowship but they prayed together experiencing changes in their inner self. By the power of the Spirit of God, they started to show signs of wonder, casting out evil spirits, healing, and spoke in tongue. If we also gather at church to study the Bible, to have fellowship and pray, we will also experience the wonderful works of the Holy Spirit as the first church had experienced.

The Growth of the First Church_Acts 3-4

Peter and John worked wonders during the growth process of the first church. A crippled beggar man was sitting at the Temple gate because his disability barred him from entry. Peter along with John saw him and said, "I do not possess silver and gold, but what I do have I give to you: In the name of Jesus Christ the Nazarene, walk!" (Acts 3:6) The cripple stood up and ran! Since the crippled beggar had been sitting in front of the Temple for many years practically every Jew knew him.

This incident became big news around town since the passersby witnessed it with their own eyes. Upon hearing the disturbing news, Annas the high priest and Caiaphas who had prosecuted Jesus in Sanhedrin Council previously arrested Peter and John. They were questioned, "By what power or in what name, have you done this?" (Acts 4:7) Filled with the Holy Spirit, Peter boldly proclaimed, "There is salvation in no one else; for there is no other name (except Jesus) under heaven that has been given among men by which we must be saved." (Acts 4:12) Realizing how difficult it was to deal against the power of the Holy Spirit, both Annas and Caiaphas released them with a warning not to preach about Jesus again. But the apostles could not stop speaking and they prayed for boldness, and their prayer was answered.

The works of the apostles of the first church were remarkable in its numbers. Thousands of people believed and repented upon hearing the message delivered by the apostles and numbers continued to grow. "Many of those who had heard the message believed; and the number of the men came to be about five thousand." (Acts 4:4) The increasing number became so big that the people gathered around the grounds of the Temple and filled up to the walls of the city of Jerusalem to give worship. The essence of a church is not the building itself but the congregation who gathers to repent in the name of Jesus through the guidance of the Holy Spirit. In other words, a building is not the main point when it comes to worship. Today, especially in connection with immigrant churches, there are instances where elders who have dedicated their service in resources and prayers in building a church and they end up acting like owners of the church resulting in divisions within the church. We must remember and reflect on how a church was born.

Due to the continuous growth, some inevitable problems also occurred in the first church of Jerusalem. Jesus had left a command before His ascension, "You shall become My witnesses both in Jerusalem and in all Judea and Samaria, and even to the remotest part of the earth." (Acts 1:8) Unfortunately, the apostles and the church members of the Jerusalem church failed to think about spreading the message to the ends of the earth. A church that experiences great revival but fails to evangelize and do missionary work will end up having internal problems. The same thing happened at the first church. But in spite of their many problems the church grew at a great speed - all because each member of the church was filled with the living Holy Spirit.

Test of Materialistic Greed: Ananias and Sapphira_Acts 5

Offering is something we give voluntarily according to the grace we have received. But in the case of Ananias and Sapphira, they got jealous when they saw Barnabas who sold off his property and offered it all to the apostles. (Acts 4:36-37) The desire to impress was so great that they hid half of the profit from their property that was sold and offered the remainder to the apostles claiming that it was all of what they had received. Even though they gave an offering voluntarily they received terrible consequences of death as a result of deceiving God.

There may be many deaths occurring, myself included, if this kind of incident happened today. When I was receiving a salary in the U.S., I deducted my medical insurance from my paycheck and was in a dilemma whether I should have given my tithing based on the total amount or not. I had to struggle off the temptation of giving less and reiterated in my head what tithing was all about. "Tithing means 9/10 of it belongs to God and He has promised to fill the rest once I give my tithes." God has always filled and provided more ever since. "Give, and it will be given to you. They will pour into your lap a good measure-pressed down, shaken together, and running over. For by your standard of measure it will be measured to you in return." (Luke 6:38)

Conflicts between Hellenistic Jews and Native Hebrews_Acts 6:1-7

The main leaders of the church at the time were obviously the 12 disciples of Jesus. They were native Hebrews. But among the members of the first church were many other foreign Jews as well. Apparently, a conflict arose relating to unfairness in the daily share between the Hellenistic Jews and the native Jews. The church was led by the apostles who were native Jews so when the food was being distributed the widows of the native Jews received two loaves of bread when the widows of Hellenistic Jews received one or if at all. Then complaints came from the Hellenistic Jews. The apostles' answer to this problem was to let them choose seven deacons of their own number to oversee these practical matters while they concentrated on the teaching.

Stephen, the First Martyr_Acts 6:8-7:60

Stephen, a Hellenistic Jew was among one of the seven deacons chosen to take care of administrative and other affairs of the church. The Pharisees and the scribes could not handle Stephen's speech filled with the Holy Spirit. They falsely charged him with blasphemy and brought before the Jewish Council, just as Jesus was.

Stephen stood up before them and preached the gospel just as Peter had done. But the response was totally different. Peter's sermon was that Jesus died not because the Jews were bad but because it was according to the will of God, and they didn't know He was handed over to the Gentiles. At that time, the people repented with "What shall we do?" (Acts 2:37) But Stephen preached against the Jews and said, "Which one of the prophets did your fathers not persecute? They killed those who had previously announced the coming of the Righteous One, whose betrayers and murderers you have now become." (Acts 7:52)

Stephen's lengthy sermon that appears in chapter 7 is actually the summary of the Old Testament. The court knows the facts but the interpretation is revolutionary. Stephen's sting was focused of Israel's old rejected prophets from Joseph and Moses onwards. "We have heard him speak blasphemous words against Moses and against God." (Acts 6:11) "We have heard him say that this Nazarene, Jesus will destroy this place and alter the customs which Moses handed down to us." (Acts 6:14)

Explaining the nation's history of boycotts of God's messengers, Stephen encouraged and warned the present generation of Israel not to reject Jesus anymore as they had in the past. He told them not to limit God's presences to the temple building, for it was more important to experience God's presence in their hearts. And he reiterated how God met Moses in the flame of a burning bush in the wilderness of Mt. Sinai instead of in a temple. His message was that the building of the Temple, the Jewish tradition was no longer effective to fill the 'new' wine (indicating Jesus). "When they heard this, they were cut to the quick, and began gnashing their teeth at him." (Acts 7:54) "They went on stoning Stephen…" (Acts 7:59)

There are some who comment that if Stephen was wiser in giving a sermon he would have bear the fruit as a result, instead of being killed. It may appear that he was too forceful and bold in delivering his message but even Peter who made thousands of people repent bearing much fruit was martyred as well. God works in different ways. If Peter had raised and revived the first church through his sermon, the persecution and martyr of Stephen helped the church to spread to all the ends of the earth.

I, in many occasions , scolded in a loud voice different elders when I was a guest speaker in various churches. And each time my wife would point out to me whether it was right for an elder to scold an elder from another church. But I seriously think I was driven by the Holy Spirit at the time without being aware of it. Early next morning I would kneel down in tears and pray. "Lord, who am I to scold them and why did you make me do it? Please comfort them and I ask you to cover this humble servant of yours with your grace." Then in 2007 at the New Year's service I heard the voice of God saying, "You have been casting your voice to clear the darkness with Light so far but from this year on your voice will be like that of a comforter and light giving warmth to the cold." From the deepest soul of my heart I felt the warmth filling up immensely. I remember streams of tears of gratitude rolling down my face. My deliverance of the Word has substantially softened and scolding had drastically diminished ever since.

"Being full of the Holy Spirit, he gazed intently into the heaven and saw the glory of God, and Jesus standing at the right hand of God and he said, 'Behold, I see the heavens opened up and the Son of Man standing at the right hand of God.'"(Acts 7:55-56) "They went on stoning Stephen as he called on the Lord and said, 'Lord Jesus, receive my spirit!' Then falling on his knees, he cried out with a loud voice, 'Lord, do not hold this sin against them!'"(Acts 7: 59-60) Having said this, Stephen endured the beatings of the stones and died feeling the joy in the kingdom of heaven.

Let us not misunderstand that God's kingdom comes only when the flesh dies on this earth. We know that the earth is a place of suffering but God has given us the Holy Spirit so that we may taste His kingdom even if we were stoned to death. That is why Jesus died on the cross. The Church is born only through the Holy Spirit and His kingdom is given to us only through the Church.

Spreading of the Early Church: 1st Persecution_Acts 8

A great revival of the early church was increasing but at that time persecutions began for the Hellenistic Jews ever since Stephen's martyrdom. It was because Stephen rebuked the native Jews. In a quick glance, the death of Stephen may appear meaningless as it didn't seem to save any soul and only sparked the persecution of the church and the believers. But the blood of a martyr is never wasted. I.t becomes a seed to many churches down the road. "On that day a great persecution began against the church in Jerusalem, and they were all scattered throughout the regions of Judea and Samaria, except the apostles." (Acts 8:1) According to this verse, it appears the apostles were not persecuted since they were native Jews.

The command of Jesus to spread the gospel to the ends of the earth is being fulfilled in Acts 1-8. The persecution that followed Stephen's death lead to the first broadening of the Church's outreach. The attack seems to have concentrated on Stephen's fellow-Hellenistic Jews leaving the apostles free to remain in Jerusalem. Wherever scattered believers went they took the message with them. Ultimately, it was God at work.

Philip and the Ethiopian Eunuch

Philip, one of the selected seven deacons in the church just like Stephen, ended up doing missionary work and evangelizing in Samaria because of the persecution. The crowds heard and saw signs of the works of Philip - casting out unclean spirits and healing many sick people. He was reaping the fruits of the seeds which Jesus had sown earlier in Samaria. (John 4:1-26) At the height of his flourishing Samaritan campaign God called him to meet the need of an individual. "Then the Holy Spirit said to Philip, 'Go up and join this chariot.' " (Acts 8:29) Philip met an Ethiopian eunuch and God knew this foreigner was ready to receive the good news about Jesus. He asked the eunuch whether he understood the book of Isaiah. "And he said, 'Well, how could I, unless someone guides me?' (Acts 8:31) "Then Philip opened his mouth, and beginning from this Scripture he preached Jesus to him." (Acts 8:35) The eunuch received Jesus and got baptized. It was through this eunuch that a church was born in Ethiopia. Peter and John also went down to Samaria and gave baptism of the Holy Spirit.

Conversion of Saul_Acts 9

Saul regarded Stephen's death as deserving and was even present at the scene. He was determined to stamp out the whole Christian movement and passionately sought out believers of Jesus and persecuted them. With a warrant issued entitling him to capture any Christians and put them in prison in Jerusalem, he was on his way to Damascus. A blinding light approached Saul and left him sightless for three days. "And he fell to the ground and heard a voice saying to him, 'Saul, Saul, why are you persecuting Me?' And he said, 'Who are You, Lord?' And He said, 'I am Jesus whom you are persecuting.' (Acts 9:4-5) Jesus made him realize that he was not persecuting people but God.

Never has any conversion brought a more radical change. Saul confessed that he was one of the Pharisees in the Council of Gamaliel which meant that he was an educated rabbi who possessed philosophic knowledge with a supremely conscious mind. Why did Saul persecute Jesus? At the time the Jews thought God could not be seen or touched according to the Law of the Old Testament. Therefore, from Saul's point of view, Jesus by right had to be killed since a mere man was claiming to be the Son of God. It was natural for him to act according to his knowledge since he had not experienced the presence of the Holy Spirit even if he was a biblical scholar.

Now the Spirit of God, the resurrected Jesus challenged him directly in a vision. When Saul fell to the ground Jesus commanded, "Get up and enter the city and it will be told you what you must do." (Acts 9:6) Prophet Ananias heard the voice of God about Saul's calling. "Go, for he is a chosen instrument of Mine, to bear My name before the Gentiles and kings and the sons of Israel." (Acts 9:15) Saul was a blessed man. God chose Saul who was a sinner among sinners. It's not that Saul was a great man but the Spirit in him.

By the time prophet Ananias reached him, Saul the persecutor had become 'Brother Saul,' a man who were to suffer much for the cause he tried to stamp out. (Acts 9:16) Ananias blessed him and immediately Saul regained his sight and got up and was baptized. (Acts 9:17-18) During his blindness days, there was nothing for him to do except probably repent and pray. Realizing the severe persecutions he had conducted towards Jesus and the believers, he may have accepted the sufferings as a natural process that he had to undertake for the sake of his wrongdoings in the past.

This incident marks a turning point - a conversion from Saul to Paul. Jesus' immense meeting with Saul changed his life completely from this point on. He became Apostle Paul and lived his life in conviction "to the end and blameless in the day of the Lord Jesus Christ" (1 Corinthians 1:8) He endured all kinds of hardship and "[ran] the race to the end." (Hebrews 12:1)

Those who have met God and received a distinct calling will not give up half way. Immense energy is given to those who have heard the voice of God enabling them to run the course to the end. "I do not consider my life of any account as dear to myself, so that I may finish my course and the ministry which I received from the Lord Jesus, to testify solemnly of the gospel of the grace of God." (Acts 20:24) This confession is mine as well and I hope that it will be the confession for all believers. Here, Apostle Paul says that as he, a persecutor and sinner, was changed and used as God's instrument, our merciful God will also meet us in the same way. (1Timothy 1:13-16)

Peter's Ministry and Meeting with Cornelius_Acts 10

Peter healed Aeneas who had been paralyzed for 8 years and also brought life back to Tabitha, a much loved Christian woman living in Joppa who had died. He did great works of the Holy Spirit. Upon death on the cross, resurrection, and ascension of Jesus, the promised Holy Spirit came down to earth not only on Peter but also on Cornelius, a Gentile. While Peter was praying in Joppa, Cornelius, a devout centurion of the Roman army was also praying in Caesarea when the presence of the Holy Spirit came upon each of them.

While praying Peter saw a vision of a sky opening up and an object like a great sheet coming down lowering into four corners to the ground. Inside were all kinds of four-footed animals and crawling creatures of the earth like snakes and a voice came to him, "Get up, Peter, kill and eat!" (Acts 10:13) Apparently, Peter was a native Jew who was strict in keeping the Jewish food laws. They were prohibited from eating anything dirty or unclean. Peter replied, "By no means, Lord, for I have never eaten anything unholy and unclean." (Acts 10:14) It is difficult to throw away old habits, concepts or traditional ways even after believing in Jesus. Changes do not happen overnight - it is gradual and takes time. Three times the vision and message came apparently instructing Peter to break the Jewish food laws. "What God has cleansed, no longer consider unholy." (Acts 10:15)

When Cornelius a Gentile but a devout man was praying, the Holy Spirit came upon him. "Now dispatch some men to Joppa and send for a man named Simon, who is also called Peter; he is staying with a tanner named Simon whose house is by the sea." (Acts 10:5-6) He followed the instructions and summoned his servants to bring Peter. God heard Cornelius' devout prayer and sent Peter who had the gospel in him to his house. The attitude of Cornelius longing to hear the Word of God is so graceful. "So I sent you immediately, and you have been kind enough to come. Now then, we are all here present before God to hear all that you have been commanded by the Lord." (Acts 10:33)

A second Pentecost occurs following Peter's teaching. The coming of the Holy Spirit on the Gentiles opened their mouth with prayer of tongue. "While Peter was still speaking these words, the Holy Spirit fell upon all those who were listening to the message. All the circumcised believers who came with Peter were amazed, because the gift of the Holy Spirit had been poured out on the Gentiles also. For they were hearing them speaking with tongues and exalting God. Then Peter answers, "Surely no one can refuse the water for these to be baptized who have received the Holy Spirit just as we did, can he?" And he ordered them to be baptized in the name of Jesus Christ." (Acts 10:44-48) This incident will play an important role later on.

Christians were scattered from Jerusalem to avoid the persecutions in Rome and finally, the first Gentile church is raised in Antioch. This event indicates the expansion of the Church. The warm response of the Greeks to the Christian message lead the Jerusalem church to dispatch Barnabas as their preacher in Antioch. Barnabas played the role of bringing Paul who was quietly residing in his hometown after his conversion to the church in Jerusalem and introduced him of his transformation.

After his conversion, Saul had actually wanted to meet the 12 disciples but they were afraid of him. Immediately after his conversion, Saul spent three years in Saudi Arabia praying and meditating, experiencing the Holy Spirit and became a faithful and powerful servant. He ultimately changed to Apostle Paul. During the Period of the

Divided Monarchy, just like healing the waters of Jericho through Elisha, God had changed Saul, a scholar of the Law, to a new person to help all the people of the world to bear fruit. Since the believers did not recognize his transformation, Saul left for his home city of Tarsus. This was when Barnabas tracked him down and brought him to Antioch to work together at the church.

Apostle Paul's recognition to the world would have been difficult if Barnabas did not bring him then. Just as the prophecy of Ananias, Paul became God's chosen instrument to spread the name of Jesus to all Gentiles, kings and the world. Both Barnabas and Paul revived the church in Antioch. Through Antioch church as the center, a new horizon of missionary work was opened. At last through the descendants of Abraham, God's blessing hands have spread out to the Gentiles.

Spiritual Search 28

The Meaning of "Temple"

The Bible starts from the Garden of Eden with Adam and Eve walking and conversing in the presence of God - "The tabernacle of God is among men, and He will dwell among them, and they shall be His people; and God Himself will be among them, and He will wipe away every tear from their eyes; and there will no longer be any death; and there will no longer be any mourning, or crying, or pain." (Revelations 21:3-4) - and ends with a new heaven and a new earth in the presence of God. From Genesis chapter 2 through Revelation 21, the 66 books in between are the stories of how people abandoned God's presence repeatedly and how God works in order to recover His presence among His loving people on this earth.

God's presence in the wilderness was the pillar of the clouds in the tabernacle and the pillar of fire; after the Canaanite conquest God received Solomon's worship of the temple as He promised David in the Promised Land of the city of Jerusalem. God in His presence filled the temple with clouds revealing to the people of Israel that He was with them.

The presence of God over Israel was the ark inside the tabernacle where the blood of the lamb was sprinkled. The temple in Jerusalem was a special place for this reason. Threader: Because Jeroboam built altars wherever he pleased in Bethel and Dan, Northern Israel was under the curse of God. The actual location of the temple was important, and that is why Solomon pleaded to God that answers be given to prayers facing towards Jerusalem.

Just as God's promise with David, Jesus came as the descendant of David, and during His ministry He proclaimed, "Destroy this temple and in three days I will raise it up." (John 2:19) and revealed that His body was the temple. In the Old Testament period, God met His people in the building of a temple but now proclaims that His presence is only in Jesus Christ. The body of the temple of Christ was torn into pieces on the cross but through His resurrection the Church, the body of Christ, was born.

God has not permitted to rebuild the temple of Jerusalem ever since it was destroyed by the Roman soldiers in AD 70. Even though God had promised David that his descendent will build a house of God no such building has been built. Instead a house of saints who have received the Holy Spirit has been raised.

God does not "dwell in temples made with hands" (Acts 17:24) but dwells in the heart of the believers of the Church in Christ. "Having being built on the foundation of the apostles and prophets, Christ Jesus Himself being the corner stone, in whom the whole building, being fitted together is growing into a holy temple in the Lord, in whom you also are being built together into a dwelling of God in the Spirit." (Ephesians 2:20-22) The presence of God is among His believers who are gathered in the name of Jesus. The Bible tells us that Jesus Himself is the temple and that we are also temples of God. "Do you not know that your body is a temple of the Holy Spirit who is in you?" (1 Corinthians 6:19)

The important fact is that Jesus, as the head of the church, and believers, as the corner stones, come together to form a community. Just as a limb is connected with a body, we must also be connected to Jesus in order for God's Spirit to dwell in the Church. The presence of the Holy Spirit will be experienced when we pray together.

In the Old Testament period, stones and rocks were cut, carved in quarries and transported to build a temple but today we are referred as "living stones" (1 Peter 2:5) to build up a spiritual house for the glory of God. Each stone must be carved in the quarry so that it may fit properly into the church building. This is one of the reason why we must be thankful for the pain and trials that we go through in our daily lives.

OPENING OF THE PERIOD OF MISSIONARIES

The Book of Acts 12-26

King Herod severely persecuted the Christians. This is the 2nd persecution. As King Herod instigated the church, thriving members of the church of Antioch began to spread the Word of God to the ends of the earth -- opening the doors of missionary work.

Beginning of the Period of Missionaries_Acts 13

A martyr is born as the 2nd persecution arises in Jerusalem. James, one of the three apostles closest to Jesus becomes the first martyr. He was the one who responded to Jesus when He asked who would drink His cup. The cup of Jesus was not a glorifying one but a cup of a cross. Shortly thereafter, Peter is captured. A maximum security prison presents no problems to Peter as the members of the Jerusalem church gathered together to pray, God sends an angel who opens the prison door and rescues Peter. In the meantime, King Herod dies of an intestinal illness, perhaps peritonitis and is expressed as "eaten by worms" in the Bible. (Acts 12)

1st Missionary Journey_Evangelistic Mission to Asia

Barnabas, Paul and John Mark had returned from Jerusalem upon the fulfillment of their mission and were praying and fasting

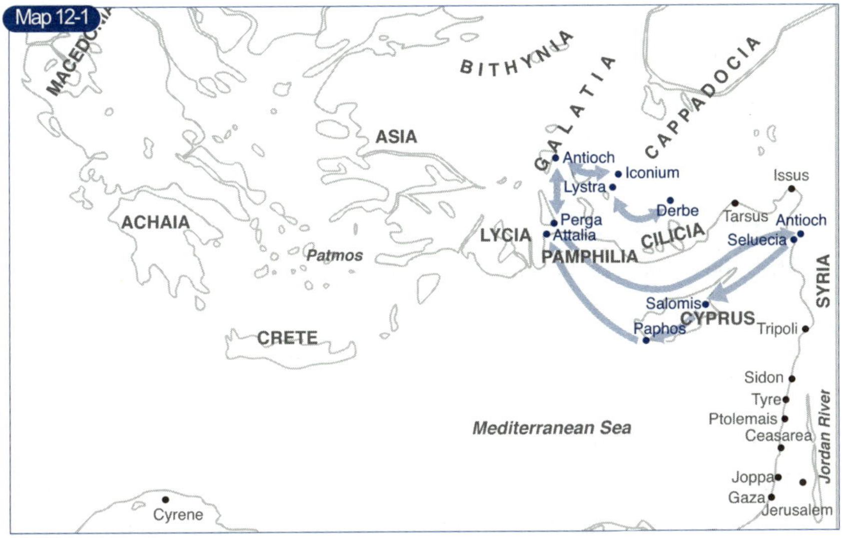

Apostle Paul's First Mission Trip. Paul and Barnabas go first to Cyprus and travel throughout the island and then head toward Asia Minor for evangelistic missions to Perga of Pamphylia, Pisidian Antioch, Iconium, Lystra and Derbe.

for the ministering of the gospel when the Holy Spirit gave a command. "There were prophets and teachers in the church of Antioch who had been brought up with Herod the tetrarch, and Saul. While they were ministering to the Lord and fasting, the Holy Spirit said, 'set apart for Me Barnabas and Saul for the work to which I have called them.' (Acts 13:1-2) It was a specific command of the Holy Spirit to send Barnabas and Paul as the first missionaries to the region of Asia. Barnabas and Paul went off for the journey taking along John Mark with them. John Mark was the man who had provided the attic room at the time of Pentecost.

Proconsul Sergius Paulus of Cyprus

Barnabas, Paul and John Mark set out on their missionary trip on a boat passing by the island of Cyprus which also happens to be where the territorial battle between today's Turkey and Greece is taking place. As he takes the lead, Paul and his company met proconsul

Sergius Paulus in Paphos, the capital of the island. They tried to evangelize him but the magician BarJesus, a false Jewish prophet who was with him, interfered to the end. So Paul cursed the magician and he became blind. Upon witnessing this, the proconsul converted and received Jesus. A high official of the island of Cyprus became the first fruit of the first pioneer mission trip.

They have barely begun their mainland journey when, at Perga, John Mark who was raised as a wealthy son returned home after realizing how difficult the missionary journey was. (Acts 13:13)

Antioch in Pisidia

Only Paul and Barnabas arrived in Galadia in Asia Minor. They started their first mission in the synagogue of Antioch in Pisidia. Threader: Jewish temples existed since the period of the exiles. The Jews were scattered throughout the world after the destruction of Jerusalem and wherever they went synagogues were built. A temple was the first place visited since it was an obvious place to meet a Jewish person. Obviously it was natural for them to deliver the gospel to the fellow country men for the love of their nation but it was also because it was evidently clear that fulfilling God's promise of spreading the gospel was easier this way.

Paul's first reported sermon in the synagogue of Antioch included a brief history of the Jews. Starting from the time of exodus, Paul talked about the journey in the wilderness, the period of Joshua's conquering of Canaan, the period of the Judges and kings up until King David who was anointed by God through Prophet Samuel. He then continued to say that Jesus was God's promised Savior, who came to earth according to David's promise (2 Samuel 7:8-16), but was rejected by the Jews who put Him to death on the cross. He cited from the book of Psalms and said that God raised Him up from the dead and that one must receive Jesus for the forgiveness of sins and justification of righteousness (Acts 13:16-39) proclaiming the core of the gospel. Through the long history of Israel, Apostle Paul focused on

Jesus and God's plan. Conclusively, it is actually God's wondrous work of salvation that we exist when Jesus is within our hearts.

By right the Jews should have believed the fulfillment of God's promise but they were against it. It was rather the Gentiles who knew nothing about God that confessed their faith in God. Due to the strong opposition from the Jews Paul proclaimed that "I am going to the Gentiles." Just as the parable of laborers in the vineyard (Matthew 20:1-16), the marriage feast (Matthew 22:1-10) and several others spoken by Jesus during His ministry, it was the Gentiles who first received the gospel instead of God's chosen people, the Jews.

The City of Iconium

Driven out of Antioch, Paul and Barnabas went to the synagogue in Iconium where the pattern is repeated. A larger number of Greeks believed but the Jews who disbelieved stirred up the minds of the Gentiles and embittered against them. Both Paul and Barnabas boldly delivered the Word of God and performed many signs and wonders through the powers received from God. They stayed in Iconium for quite a long period of time carrying out the works of God. But after an attempted stoning from the Jews and the Gentiles they escaped to another destination.

Lystra

Paul and Barnabas now went to Lystra. A cripple who had been listening attentively to the words of Apostle Paul was commanded, "Stand up on your feet." (Acts 14:8-10). Witnessing the healing of a cripple lead the Turkish people who were educated with the Greek mentality acclaimed Barnabas as Zeus (chief god of the Greeks) and Paul as Hermes (the messenger-god) and wanted to offer sacrifice towards them. Shocked and alarmed by their reaction, both Barnabas and Paul clearly indicated that they were no different from them and were also men of the same nature. They turned the focus to Jesus urging them to turn to a living God who made the heaven, earth, the sea and all that was in them from the vain things of the world. (Acts 14:11-15)

Many people believed in Jesus "but the Jews came from Antioch and Iconium and having won over the crowds they stoned Paul and dragged him out of the city, supposing him to be dead." (Acts 14:19) At this time, Paul was raised up to the throne next to Jesus in heaven. "I know a man in Christ who fourteen years ago-whether in the body or out of the body I do not know, God knows such a man was caught up to the third heaven." (2 Corinthians 12:2)

Bearing the incident of Lystra in mind, Apostle Paul said death could also be regarded as beneficial to us. "For we know that if the earthly tent which is our house is torn down, we have a building from God, a house not made with hands, eternal in the heavens." (2 Corinthians 5:1) The "earthly tent" is our flesh and life in this world is a temporal journey. We must, therefore, long for the eternal house in heaven. Let us understand that to overcome the earthly tent means to deny the fleshly things of the world. It does not mean physical death. "If anyone wishes to come after me, he must deny himself, and take up his cross daily and follow Me." (Luke 9:23) "I die daily." (1 Corinthians 15:31) "Dying daily" means to crush our fleshly thoughts. Instead of focusing on 'self' we must deny ourselves. The times when our self dies are when we get reprimanded by our immediate boss at work or when we get rejected in relationships.

Paul must have thought of Stephen's martyr when he was getting stoned and being dragged out of the city. Upon waking up from his faint, he didn't leave Lystra but instead went into the city again to preach the gospel. Timothy decided to become a disciple of Apostle Paul after receiving grace from witnessing what his teacher did. Further trouble from the Jews brought Paul and Barnabas on to Derbe, the furthest point of Paul's first mission. They returned to Antioch via Caesarea ending Paul's first missionary trip to Asia Minor.

Conference of Jerusalem Church_Acts 15

A meeting is held at the church of Jerusalem after the first mission trip. Certain leaders of Jerusalem church came to Antioch church and gave warnings: "you cannot receive salvation if you do not keep the laws of the Jews in spite of your belief in Jesus" and saw the red light and openly opposed Paul's teaching. "Some men came down from Judea and began teaching, "Unless you are circumcised according to the custom of Moses, you cannot be saved." (Acts 15:1) There were many Gentiles including Luke, the doctor and author of the gospel of Luke in the Antioch church. Just imagine how confused they must have felt since Paul's teaching was that the only way to reach God's salvation was through faith in Jesus Christ. The leaders of Jerusalem church was opposing Paul's teaching and probably threw a question like, "We are the actual disciples and apostles who followed Jesus, and what right does he have to teach that it is not necessary to keep the laws when he is not an apostle himself?"

On the other hand, Paul claimed that he had become an apostle of Christ upon His direct calling to become the light to the Gentiles. Threader: Paul realized that "salvation is reached by faith and not by keeping the laws" through the presence of the Holy Spirit which is the theme and message of the book of Romans and Galatians that follow hereafter. Among the letters of Paul, we assume that the first letter was sent to the church in Galatia where his successful campaign took place. He introduces himself in the book of Galatians as, "Paul, an apostle not sent from men nor through the agency of Man, but through Jesus Christ and God the Father who raised Him from the dead." (Galatians 1:1)

On such a vital matter, an authoritative decision by the apostles and elders were essential to avoid a complete split so Antioch church sent Paul and Barnabas to the church in Jerusalem. Paul left for Jerusalem with a heavy heart and there the Holy Spirit reminded him of Peter's earlier events and made him to give the account of God's work among the Gentiles. "Now therefore why do you put God to the test by placing upon the neck of the disciples a yoke which neither our fathers nor we have been able to bear?" (Acts 15:10)

Peter's attitude had changed since he realized that it was the Holy Spirit's work that he met Cornelius. When he heard the words of Cornelius, a Gentile, he experienced the Holy Spirit and testified about the prayers of tongue. The Bible clearly tells us that it is the work of the Holy Spirit that confirms our salvation and certainly not by keeping the laws.

The general acceptance was finally summed up after the verdict was given by James, the brother of Jesus and leader of the Jerusalem church. The Gentiles are asked, simply to accommodate the Jewish Christians, by respecting Jewish food laws, "that they abstain from things contaminated by idols and from fornication and from what is strangled and from blood." (Acts 15:20) so that Jews and Gentiles can share the same table and the church can meet together as one.

The Jerusalem conference is a turning point for opening the gate of missions to the Gentiles and new churches. Now Paul proclaims in confidence that "salvation is by faith and not by the actions of the Law." The good news was now relayed to the places Paul visited during the first missionary trip and the second missionary trip was to be unfolded in Asia Minor to Europe.

2nd Missionary Journey_Mission to Europe

Silas and Timothy - Paul's New Co-Workers

A sharp argument between Paul and Barnabas took place at the beginning of their second missionary trip. Barnabas encouraged that John Mark should accompany their trip but Paul refused recalling John Mark had left to go back home because of lack of enduring hardships during their 1st missionary trip. As a result of the argument, Paul took Silas on his 2nd missionary trip and revisited the mainland cities of the first campaign.

There are occasions where ministers also argue over other problems unrelated to the gospel. We are actually comforted by the fact that even Apostle Paul who was like Christ in many ways had a similar experience. In some instances, there are believers who contemplate in leaving the church after witnessing the flaws of a minister. When confronted in such a situation we must focus on Jesus and pray so that He may correct His servant at an appropriate time. Alternatively, praises must be directed to God when positive things occur through the minister.

Apostle Paul met Timothy at Lystra, a church first founded during his first missionary trip, and baptized him. Timothy was added to the evangelical journey. When Paul was staying in Derbe, a vision appeared in the night telling him to go to Macedonia. "A vision appeared to Paul in the night: a man of Macedonia was standing and appealing to him, and saying, 'Come over to Macedonia and help us.' (Acts 16:9) Guided by the Holy Spirit, Apostle Paul crossed the sea and set his first entry to Europe.

During our lifetime we experience difficulties when things don't happen according to our plans. Even if so we must not complain but instead be aware that it is the Spirit of Jesus blocking our plans. Be thankful towards God since He knows best and guides us to a better path. This is what we refer to as "spirituality." God gives spirituality as a gift to those who pray.

The Work in Philippi _ Acts 16

The 2nd mission trip opened the doors of evangelism in Europe. The first place that Apostle Paul went was Philippi. In each place he visited, Apostle Paul usually went first to synagogues but in Philippi there was none. So on the Sabbath day he went to a riverside hoping to find a place of prayer there. Threader: After the period of exile, the Jews prepared a place of prayer near a riverside if there were no synagogues around. Paul met a woman named Lydia, a worshiper of God and a local businesswoman there. As Paul was speaking, the

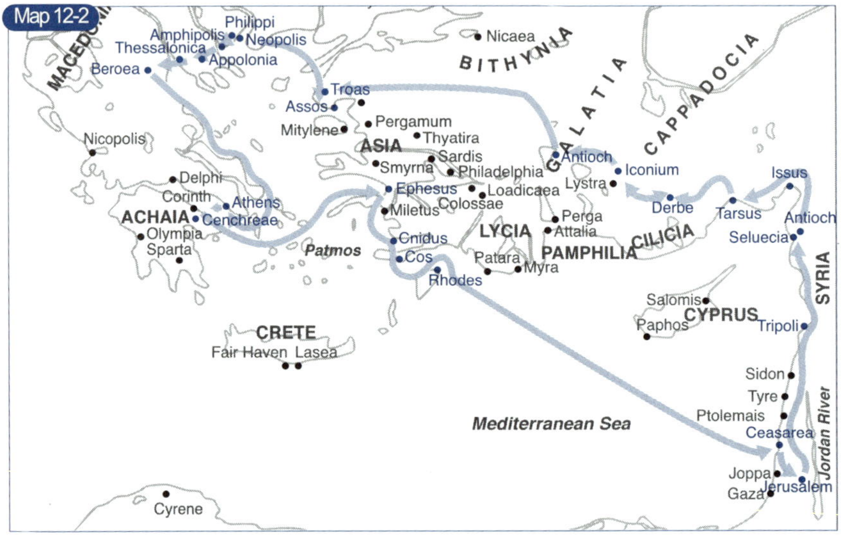

Apostle Paul's 2nd Missionary Journey The 2nd evangelical trip covered a large area as a result of Jerusalem's conference. Meeting new co-workers, Silas and Timothy, Paul started from Philippi and traveled onwards to Thessalonica, Berea, Athens and Ephesus.

Lord opened her heart to respond to receive Jesus. So the church at Philippi began with this woman as she opened her place for worship.

When Paul freed a slave-girl whose psychic powers earned her owners easy money, trouble quickly arose. Philippi was a Roman colony and the owners reported Paul and Silas to the authority. Even after their arrest, Paul and Silas sang praised and prayed in prison. Shortly thereafter followed a dramatic conversion of their jailer after an earthquake opened the prison doors and parted the prisoner's chains. (Acts 16:25-26)

It is quite easy to sing praises when things go merrily but once you get beaten up and falsely accused, complaints or resentments quickly set in. On a personal level, I have witnessed many believers being disappointed when things do not work out as they had expected after earnestly serving God. We must realize that even after serving God and sacrificing ourselves in many ways negative things can happen to us. True believers will praise God even when things don't work out favorably for them. God loves such believers and will reveal His presence to them. During tough times, we must neither complain nor worry but instead praise God. Then we will experience a remarkable miracle just as Paul did. I can attest to this in confidence since I have received such grace many times.

When the jailer awoke and saw the prisoners had escaped, he tried to kill himself but Paul cried out with a loud voice, "Do not harm yourself, for we are all here!" (Acts 16:28) Overwhelmed with emotion, he fell down before Paul and Silas and said, "Sirs, what must I do to be saved?" (Acts 16:30) They replied, "Believe in the Lord Jesus and you will be saved, you and your household. And they spoke the word of the Lord to him together with all who were in his house." (Acts 16:31-32) Through one jailer's conversion of faith his entire family received salvation. Along with Lydia, they raised the church of Philippi.

Are you praying earnestly for your family's salvation? If you believe in Jesus wholeheartedly, believe in the fulfillment of God's promise "you and your household will be saved." It is only natural for your entire family members to receive salvation if you truthfully believe in Jesus.

The members of Philippi church supported Apostle Paul in finance and prayer, enabling him to do God's work. Apostle Paul also had a special affection for this church. He confessed, "For God is my witness, how I long for you all with the affection of Christ Jesus." (Philippians 1:8)

The Work in Thessalonica and Berea

Paul and Silas traveled to Thessalonica since the persecution of the Jews in Philippi had begun. The response to Paul and Silas' preaching at the synagogues in Thessalonica was extremely favorable. Many people received the gospel. The Thessalonians particularly had great interest in the 2nd coming of Jesus and with this, a church of Thessalonica was raised.

The church members of Thessalonica asked Apostle Paul, who was in Corinth at the time: "Why is it that we are not experiencing joy and thankfulness in our hearts in spite of our belief in Jesus?" In response to this, Paul sent a letter to the church of Thessalonica which is the book of Thessalonians. Threader: Like this, majority of the letters Paul wrote was sent to the pioneer churches that he raised during his evangelical trips. In this letter, Paul advices his fellow believers saying, "Always be happy, pray and give thanks in everything for this is God's will for you in Christ Jesus." (1 Thessalonians 5:16-18) After receiving Jesus, those believers who pray at all times can be happy and be thankful regardless whatever their circumstances.

I was not able to comprehend what this verse meant during my elementary stage as a believer. But as I started to pray daily at dawn break I realized the change in myself as I grew in faith. I began to be thankful and joyful in whatever circumstances that confronted me. Quite frankly, as an ordinary human being, I also fell down when sudden trials occurred in my life. But when I knelt before God at dawn break, the Holy Spirit who penetrated into my deepest soul prayed in spirit on my behalf. The presence of the Holy Spirit began to touch and comfort me with love. Feeling His presence within me, uncontrollable tears started to pour down on my face and as I woke up an enormous joy and comfort overwhelmed me.

The Jews of Thessalonica started to become jealous because Paul and Silas won over the devout Greeks here as elsewhere. So with the guidance of the Holy Spirit, they set out for Berea. The Jewish group in Berea was notable for their open-minded study of the Scriptures. "Now they were more noble-minded than those in Thessalonica, for they received the word with great eagerness, examining the Scriptures daily to see whether these things were so." (Acts 17:11)

Just because we have believed for a long time it does not make us read the Bible every day with an earnest heart. There are many first-time believers who are eager in receiving the Word of God in their heart and study the Bible every day. As the people of Berea who were open minded in receiving and studying the Bible, no matter how long one has believed that person will definitely become a loyal and wise servant of God.

The Work in Athens

Some Jews in Thessalonica persecuted Paul, and escorted by believers, he moved to Athens the capital of Greece. Paul was a strategist and raising a church was his purpose wherever he went, so he left Timothy and Silas behind to teach the Scriptures to the church members of Berea.

Athens was a city full of altars of foreign gods to a degree that there was an altar with an inscription, 'To an Unknown God.' Paul was revolted at the sight of a city given over to idolatry. "So Paul stood in the midst of the Areopagus and said, 'Men of Athens, I observe that you are very religious in all respects. For while I was passing through and examining the objects of your worship, I also found an altar with this inscription, 'To An Unknown God.' Therefore what you worship in ignorance, this I proclaim to you.' (Acts 17:22-23) Paul encourages them to know what their belief was.

There are many people who proclaim to believe in Jesus and yet do not know Jesus at all. There are also many people who think they believe in Jesus but have no knowledge of the Holy Spirit. There are even those who do not want to know about the Holy Spirit. Unfortunately, Jesus cannot be with this kind of people. Jesus whom God has raised from the dead is sitting next to the heavenly throne. It is the Holy Spirit that delivers Jesus' heart, His breath and love for us to meet Him.

Paul addressed the Greek philosophers in Athens and gave the message that they will be forgiven although they didn't know Jesus. "Therefore having overlooked the times of ignorance, God is now declaring to men that all people everywhere should repent, because He has fixed a day in which He will judge the world in righteousness through a Man whom He has appointed, having furnished proof to all men by raising Him from the dead." (Acts 17:30-31) A different audience calls for a different presentation. Athens proved to be a hard ground for the gospel.

The Work in Corinth

Paul and his company went to Corinth. Corinth was one of the largest commercial and a thriving cosmopolitan city in Greece at the time. Tentmakers Aquila and Priscilla became staunch friends of Paul whom God had prepared in Corinth. Being in the same trade as they were (Acts 18:3), during the day Paul became a tentmaker to support himself as well as for his missionary work.

Apostle Paul performed many signs and wonders in Corinth. People were healed by only touching Paul's apron and towel. The hospitable pair, Aquila and Priscilla, were great supporters to the young churches as they traveled together with Paul to Corinth and Ephesus. They were truly a role model for the co-workers of God at the time.

As Christians, it is difficult to keep our faith alone. We need people to keep us accountable and help us not to fall into temptations of the world. We must become 'Us' in Christ and not insist on 'Me' in Christ. We must humble ourselves in front of God's given gifts. We should not feel envious towards a person who delivers the message of God better than ourselves. Instead, we must be able to pray for our co-worker like this: 'As long as the Good News of Christ is spread to many people, please use my co-worker who is better equipped than myself to carry out Your work.' When we humble ourselves in front of God the Holy Spirit will then comfort us and fill all the gaps in our heart.

Paul got thrown out as he was teaching in the synagogue. That very night, the Holy Spirit appeared to Paul and comforted him. "The Lord said to Paul in the night by a vision, 'Do not be afraid any longer, but go on speaking and do not be silent; for I am with you and no man will attack you in order to harm you, for I have many people in this city.' (Acts 18:9-10) Just imagine how Paul must have felt when the Lord came directly to comfort him!

Paul continued teaching for 18 months in Corinth and the uproar of the Jews took him to court. The proconsul Gallio was swift to judge that Paul had committed no crime and hustled them away. As Paul left Corinth, he vowed to spread the gospel from Cenchrea to Rome. On their way back to Jerusalem from Corinth, Paul and his companions stopped momentarily in Ephesus.

Visit to Ephesus

People of Ephesus were overjoyed when the gospel was preached by the companions of Paul. An eloquent man named Apollos from Alexandria of Egypt visited Paul in Ephesus. He was a biblical scholar at the time and evangelized many people after believing in Jesus. Paul sent Apollos to Aquila and Priscilla. Eventually Apollos became a man of great influence and leader in the Corinthian church.

The people of Ephesus wanted Paul to stay longer so that they may listen to more of his teachings. But promising them he would return if it was God's will, Paul left for Antioch via Caesarea.

3rd Missionary Journey: School of Tyrannus

Study Hall of Tyrannus in Ephesus

Paul begins his 3rd missionary work in the regions above the Antioch church which is in fact the area of Galatia where the 1st missionary trip took place. "It happened that while Apollos was at Corinth, Paul passed through the upper country and came to Ephesus and found some disciples." (Acts 19:1) Paul visited the pioneer churches in the area of Galatia and taught the church members the Scriptures with prayers to form a solid foundation.

Then Paul and his companions settled in Ephesus, the biggest city of Asia Minor, also known as the worldly cultural center of self-

Map 12-3

Apostle Paul's 3rd missionary trip. Paul's third mission started in the regions of Galatia where the first pioneer church that was raised during his 1st evangelical trip. He conducted evangelical work through the school of Tyrannus.

indulgence at the time. Finding some disciples there, Paul asked them "Do you know the Holy Spirit?" They responded 'no'. Apparently they only knew of John's baptism but had not heard anything of the Holy Spirit. Paul realized the urgency to teach not only the Scriptures but also the movement of the Holy Spirit to the believers of Jesus who had received salvation already. He then borrowed a place to teach and the real work of ministry began.

Why did Jesus shed blood and die on the cross, resurrect and ascended into heaven? It was because He wanted to send the Holy Spirit to us so that we could feel and meet Him in our hearts. "Hope does not disappoint because the love of God has been poured out within our hearts through the Holy Spirit who was given to us." (Romans 5:5) But today many believers of Jesus go to church but have neither any knowledge of the Holy Spirit nor any interest in knowing it. I have witnessed this frustrating situation through various churches in Korea and America and therefore, feel compelled to deliver boldly of the Holy Spirit.

Paul settled in Ephesus and borrowed the study hall of Tyrannus. This school was operated by a famous Hellenism philosopher "Tyrannus." There is an afternoon nap time called "siesta-time" in the Middle Eastern countries (in Ephesus it was from 11am-3pm). Paul took advantage of these hours and taught the Scriptures and evangelized in the study hall of Tyrannus. During his two years of mission in Ephesus, powerful works of the Holy Spirit came through Paul.

The head minister of Onuri Church in Korea, Yong Jo Ha had been diagnosed with cirrhosis of the liver at a young age of 30. The doctor told him that he would die if he didn't stop ministering in his condition. With fervent efforts, Minister Ha served and founded the Church of Entertainers and with his retirement fund (8,000,000 won = approx. US$8000) purchased a small bookstore in front of Ewha Women's University. There he began his mission of evangelical publications and bible lectures. That small bookstore is today Korea's main representative institution of evangelical publications and educational Bible center called "Study Hall of Tyrannus."

During his two years of teaching, Paul heard about the news of two divisions in the church of Corinth-namely, Paul and Apollos. Upon hearing this, Paul confessed, "I planted, Apollos watered, but God was causing the growth." (1 Corinthians 3:6) This meant that it was the Holy Spirit that caused the growth. In other words, there should be no reason for any argument or competition between fellow workers.

The duties or calling that we have received are to plant (evangelism and mission) and water (teach), and bearing of the fruit is done by God. We are merely His tools. We are only His channels delivering the seed of life. For this reason, there is no need for any divisions, conflicts or acting as the master of the church. Under no circumstances or whatever special works you carry out, do it with "humility of mind and regard one another as more important than yourself" (Philippians 2:3), "one Lord, one faith, one baptism, one God and Father of all who is over all and through all and all" (Ephesians 4:5-6) and that "we are being built together into a dwelling of God in the Spirit." (Ephesians 2:22)

Threader: Many problems arose especially in the church of Corinth regarding the special gifts of the Holy Spirit. Upon hearing this from Ephesus, Paul wrote letters to the church of Corinth, which is the 1st book of the Corinthians. We have actually benefited from this letter since explicit explanations were given with regard to the special gifts of the Holy Spirit.

Teaching and healing go together, and the news of remarkable exorcism spread like wildfire through the city. So effective was Paul's ministry in communicating the message that magicians were captivated by the power of the Holy Spirit and burned all of their magical papyrus scrolls of spells. This resulted in putting the silver-smiths of idol makers out of business, so they stirred the whole place to uproar. Shortly after the riot had been ceased, Paul left Ephesus.

Visit to Corinth

Instead of returning to Antioch church, Paul decided to visit the church of Corinth. He had spent the longest time in the church of Corinth during his 2nd missionary trip and was curious to find out how they had changed after receiving a letter from Ephesus. While spending three months in Corinth, Paul was determined to go to Rome for the purpose of spreading the gospel to the ends of the earth. He wrote a letter to the Roman church requesting for their cooperation and simultaneously introduces himself which is the book of Romans.

Paul and his companions wanted to stop again in Ephesus on their way back to Antioch church from Corinth but because of the uproar they arrived in Troas which was right underneath Ephesus. In Troas, Paul received great wisdom through the Holy Spirit that he spent long evenings giving sermons. The effort to listen for so long late at night was too much for a young weary man that he dozed off into a deep sleep and fell off the window sill and died. Apostle Paul brought the man alive.

There were five additional people other than Jesus who were raised from the dead in the New Testament. Jesus raised the daughter of a synagogue official Jairus, raised the widow's son of the city of Nain and raised Mary's dead brother Lazarus; Peter raised his female disciple Tabitha and Paul raised Eutychus in Troas. The people who were raised from the dead had something in common. All of them died young from an unknown reason. Many people gather whenever a miracle of healing takes place even today or in the past. But be mindful that signs and wonders (miracles) do not bring you salvation. The glory of God is definitely revealed through the wondrous miracles but it does not necessarily connect to salvation. We must go beyond miracles and remember that salvation does not occur without the 'blood shedding of redemption.'

Paul's Farewell Sermon in Miletus

Apostle Paul was unable to visit Ephesus due to the blockage of the Gentiles. So before heading towards Jerusalem Paul and his companions gathered the elders of Miletus (leaders of each church at the time). Paul then reported of his work done in Asia Minor and proposed the vision of missionary work ahead and gave a farewell sermon. He foresaw so clearly the internal troubles the church will face and warned them to be on their guard. "I do not place any value on my own life, provided that I complete the mission the Lord Jesus gave me - to bear witness to the good news of God's grace." (Acts 20:24) Fully aware of the dangers ahead, Paul reconfirmed his commitment, in front of his companions, saying that he was fully prepared to risk his life for the work of God.

The Holy Spirit had been revealed not only to Paul but also to his companions so they knew that Paul would suffer and receive hardships if he went to Jerusalem. But Paul knew that it was the only way to spread the gospel to the ends of the earth and said, "I must complete the mission." (Acts 20:24)

"I am earnestly serving God but why is it that trials and tribulations keep coming to me one after the other!" If there are any believers who complain and hold a grudge towards God like this, I urge you to repent and hold on to Paul's conviction and proclaim it with your lips. Even an inadequate person like me has been called by God to deliver the Word. Wherever I go to deliver or teach the Word, I make Paul's confession as my very own and offer it to the Lord on a daily basis. It is a blessing indeed to realize that God has given us works to do on His behalf.

Many believers misunderstand that if they truly love God and do His work that they will be rewarded with worldly blessings. Naturally there will be blessings if we live in obedience to God's way and if we abandon God for idolatry then curse follows according to Deuteronomy 11. Occasionally we are confronted with hardships or disadvantages in a worldly sense when we testify God's will.

In January 2005, I had started a seminar in New York called "Threading the Bible" under joint sponsorships of the Council Association of the Church of New York and Study Hall of Tyrannus (Korea). Every Sunday afternoon 1,200 believers gathered together passionately to study and sing praises with their raised hands. My heart went out to those believers who were clearly thirsty for the Word of God. So I led the study with a heart of revival and my heart was burning with fire. But then an unexpected trial and affliction came upon me. I was confronted with great accusations in the media and negative slanders from various religious institutions along with Buddhist organizations during the 5-week period of my seminar. They profoundly expressed personal attacks towards me stating that a government official was delivering the teachings of Christianity and pointed fingers at me for doing so. Shortly after various religious groups submitted appeal letters to each department in Seoul, Korea with the intention to put pressure that either the seminar be stopped or I should be removed from the government office. Quite frankly, my position in the government office was influenced through this incident. Through this experience, I learned that I also have to carry the Lord's cross as well in order to participate in the power of the Lord's resurrection.

Paul's speech was deeply personal towards the elders as he commended them. "Therefore be on the alert, remembering that night and day for a period of three years I did not cease to admonish each one with tears. And now I commend you to God and to the word of His grace, which is able to build you up and to give you the inheritance among all those who are sanctified." (Acts 20:31-32) His words moved them to tears as they put their arms around him in farewell.

Evangelism in Jerusalem_Acts 21-26

Imprisonment

After giving his farewell sermon in Miletus, Paul left for Jerusalem. Fellow Christians of the Jerusalem church accepted Paul's teaching which was "salvation is obtained by faith." But in order to undo the misunderstanding of the Jews, Paul openly identified with a group of men under a strict vow and performed purification of the law for one week. Before the week of the vow was over, a group of conservative Jews seized Paul in the temple of Jerusalem. (Acts 21:30)

Bounded in chains by the soldiers, Paul defense began - first before the Roman commander and then before the Jewish Sanhedrin Council. During life threatening moments and at low points, Paul was given a word of encouragement by the Holy Spirit. "The night immediately following, the Lord stood at his side and said, 'Take courage; for as you have solemnly witnessed to My cause at Jerusalem, so you must witness at Rome also.' (Acts 23:11) The conspiracy of the Jews to kill Paul ignited an emergency transfer to take place from Jerusalem to Caesarea (the base of the Roman governor's infantry at the time).

Paul served two-year imprisonment in the basement prison cell of

Caesarea and delivered the Word of God to various people. Among them were highest officials like Governor Felix, his successor Festus and even King Agrippa who was paying his respects to the new governor. "Some days later Felix arrived with Drusilla, his wife who was a Jewess daughter of Herod, and sent for Paul and heard him speak about faith in Christ Jesus. But as he was discussing righteousness, self-control and the judgment to come, Felix became frightened and said, 'Go away for the present and when I find time I will summon you.' (Acts 24:24-25) After hearing Paul's speech about justice and self-control and future judgment, Governor Felix, who was keen on receiving fat bribes, was scared. His conscience was bothered and it is said that he had called upon Paul frequently to listen to his teachings thereafter. For whatever purpose there was for Governor Felix, God had given him frequent opportunities to listen to the Word of God.

Felix's successor Governor Festus and King Agrippa received grace from listening to the words of Paul as well. The central issue was resurrection - "Why does it seem incredible to you that God should raise the dead - especially when Christ was the first to rise from the dead?" At this point, Paul was interrupted by Festus who shouted, "You are out of your mind! Your great learning is driving you mad." (Acts 26:24) Agrippa laughed it off by saying, "In a short time you will persuade me to become a Christian." (Acts 26:28) He couldn't afford to lose face with Festus or to offend the Jews. In spite of their grace they refused to receive Jesus. But surely they must have felt fear in their hearts afterwards.

Apostle Paul challenged the powerful two figures at the time, the governor and king. "I would wish to God that whether in a short or long time, not only you but also all who hear me this day might become such as I am, except for these chains." (Acts 26:29) What a fantastic remark! He dared them (governor and king) to become like him, a prisoner. Even when physically bounded in ropes, Paul could taste the kingdom of heaven which was unknown to the king or the governor who had all the worldly power. God used Paul, a prisoner and lowest of all positions and had him deliver the gospel to the high officials of Israel, governors and king. This is God's way and God's method. Whatever capacity we believers of God may have whether of a high position or a lesser position in the society as long as we are used as His tool to deliver the gospel we must be thankful.

Paul in his dark prison cell spoke out to the people who were free, "Rejoice in the Lord always; again I will say, rejoice!" (Philippians 4:4) How was he able to say this? Even though his environment was harsh and difficult, he was able to focus in the rewards to receive in God's world. A person with faith can be filled with joy and thankfulness.

Violent Wind "Euraquilo"

Paul as a Roman citizen insisted upon Governor Felix that he wished to appeal to Caesar. Rome was ruling over the world at the time. If a Roman citizen committed a crime they went to Rome to be judged directly by the Emperor. So along with other prisoners Paul was shipped to Rome. The voyage to Rome was made in three trips: a coaster from Caesarea to Myra (on the south coast of Turkey), a cargo vessel from Myra to Malta; and another from Malta to Puteoli in the Bay of Naples. For 14 days they were caught in a violent wind called 'Euraquilo' and suffered tremendous hardships with no means of knowing where they were. During this midst the angel of God promised safety and comforted Paul. "Do not be afraid, Paul; you must stand before Caesar; and behold, God has granted you all those who are sailing with you." (Acts 27:24) God raised Paul as a shining light for the Gentiles and appeared three times giving comfort, hope and encouragement at the most crucial moments of his ordeal during his missionary journey. God not only protects His children but also the people around His children as well.

Evangelism in Rome

Citizens of Rome brought their cases to be heard by the Roman Emperor which constantly resulted in full prison cells. For this reason, those who were able to financially support themselves were under house arrest while waiting for their case to be heard by the Emperor. In the meantime the palace guard would stay with someone under house arrest around the clock. Their shifts would take place in the morning which meant that the guard would lock his wrist along with Paul's and stay with him throughout the day. What do you expect they did all day long? Paul witnessed God to the guard whether he liked it or not. The Roman guard had no choice but to listen to Paul's message and by night his heart was full of grace and probably went home in tears. This applied to the night guard as well. "So that my imprisonment in the cause of Christ has become well know throughout the whole praetorian guard and to everyone else, and that most of the brethren, trusting in the Lord because of my imprisonment have far more courage to speak the word of God without fear." (Philippians 1:13-14)

Paul invited leaders of the Jews to his lodging place and eventually they came to him in large numbers. Then Paul "solemnly testified about the kingdom of God and tried to persuade them concerning Jesus from both the Law of Moses and from the Prophets from morning until evening." Paul earnestly and boldly taught of God's kingdom to all those who came to his lodging during his two years of house arrest. Whoever is full of the Holy Spirit will have the power to overcome difficult circumstances, just like Paul who was under tremendous hardship, and share the good news with others.

Paul was practically in and out of prison delivering God's message during his stay in Rome. While he was momentarily released from prison it is said that he was beheaded in execution and died as a martyr. Even though he was not able to fulfill his mission to spread the good news to the ends of the earth but in fact, under the direction of

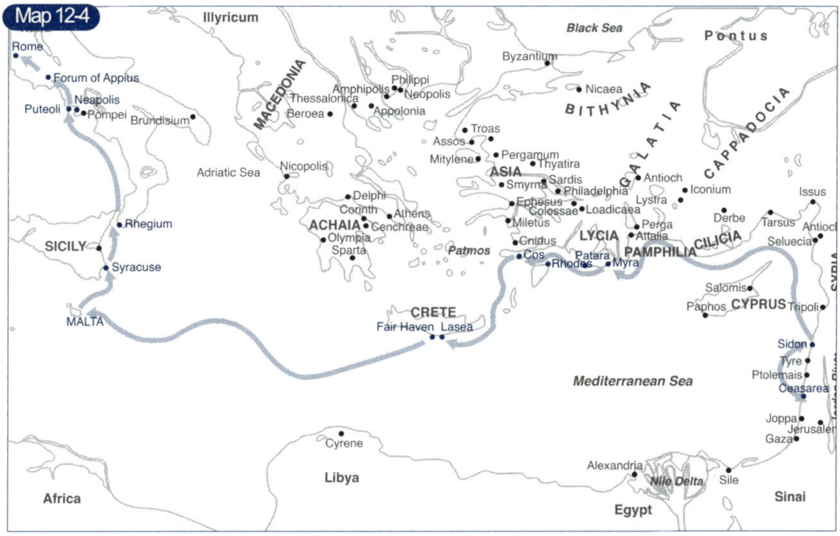

Apostle Paul's Evangelical Journey to Rome. Even though Paul was a prisoner he boldly testified God's message in confidence. Unable to fulfill his hope of missionary to the remotest place of the earth which was Spain at the time due to his death as a martyr, eventually the Roman church delivered the message to Spain on his behalf.

the Holy Spirit, a new born church bursts through the national frontiers of Israel to become an international, worldwide movement.

Spiritual Search 29

The Role of the Holy Spirit

Through the four Gospels we have covered how God the Father fulfills His promise with Abraham and David by sending His Son Jesus Christ to the world who died on the cross and resurrected so that salvation is given to us.

Through the book of Acts we have learned that, as promised by Jesus, the Holy Spirit was sent for us to enjoy God's kingdom on earth until His 2nd coming. The eternal love that was fulfilled through the Holy Spirit between God the Father and the Son of God before creation has been made known to the believers of God with the help of the Holy Spirit. We have learned the love pattern: upwards with Jesus and sideways with neighbors. So that is why we have been taught to pray as - "Thy kingdom come (let the kingdom of heaven be enjoyed on this earth)" "Thy will be done on earth as it is in heaven (let the cycle of love fulfilled in heaven be also created in the earth among others)."

Through baptism and the communion, as believers we have given our promises to partake in the cross of Jesus and His resurrection. And also taking on the baton of Apostle Paul, we are the people to continue on with chapter 29 of the book of Acts. A Christian empowered with the Holy Spirit is not some abstract power but a person who undergoes self denial, sacrifice (giving in) self and considers disadvantages to self for others on a daily basis and carries the burden of the cross through his/her life. We must also bear witnesses of God to the ends of the earth until His 2nd coming. Apostle Paul is our perfect role model who was empowered by the Holy Spirit and lived like Christ throughout his life.

The following are the roles of the Holy Spirit.

First, the Holy Spirit reveals our sin and makes us repent.

"I tell you the truth, it is to your advantage that I go away for if I do not, the Helper will not come to you; but if I go I will send Him to you. And He, when He comes, will convict the world concerning sin and righteousness and judgment." (John 16:7-8) Those who feel the presence of the Holy Spirit through prayer and the Word of God are sensitive towards sin. Each day you kneel and confess admitting yourself as a helpless and a weak sinner in front of the Lord. By doing so, the Holy Spirit purifies your soul with the overflowing stream of life. Just as a person becomes dirty without doing anything around the house, even Christians who have received salvation by believing in Jesus continue to sin whether big or small throughout our lives. That is why we must humbly kneel before the Lord and receive purification by the Holy Spirit on a daily basis. Those who do not know the Holy Spirit lie, cheat, gossip, drink, commit adultery and do all kinds of other immoral things and continue to live shamelessly. Some may claim that "they have no sin" because Jesus had spoken on the cross, "it is completed." We must not forget Jesus' teaching of the Lord's Prayer to His disciples - "forgive our sins."

Second, the Holy Spirit is the agent of Christ.

"But when He, the Spirit of the truth, comes He will guide you into all the truth; for He will not speak on His own initiative but whatever He hears, He will speak; and He will disclose to you what is to come. He will glorify Me, for He will take of Mine and will disclose it to you." (John 16:13-14) "But the Helper, the Holy Spirit, whom the Father will send in My name, He will teach you all tings and bring to your remembrance all that I said to you." (John 14:26) The Holy Spirit testifies of Jesus. The Holy Spirit does not speak on its own but only speaks of what Father wants to be witnessed of His Son. So whoever received the Holy Spirit cannot be still but has to become witnesses of Jesus. (Acts 1:8) Once the Holy Spirit works in us, the Word of God comes into our mind and we begin to understand it. The entire Bible is written through the inspiration of the Holy Spirit and without the inspiration of the Holy Spirit, one cannot understand the meaning of it. This is primarily the reason why Jesus cannot be acknowledged as the Lord without the help of the Holy Spirit, since the Holy Spirit is the Spirit of Jesus.

Third, the Holy Spirit unites - the Lord and me as one (meet).

"The Spirit of truth, whom the world cannot receive because it does not see Him or know Him, but you know Him because He abides with you and will be in you." (John 14:17) "I am the vine, you are the branches; he who abides in Me and I in him, he bears much fruit, for apart from Me you can do nothing." (John 15:5) The Lord meets us in Spirit and caresses us. He has loved us even before the creation of the world and has worked for a long period of time to come into our heart. Let us give our praise, honor and glory to the Trinity of God!

. . .

in no way alarmed by your opponents--which is a sign of destruction for them, but of salvation for you, and that too, from God. For to you it has been granted for Christ's sake, not only to believe in Him, but also to suffer for His sake,

Philippians 1:28-29

LIFE BECOMING LIKE CHRIST

The 13 Letters of Paul

The Letters make up about a third of the New Testament-out of 27 books excluding the book of Acts the rest of the 22 books are all letters. There are 13 letters under Paul's name which falls naturally into four groups, one anonymous letter (Hebrews), one by James, two under Peter's name, three under John's and one by Jude. The historical story of the four gospels and the book of Acts of the New Testament carry the message of "believe in Jesus Christ then you and your household will receive salvation" which is referred to as the 'salvation of justification.' In the meantime, the 22 letters carries the message in detail the ways and method of how a believer must conduct a Christian living (process of sanctification).

Paul's 13 Letters

The 13 letters of Paul went under the name of the receiver in each book. Among his letters, there were 9 letters sent to churches and 4 pastoral letters.

Apostle Paul wrote letters during his 1st missionary trip to the church in Galatia and during his 2nd mission trip to the churches of Corinth and Thessalonica. In his 3rd mission, he also wrote to the Roman church requesting for their cooperation. And during his house arrest in Rome, he wrote to the churches of Philippi and Colossae as well as to the deacon, Philemon. The letters written during his imprisonment are referred to as the 'Prison Letters.'

Chart 4 The Core Structure of the New Testament

Historical Books	The Letters		
	Pauline Letters (13)		General Letters (9)
Matthew, Mark Luke, John	To Church	Romans, 1 & 2 Corinthians Galatians, Ephesians, Philippians, Colossians, 1 & 2 Thessalonians	Hebrew, James 1 & 2 Peter 1 2 & 3 John
	To Pastor	1 & 2 Timothy, Titus & Philemon	Judah & Revelation

1 & 2 Timothy, Titus and Philemon are pastoral letters. It would be more accurate to refer to Philemon as a deacon rather than a pastor.

The Book of Romans-Receive Salvation

Salvation by Faith

After completing his 3rd missionary trip and before returning to Jerusalem, Paul sent a letter to the members of the Roman church for their cooperation in delivering the gospel to Spain which for them was the remotest place on earth at the time. This is the background of the letters written to the church in the book of Romans.

The teachings of salvation in Christianity are theologically well organized in this book. Paul explains precisely of the salvation of justification and salvation of sanctification in a systematical way.

First, justification of salvation is obtained through faith. It means whoever believes in the gospel becomes privileged to become a child of God. Paul was commissioned to preach in his letter that God treats all people alike, a Jew and Gentile. Everyone is in the grip of sin and we are all sinners before God, therefore, we must seek salvation. (Romans 3:9) And the heart of the Christian message is that all who acknowledge Jesus as Lord and believe that God raised Him from the dead will find salvation. "For in the gospel a righteousness from God is revealed, a righteousness that is by faith from first to last, just as it is written: "The righteousness will live by faith." (Romans 1:17) God's righteousness is revealed in the gospel, so that is why from the beginning to the end salvation is obtained by faith.

Salvation of Sanctification

We must understand the justified salvation is only the beginning. Paul explains in the book of Romans how a believer is set free from sin, law and death. We believers must be alert at all times to experience the Holy Spirit through daily prayers and the Word, so that we partake in the death of Christ and His resurrection.

Paul teaches us the principle of prayer: "With the heart a person believes, resulting in righteousness, and with the mouth he confesses, resulting in salvation." (Romans 10:10) This means that once we confess that Jesus is Lord your God it is not the end and that salvation must be experienced endlessly throughout our lives - believing in our heart and then confessing through our lips (by praying). "For by grace you have been saved through faith; and that not of yourselves, it is the gift of God." (Ephesians 2:8) Not only is the acceptance of the gospel enough but it must also include our commitment of daily prayers to meet God. We must realize that it is God's intention that every one of us should be like Christ; like Him in character now; like Him in glory eventually - recreating us 'in His image.' Every little circumstance of our life is worked into this great overall purpose.

Humans are made of spirit and flesh. The physical needs are filled up with food (physical food) but in order to fill our spirit (spiritual food) we need the Word of God. God has created humans in spirit and flesh and left empty space (void) with an intent to be filled with something. Just as Jesus spoke about the parable of a mustard seed, the minute we receive the Word of God Satan blocks it from growing within us, and that is why we must be determined to keep it with every effort through reading the Word and prayer. It would be almost impossible to bear good fruit without receiving the Word and prayers on a daily basis. With continuous confession through our lips, we must be able to fill our inner self with God's spirit and love. That is the way to achieve the salvation of sanctification. (Romans 10:10)

"I see a different law in the members of my body, waging war against the law of my mind and making me a prisoner of the law of sin which is in my members." (Romans 7:23) There are constant battles within ourselves between the law of the Spirit and the law of sin even after we receive salvation by believing in Jesus. Though we desire to follow God's way our sinful nature brings us down. As holy as Apostle Paul was, he confessed "Wretched man that I am! Who wills et me free from the body of this death?" (Romans 7:24)

But then again, we can overcome it through Jesus Christ. "There is no condemnation for those who are in Christ Jesus. For the law of the Spirit of life in Christ Jesus has set you free from the law of sin and of death." (Romans 8:1-2) The Holy Spirit of Jesus sets us free from the authority of death since the Spirit of God is alive and actively at work in everyone who belongs to Christ.

Apostle Paul gives advice to the believers of Jesus who have received salvation, "If you are living according to the flesh, you must die; but if the Spirit you are putting to death the deeds of the body, you will live." (Romans 8:13) It tells us that we will die if we live according to our fleshly means after receiving believing in Jesus. As believers of Christ, we must make a decision between the law of the Spirit and the law of sin. In other words, whether we will follow the Holy Spirit as it leads us or follow instincts of human nature.

Why does God permit Satan's activities? We must not forget that Satan is only permitted to act within the boundaries of God's plan and providence. (Job 1:12) Satan gives us pain but God tells us in the Bible that suffering is a beginning of a blessing. It is because Father's love can be realized while going through pain. Satan tempts us with visible things and urges us to abandon God's love which is invisible. Suffering may come because of our wrongdoings and blessings come to us when we cry out to God through the guidance of the Holy Spirit. A person who knows the love of God can make the right decision between the fleshly temptation and the calling of the Holy Spirit.

"We know that God causes all things to work together for good to those who love God, to those who are called according to His purpose." (Romans 8:28) Not all churchgoers necessarily experience this verse. Those who receive and experience God's love as they live are able to work out any differences that might arise among people and work harmoniously with one another. In order to receive God's love, we must live according to His ways. "If anyone loves Me, he will keep My Word; and My Father will love him, and We will come to him and me Our abode with him. He who does not love Me does not keep My words; and the word which you hear is not Mine, but the Father's who sent Me." (John 14:23-24)

The core teachings of salvation and the process of becoming sanctified contained in the book of Romans are as follows: It teaches human responsibility. It teaches us to attend church as believers of Jesus and to abide in the power of the Holy Spirit through the Word and prayer holding on to God's sovereignty. It teaches us to choose to live according to the laws of the Spirit. [Note: I have not put any efforts in listing detailed explanations of the Letters theologically. Rather being an ordinary believer myself, I have tried to simplify the overall commonality flow of the message in the 22 letters for easy understanding.]

1 Corinthians - Distinguish the Problems of Life

When working in Ephesus during his 3rd missionary journey, Paul had heard of the various problems in the church of Corinth through the people who visited him. The church members of Corinth wrote a letter to Paul asking for advice on how to resolve the problems. Paul wrote this letter (1 Corinthians) from Ephesus.

In the letter, Paul gives advice in response to a number of reports and questions. He is primarily concerned with correcting their keeping the same social life even after becoming a Christian.

Paul talks about adultery. "Do you not know that your body is a temple of the Holy Spirit who is in you, whom you have from God, and that you are not your own?" (1 Corinthians 6:19) Christians have been jointed to Christ's body so we must honor God in the way we use our own bodies. To think a body is not important is wrong. For Christians, the body cannot be separated from the whole personality. Our body is where Jesus dwells s and a place where He meets us. We must realize that our body is precious, and it is the reason why we are healed through His mercy when we get sick. "The body is not for immorality, but for the Lord and the Lord is for the body." (1 Corinthians 6:13)

The early church of Corinth displayed strong works of the Holy Spirit. Spiritual gifts like speaking in tongue, prophecy, casting out evil spirits, healing the sick, etc. were exhibited among its members and the disorder in the church came about when they claimed their gift was more important than others. Upon hearing this, Paul stressed the need for order within the church and gave them instructions.

Paul lists different types of spiritual gifts. (1 Corinthians 12-14) He explains that these spiritual gifts come from a single source, the Holy Spirit and are given for the good of the whole church. Every individual has an indispensable part to play in the life of the one body, and the important thing is not which gifts are most impressive but how they can best serve to build up the church. (1 Corinthians 12:4-31) Spiritual gifts are temporary, and at the 2nd coming of Christ they will be gone so it is more important to bear fruit of the Spirit. The fruit does not bear on its own. It only bears open when we live according to God's way which is the process of becoming sanctified.

There were other various problems concerning lawsuits between Christians, arguments and questions relating to jealousy. Paul warns them that they will not inherit God's kingdom if disorderly acts are conducted in the church. (1 Corinthians 6:6-9) Dealing with similar problems, Paul writes to the church in Ephesus: "With all humility and gentleness, with patience, showing tolerance for one another in love, being diligent to preserve the unity of the Spirit in the bond of peace." (Ephesians 4:2-3)

Problems in the church arise because the Word of God is known intellectually rather than acknowledged and confessed through the lips. Without opening of the heart to God how can the Holy Spirit work in you? Even though you may know the Word of God, without experiencing God's love you will live just like the worldly people-arguing and hating, etc.

The characteristics of sanctification can be found in 1 Corinthians. "And that which you sow, you do not sow the body which is to be, but a bare grain, perhaps of wheat or of something else." (1 Corinthians 15:37) When we spread the gospel it is the seed that we are spreading. The seed of the gospel must grow and God makes sure of it. "But God gives it a body just as He wishes and to each of the seeds a body of its own." (1 Corinthians 15:38) A believer must live a life filled with the Holy Spirit through the Word and prayer at all times until the seed grows to bear fruit. We must be able to change ourselves by displaying to others with the fruit of the Holy Spirit which is love, gentleness and moderation.

2 Corinthians - Make a Decision to Become Holy

"Therefore, having these promises, beloved, lest us cleanse ourselves from all defilement of flesh and spirit, perfecting holiness in the fear of God." (2 Corinthians 7:1) Those who fear God will become holy and be purified from the dirtied spirit and flesh. It would be misleading if you bring someone to church and teach, "You have received salvation by believing in Jesus and so you will now go to heaven so do not worry anymore. There's nothing more for us to do." What God wants us to do is to subdue our fleshly desires and make a conscious decision to become holy through the Word of God and prayer on a daily basis to fulfill (become sanctified) the salvation received from the Lord, which is the theme of all the letters.

Galatians
- Follow the Instincts of the Holy Spirit

The basic theme of Galatians follows the similar message of the book of Romans to the church members to address the teachings of salvation. Not long after Paul's return to Antioch church from his 1st missionary trip, other Jewish-Christian teachers arrived in Galatia and insisted that non-Jewish converts must also be circumcised and observe the Jewish law. When Paul heard this he was distraught and emphasizes in his letter to the Galatians the roots of the Christian message. Salvation-new life is God's gift to all who believe.

Paul reiterates that it is faith, from first to last salvation of justification. "Nevertheless knowing that a man is not justified by the works of the Law but through faith in Christ Jesus, even we have believed in Christ Jesus, so that we may be justified by faith in Christ and not by the works of the law since by the works of the Law no flesh will be justified." (Galatians 2:16) He emphasizes further on the importance of leading a sanctified life. "For you were called to freedom, brethren; only do not turn your freedom into an opportunity for the flesh, but through love serve one another." (Galatians 5:13) Freedom is much too precious to throw away. It would be a big mistake to think that whatever sin you commit through your actions has nothing to do with salvation, since salvation is obtained through faith.

Christians are not to be subject to the law but led by the Holy Spirit. God's life giving Spirit gives us the power to overcome sin, hurt and circumstances around us. But then again, the issue is that even after believing in Jesus there are people who go all the way and emasculate themselves taking advantage of this so-called 'freedom.' Freedom has been given to us so that we serve one another.

If a person is burdened with one's own sin or hurt, obviously there's no chance that person will look out for others. With His blood, Christ has set us free from our sins enabling us to serve others who are more in need. Salvation by faith is given to us so that we may bear fruit of the Holy Spirit and eventually do good to everyone, especially to those who belong to our family of the faith with the love of Christ. "But the fruit of the Spirit is love, joy, peace, patience, kindness, goodness, faithfulness, gentleness, self-control; against such things there is no law." (Galatians 5:22-23)

"For the flesh sets its desire against the Spirit, and the Spirit against the flesh; for these are in opposition to one another so that you may not do the things that you please." (Galatians 5:17) The desires of the flesh and the Spirit are constantly battling with one another, so that is why whatever your heart tells you the body resists. A living proof of a Christian service can only be accomplished through daily medication of the Word. We must confess our weaknesses and seek help of the Holy Spirit to transform our lives in the name of love. Let us lead our lives in sanctification by kneeling before the Lord on a daily basis.

Ephesians - Relationships between the Church and Saints

The Church is a Heavenly Place on Earth_Ephesians 1-3

The first three chapters of Ephesians relate to the theory of the church. "I pray that the eyes of your heart may be enlightened so that you will know what is the hope of His calling, what are the riches of the glory of His inheritance in the saints." (Ephesians 1:18) The inheritance given to the people of Israel was the land of Canaan and for believers - it is the Church. When our spiritual eyes are opened through the help of the Holy Spirit we will realize that the Church is a secret channel for God's blessing.

The Church became the glorified inheritance because Jesus died on the cross, and it is the Church that carries out Christ's work in the world. The power God exercised in raising Christ from the dead and setting Him in the supreme control over the universe is at work in us, too.

"He brought about in Christ, when He raised Him from the dead and seated Him at His right hand in the heavenly places far above all rule and authority and power and dominion, and every name that is named, not only in this age but also in the one to come. And He put all things in subjection under His feet, and gave him as head over all things to the church which is His body, the fullness of Him who fills all in all." (Ephesians 1:20-23)

Jesus fills the heart of His believers in all different ways. The church is filled with Jesus, therefore it is the source of all blessings. Blessings cannot be received when you leave the Church. "Blessed be the God and Father of our Lord Jesus Christ, who has blessed us with every spiritual blessing in the heavenly places in Christ." (Ephesians 1:3) God has poured out His love on us, blessing on blessing.

When we give worship at church, God gives His spiritual blessings to the heart of the minister through the Word. The spiritual blessings then form into an active material, health, happiness and visible blessings on earth. "I pray that in all respects you may prosper and be in good health, just as your soul prospers." (3 John 1:2) The advice from Apostle John is referring to the blessings of the church.

No matter how successful a person might be in the world there are certain things that cannot be resolved with worldly things - for instance, a broken home or health. Even though one may have failed in the world, when that person succeeds in giving worship to God at church the spiritual riches can turn into earthly blessings. Since Christ stands at the very heart of God's plan, the Church is the only place that wins over the world and becomes our only refuge and hope.

Put On the Armor of God_Ephesians 4-6

How Christians should lead their lives (process of sanctification) is covered under chapters 4-6 in Ephesians. One missionary who was transferred to China from the U.S. referred to these chapters as "put on the armor of God wherever you go and stand up against the wrongdoing."

"With all humility and gentleness, with patience, showing tolerance for one another in love, being diligent to preserve the unity of the Spirit in the bond of peace." (Ephesians 4:2-3) Christians are bound together by a common faith, a common life, common loyalty, and a common purpose. We serve one Master. The bond must constantly be cemented by a loving, forbearing attitude towards one another and by using the different gifts for the common good.

The phrase that describes the attitude of a Christian is "Put on the Armor of God." Like a Roman soldier, we have a belt and breastplate, shoes and shield, helmet and sword. God fits us with all the armor we need for defense and protection. (Ephesians 6:14-17) We are told to put on the armor of God daily in order to overcome the traps and temptations of Satan in our daily lives.

One's strength comes from the waist. We need spiritual weapons and these God provides. With the truth of God around our waist we prepare ourselves to fight against Satan. We arm ourselves with merciful love and put on the shoes of the gospel to prepare for evangelism. We hold our shield of faith to block off any kinds of trials that may confront us. We then wear the helmet of salvation to shrug off evil thoughts that might hinder us. Ultimately we attack with the Holy Spirit which is like a pierce of a sword.

Most important of all is the unseen weapon of prayer. The shield of righteousness and faith comes out from the power of prayer and the rest belongs to the Word of God.

But then, why is it that many believers have a hard time praying? The book of Ephesians teaches us how to pray. "With all prayer and petition at all times in the Spirit" (Ephesians 6:18a) Whatever you pray for, always do it in Spirit and through the guidance of the Holy Spirit. What this means is that you must pray in tongue.

God has said that whoever seeks the prayer of tongue it will be given. Paul's closing prayer for his brothers and sisters in Christ is not to wait but to "be on the alert with all perseverance and petition for all the saints." (Ephesians 6:18b) Jesus has promised that the Holy Spirit will be given as a gift to those who fervently ask. For this reason, we must always be on alert and seek. (Luke 11:5-13)

Philippians - Always Rejoice

The keynote of this letter is joy. Paul was in chains awaiting sentence when he wrote this letter to a group of Christian supporters in Philippi who had a special place in his heart. Before going to Rome, Paul spent two years in the basement prison cell of Caesarea. At that time, Paul said to Governor Festus and King Agrippa, "I would wish to God, that whether in a short or long time not only you, but also who hear me this day, might be come such as I am, except for these chains." (Acts 26:29)

Paul's message in the book of Philippians is "Rejoice! Rejoice in the Lord always!" He has learned to fill his mind with the Holy Spirit. The secret of contentment whatever his circumstances may have been was in Christ's strength. Just as martyr Stephen was able to off-load all his mind with joy, focusing on Jesus who was sitting next to the heavenly throne, when he was stoned to death and suffered physically, we must also live in joy and peace while on this earth and eventually go to heaven.

The book also states that without leading a sanctified life on this earth one cannot be happy. The Lord is equal to God the Father but

He emptied Himself to the point of death out of obedience and rejoiced in the reward of the cross. "Have this attitude in yourselves which was also in Christ Jesus, who although He existed in the form of God, did not regard equality with God a thing to be grasped, but emptied Himself, taking the form of a bond-servant and being made in the likeness of men. Being found in appearance as a man, He humbled Himself by becoming obedient to the point of death, even death on a cross." (Philippians 2:5-8)

Those who insist upon 'self' have to control everything but the reality of the world doesn't allow that, so as a result they can never experience peace or joy. When you realize that the ability to do everything comes from the One, no matter how other people treat you, feel rejected or go hungry, you are still able to feel joy and satisfaction. "I know how to get along with humble means, and I also know how to live in prosperity; in any and every circumstance I have learned the secret of being filled and going hungry, both of having abundance and suffering need. I can do all things through Him who strengthens me." (Philippians 4:12-13) To be able to do all things means having the ability to become humble and ability to carry the cross.

This ability comes from a person who is filled with the Holy Spirit. Pray and seek for the power of the Holy Spirit. Apostle Paul continuously gives advice and encouragement to us always to be alert and pray for the power of the Holy Spirit.

Colossians - Who is Jesus?

Paul writes urgently to the Colossian church from the prison of Rome. He has heard that the church was adopting a heresy and losing sight of Christ.

There is a simple method of distinguishing the true faith from heresy. Surprisingly enough, the Mormon Church is referred to as the Church of Christ. But in fact, they deny the Trinity of God.

Outwardly they talk about Jesus but once you follow their teaching it is the founder of the Mormons who has taken over Jesus' seat. This is the same act of the proud angel, Satan (aka Lucifer) who wanted the seat of God. Heresy can easily be noticed if you go in slightly and glimpse through their teaching.

With this in mind, we notice that the evident theme of Colossians is 'Who is Jesus?' "He is the image of the invisible God, the firstborn of all creation." (Colossians 1:15) Jesus is invisible Spirit and the living expression of God Himself - active in creation, upholding all that exists, in power and in position. It is Jesus who has revealed the invisible love of God to mankind. "For by Him all things were created, both in the heavens and earth, visible and invisible, whether thrones or dominions or rulers or authorities all things have been created through Him and for Him." (Colossians 1:16) This means that Jesus is the Creator and "all things have been created for Him." This book testifies that Jesus Christ is the Creator who revealed the invisible love of God and that He is God of Trinity who rules over all creation and the universe.

A challenge thrown to the world by Reverend Rick Warren, author of The Purpose Driven Life, that all mankind has been created by Jesus for the purpose of God the Father is based on the first chapter of Colossians.

1 & 2 Thessalonians - Have a Correct Understanding of Jesus' Return

When Paul and Silas spent three weeks preaching in the Thessalonica synagogue the Jews stirred up trouble, because Paul was preaching about another king other than the Roman Emperor. Not having sufficient time to fully explain the gospel, it is assumed that Paul must have emphasized of the glorifying 2nd coming of Christ.

The new believers in the Thessalonica church faced some problems regarding this issue. It was evident that they didn't know how to lead their lives properly as Christians and asked questions like, "Why is it difficult? We thought that things will be smooth after believing in Jesus but it's very difficult!"

Paul was concerned after hearing the news from Timothy and sent a letter to the Thessalonians during his 2nd missionary trip. As the time for Jesus' return draws near, he emphasizes the attitude of living for God and that people must act out their Christian love to families and neighbors. (1 Thessalonians 4:1-12) Even where love already exists there is always room for more. "Rejoice always; pray without ceasing and in everything give thanks." (1 Thessalonians 5:16-18) Paul advises that this must be the standard practice of a Christian.

Are we able to give thanks when our business goes bust; we get fired from a job; we are diagnosed with cancer? Can we confess? "Lord what you do to me is complete. O perfect and faithful God, I thank you deeply." Are we able to kneel down before God thanking Him when our future seems so unpromising? As Christians, these are the times when we must truly thank God and rejoice in Him. Why? Because through our trials God is trying to transform us into a blameless and holy being and has chosen the kindest path for our sake.

Apparently the Thessalonians had keen interest in the 2nd coming of Christ. Jesus spoke to His disciples, "But of that day and hour no one knows, not even the angels of heaven, nor the Son, but the Father alone." (Matthew 24:36) Paul clearly stated "the day of the Lord will come just like a thief in the night." (1 Thessalonians 5:2) We must always be alert and pray since we do not know when Christ is coming. Let us hold on to the Word and pray at all times. Having the privilege of being God's children, we must prepare to transform ourselves into a holy being. This way, whenever He comes we will be ready to meet Him. "Therefore be on the alert, for you do not know which day your Lord is coming." (Matthew 24:42) We have been taught explicitly through the sermon given by Jesus on Mount of Olives. (Matthew 24-25)

At the time, the church members of the Thessalonica church thought that they didn't have to work hard since Jesus was going to return. But Paul instructs them to get on with their work, whatever it might be, and tells them not to put their tools down and wait for Christ's coming. He warns against the anti-Christ and the false teachings and adds, "If anyone is not willing to work, then he is not to eat either." (2 Thessalonians 2:10) In other words, as an excuse of Jesus' return, do not call out 'Hallelujah' in the mountains. Take a look at Apostle Paul's life. During the day he earnestly attended to tent-making and when people took naps in the afternoon he took the advantage of those hours as well as evenings to preach the Word of God. God's command to us is to 'go into' the world and teach the Word - "Go therefore and make disciples of all the nations" (Matthew 28:19)

1 Timothy - Fight the Good Fight with Faith

Along with Timothy, Paul was leaving Ephesus for Macedonia when he heard the troubled news at the Ephesus church. They were getting side-tracked away from Jesus' love with false teaching which was misleading them to idle speculation and Jewish legends. This was a wrong approach to the Old Testament law, so Paul sent Timothy to stop it from spreading. The Christian message must result in faith, love and a clear conscience. The Ephesus church was a big church founded by Paul where he opened the study hall of Tyrannus.

The book of Timothy is Paul's letter warning Timothy of the dangers of false teaching and telling him how to choose the right kind of leaders while giving him personal guidance for his own leadership role in Ephesus church. Paul stresses that if the church leader does not stand by the teachings of Jesus Christ, his/her heart will become corrupted resulting in unnecessary arguments and endless disputes. (1Timothy 6:3) As dedicated as Timothy he will steer clear of the pitfalls of money (1 Timothy 6:10) and his goals are faith, love, perseverance and gentleness in the good fight of faith. This verse and advice not only apply to the leaders (pastors) of the church but also to ordinary believers. Those who are totally committed to their transforming to godliness like Christ must always remind themselves of this message.

2 Timothy - Endure Suffering and Testify

When Paul was momentarily released from prison in Rome, he visited the churches of Philippi and Corinth. He then passed through Troas and headed towards the Ephesus church where Timothy was working. While in transit Paul was captured again and was brought back to the prison in Rome. This is Paul's last and moving letter to his son of faith, Timothy, realizing that his death was approaching. (2 Timothy 4:6) Deep thankfulness fills Paul's heart as he thinks of Timothy and he longs to share his own confident faith with him. In this letter, Paul asks Timothy to come and visit him in Rome. He has a last charge for Timothy to go on declaring God's message; "preach the word; be ready in season and out of season; reprove, rebuke, exhort with great patience and instruction."(2 Timothy 4:2) In spite of being aware of the troubled times ahead of him, he encourages them to carry out their works as good soldiers of Christ Jesus to the very end.

Titus - To the Leaders

Just as Paul had left Timothy behind to resolve problems in the church of Ephesus he placed Titus in charge of an unruly and difficult group in the church of Crete. The book of Titus is Paul's pastoral letter to him when he was faced a situation very similar to Timothy's at Ephesus.

Paul stresses the qualifications of church leaders and the requirement that any leader must hold - warning them about false teachings as well as instructing them that the Christian life calls for discipline, obedience and respect for others. He also teaches how a relationship between a pastor and a church member must be. The church of Titus was founded in the island of Crete where the locals were known as habitual liars, so Paul emphasizes that Christians must clearly be distinguished from the Gentiles.

Philemon - Change the Society with the love of Jesus

When Apostle Paul was imprisoned he came into contact with Onesimus, one of Philemon's runaway slaves who became a Christian through him. Paul loved this young man like a son but he was Philemon's legal property. Knowing that Onesimus was liable to terrible punishment, Paul wrote a letter to Philemon which is the book of Philemon. Paul writes in his letter that Onesimus is now a different man and appeals to Philemon to treat his slave as a brother in Christ and set him free as if he were the apostle himself.

Slavery in Rome was universally accepted when Paul's letter to Philemon was written. And in the eyes of Paul everyone is specially predestined to be God's children. This letter provides the clearest evidence that Christian community should be an example of what the world should be like with the foundation of love - both spiritually and socially.

Spiritual Search 30

Why are Letters Necessary?

The New Testament consists of four gospels: Matthew, Mark, Luke and John. In addition to Acts that follows these gospels, there are 22 letters. Apostle Paul wrote letters to the early church and pastors. This indicates that the letters were written primarily to the believers of Jesus and not necessarily for the purpose of evangelizing non-believers. Not only did the four gospels present Jesus as Christ but also that He was the only way to receive salvation. The letters was another way of teaching how a believer must conduct a Christian living (sanctified lifestyle). After all, if one were to believe in Jesus and receive salvation, then by right there must be a difference in their attitudes than before.

If living a religious life was all about believing in Jesus and going to heaven after we die, there would be no use for these letters. If we are already reserved to go to heaven, what's the point? It won't matter how we live.

Many people think that blessings come automatically once we believe in Jesus. This assumption can be derived from Deuteronomy (Deuteronomy 11:26-28) in the Old Testament. But once you start reading the letters, you will begin to realize that it is not just good things that happen to those who believe in Jesus. In spite of our strong faith, hardships and difficult situations occur at times. But we are able to overcome and experience God's kingdom through Jesus. The letters teach us the way to achieve this. Tough times like being laid off at work, discovery of terminal illness, or no roof over your head due to bankruptcy, your faith (Habakkuk 3:17) allows you to overcome and praise God even in such critical times, and this is the gospel message found in the letters.

There is a reason why God gave spiritual gifts to believers. It is because of the rule of human relationships. Human relationships are a two-way street: give and take.

Why do children study? It is to give and take. For instance, you study law in order to provide legal service and in return you receive service. "If you want to be entertained then entertain first." You give one and you receive one back - that's the principle of life.There's no such thing as freebies in the world.

But Jesus commands us to "Love your neighbor as you would love yourself." If we were to obey God's command, then we will experience losses at times. That is why God gave us spiritual gifts. Spiritual gifts give you the power and ability to share with others in need. The 21 spiritual gifts mentioned in the Bible are essential tools that enable us to serve others.

The more you give the more you receive God's spiritual gifts. In my case, the more I deliver the Word of God to people the deeper my understanding of the Word becomes. This is strictly God's doing. After Peter and John received the Holy Spirit, they felt compassionate towards the crippled beggar sitting in front of the Temple's gate. They wanted to give him something but there was nothing to give. Then Peter said, "I don't have any silver or gold for you. But I'll give you what I have. In the name of Jesus Christ the Nazarene, get up and walk" and a miracle happened. Surely this gift cannot be exchanged with silver or gold. Someone who has utilized the gift of healing is just as overjoyed as the one who has been healed. Greater joy is filled in the heart when one shares spiritual gifts received from God. For this reason alone, believers are rich in Christ even though they may not have the world's riches.

Secular people are busy working but they are limited in giving only what they have. On the other hand, people who have received heavenly blessings can give sparingly to others. By doing so, you are filled with abundant joy in return. The Bible is filled with stories about people who shared their spiritual gifts with others.

. . .

But the fruit of the Spirit is love, joy, peace, patience, kindness, goodness, faithfulness, gentleness, self-control; against such things there is no law.

Galatians 5:22-23

TRANSFORMATION OF OUR INNER SELF

9 General Letters

Apart from Pauline letters, the letters addressed to groups of Christians in different parts of the Greco-Roman world by the apostles and the two brothers of Jesus are referred to as 'general letters.' They also teach practical guidance on Christian conduct, covering various topics. We are now approaching the end of the lengthy 66 books of the Bible. Do you have a better grasp of the Bible? If you have committed to changing your inner self and living a sanctified life by meditating and praying daily, you have clearly grasped the 'thread' of the Bible.

The 9 Letters of the Apostles

There are nine books in the general letters. Each letter has been named after the author. James who was the brother of Jesus wrote the book of James; Judah, also the brother of Jesus, wrote the book of Judah; Peter wrote 1 & 2 Peter, and Apostle John wrote 1, 2 & 3 John as well as Revelations which is the conclusion of the Bible. The book of Hebrews has been included in the general letters since the author is not exactly known.

Hebrews - Act Upon Your Faith

The book of Hebrews compares and contrasts the person and

the achievements of Jesus with the Old Testament priesthood and sacrificial system. Nowhere else but in Hebrews it expresses Jesus as the high priest in the Bible. It also explains theology behind how God has made a new covenant in which sacrifice and priesthood take on a revolutionary meaning.

Today's church no longer needs to sacrifice as in the Old Testament period, since what the law could not do, Christ has done. His offering is effective forever. "Not through the blood of goats and calves but through His own blood He entered the holy place once for all having obtained eternal redemption." (Hebrews 9:12) Jesus has opened access to the presence of God.

It also emphasizes that Jesus' priestly work of redemption is far superior than all the high priests appearing in the Old Testament such as the prophets, angels, Moses or Aaron; as the perfect high priest Jesus offered Himself as the perfect sacrifice. (Hebrews 8:1-10:18) So we must come near to God (Hebrews 10:19-13:25) and lead a better devoted life than the period of the Old Testament, which ultimately leads us into sanctification. (Hebrews 11) Majority of the people refer to Hebrews 11 as the chapter of faith, but I think it can be referred to as the chapter of action. According to this chapter, faith is shown through actions. Abel's offering showed his faith; Abraham's trusting obedience to God's call took him away from his settled life at home in Ur of the Chaldeans. Those who have faith lead their life in obedience to God.

James - Bear Fruit Through Deeds, not Words

The book of James is known as the Proverbs of the New Testament. James stresses that real faith shows in the way Christians behave and that it is important to live them out. If Paul had fought against lawmakers who believed the doctrine of salvation by works,

James fought against law breakers who lived as they pleased assuming they would go to heaven after receiving salvation by faith. James reminds us of the need for genuine Christian standards and values in every area of life. The Christians were suffering politically and financially due to King Agrippa's persecution at the time, so their excuse for not putting faith into practice was that they had received salvation by faith.

So James warns if our faith does not show in what we do and the way we behave, it is dead! He writes, "If a brother or sister who is without clothing and in need of daily food, and one of you say to them, "Go in peace, be warmed and be filled" and yet you do not give them what is necessary for their body, what use is that?" (James 2:14-17) He further gives advice saying, "But prove yourselves doers of the word, and not merely hearers who delude themselves." (James 1:22) Christians with genuine faith will care for others and show them respect regardless of appearances and social status. Faith without action is dead. One who has faith acts upon it. At the same time, let us not forget that it is not through action that we are saved but through faith that makes us act. James also teaches us to control our tongues. To master this most uncontrollable and contradictory member of the body is to have perfect self-control. One single word can be just as destructive as deadly venoms. The same tongue can bless and curse, do good and do untold harm. (James 3:8-10) He reminds us that those who want friendship with the world become an enemy of God. A warning to the rich is followed. James commands the rich to share their wealth with the poor and to intercede on behalf of one another. (James 5)

1 & 2 Peter - Have Hope Even Through Suffering

Peter wrote 1 & 2 Peter to the scattered groups of Christians enduring persecution in the reign of the sadistic Emperor Nero giving them hope and encouragement.

At the time Christians were in hiding in Catacombs, public cemeteries, in order to keep their faith. Peter says to his readers, "You are a chosen race, a royal priesthood, a holy nation, a people for God's own possession, so that you may proclaim the excellencies of Him who has called you out of darkness into His marvelous light." (1 Peter 2:9) These words were great comfort and hope to these Christians who were in terrible predicament hiding quietly in the graveyards enduring severe persecutions.

These same words apply to believers today as well. After receiving Jesus, there are times when we get persecuted by our worldly friends or neighbors who tempt us to go back to the 'old days.' Whenever you struggle with such situations, I urge you to remember this verse which will help you overcome the temptation.

"For you have been born again not of seed which is perishable but imperishable, that is, through the living and enduring word of God." (1 Peter 1:23) Even in times of suffering there is so much to be thankful for because after enduring it we will participate in God's glory. Therefore, as Christians we must spread and testify the Good News of our Savior and His glory. Peter encourages us to enjoy trials and sufferings since they test our faith and prove it genuine. The dark days are short in comparison with the joy to come.

Among the 12 disciples Peter was the only one who was married. For that reason he emphasized the importance of husband and wife's love for one another. A good relationship is vital not only for their happiness but for spiritual health too. He indicates that friction in a marriage relationship can block prayers from being answered. (1 Peter 3:1-7) It gives us an insight into how the entire congregation's prayers may be jeopardized if there was a problem in the pastor's family. Peter teaches about the spiritual blessing that comes with suffering (1 Peter 4) and a true shepherd spirit for pastors (1 Peter 5) and how church members must respect their authority. Christians need to acquire a genuinely humble spirit while being alert and level-headed to face formidable and unrelenting oppositions of the devil.

In 2 Peter, the 2nd coming of Christ is mentioned to the Christians who were being persecuted by the well strategically organized Roman government. Peter urges them to live with hope of Jesus' return and in a godly manner. As Christians, there must be progressiveness in the lifestyle they lead in a godly way. "Seeing that His divine power has granted to us everything pertaining to life and godliness, through the true knowledge of Him who called us by His own glory and excellence." (2 Peter 1:3) The second letter indicates that at end times believers will be persecuted but Peter encourages them to overcome it with the hope of the 2nd coming of Christ.

1, 2 & 3 John - If You Love God Love Your Brethrens

Among the 12 disciples it is well noted that Peter was one that loved Jesus the most. He was the one who expressed his love frequently to Jesus, and even Jesus, upon His resurrection confirmed Peter's love personally. On the other hand, Apostle John was one of the 12 disciples who boldly expressed that he was the one whom Jesus loved the most. So that is why 1, 2 & 3 John is referred to as love letters.

Theologically, John's purpose in writing these letters was to warn the readers against false teaching, calling on them to hold to the truth that "God is love," requiring His children to love one another. (1 John 4:16) These words are a strong weapon to defend us against heresy. We must realize that heresy is intellectually appealing and possesses superior knowledge of God but what it lacks is deep understanding of the love of God. It is because someone else (founder of a religion) other than Jesus has taken over the seat.

The book of 1 John makes a distinction between true and false believers and provides the reader with three standards for making that distinction. First, whether they believe sins were forgiven by the death of Jesus and His resurrection; Second, whether they have brotherly love; and Third, whether they are living in a godly manner rather than breaking God's law deliberately and habitually. John reiterates that it is important to live as the children of God and that by abiding with God's Holy Spirit they will stay with the Son and God the Father — which means eternal life. The essence of John's message must be carved into our hearts that to know God is to obey and love one another. Remarkably in 1 John, it delivers God's promise that He will give answers to our prayers. "This is the confidence which we have before Him, that if we ask anything according to His will, He hears us. And if we know that He hears us in whatever we ask, we know that we have the requests which we have asked from Him." (1 John 5:14-15)

In 2 John, emphasizes not to casually settle with the wrong teachings and heresies. "If anyone comes to you and does not bring this teaching, do not receive him in your house, and do not give him a greeting; for the one who gives him a greeting participates in his evil deeds." (2 John 1:10-11)

In 3 John, God promises blessings of prosperity and health to believers when their soul prospers. "Beloved, I pray that in all respects you may prosper and be in good health, just as your soul prospers." (3 John 1:2) Let us not misunderstand this verse by thinking that once you believe in Jesus everything will be great. We must remember that the core message of the gospel is the doctrine of the cross which represents enduring trials and sufferings for the Lord, self-denial and sacrifice for others' sake.

Let us not forget the true attitude of a Christian reflecting on Jesus who carried the cross for His love for us. "When Jesus saw the crowds, He went up on the mountain; and after He sat down, His disciples came to Him." (Matthew 5:1) Among the crowds were His disciples. The crowds had heard of Jesus' healing the sick, so they were basically there to get healed whereas the disciples were there to participate in carrying the cross together with Jesus. Let us take a moment and ask ourselves - whether I am a disciple or merely a person in the midst of the crowd.

Jude - Hold Fast to the Truth and Build on the Faith

Jude, the younger brother of Jesus and James, writes to urge the Christians to hold fast to the truth, so that they may resist against the false doctrine by false teachers. "My beloved, build yourselves up on your most holy faith, praying in the Holy Spirit." (Jude 1:20) This is actually the emphasis of all the letters and the goal of the process of godly life for the believers. The warning goes further, saying that one must guard oneself against the false teachers who deny Christ and have sneaked into the church premises turning God's grace into a sexual market. Jude encourages his readers not to fall into the temptation of being the children of flesh by giving themselves up to pride or lust but commands them instead to become the children of the Holy Spirit.

The Revelation to John - Hope for the New Heaven and a New Earth

The book was written during the peak of persecution by Emperor Domitian when aged Apostle John was in exile on Patmos Island. It records the events that the Holy Spirit revealed to him, which he sent out as a circular letter to the seven churches in Asia.

Frequently when revelation is mentioned, many people show interest assuming that it is about the judgment of mankind at the end times. But in truth, John's message is a message that contains comfort and hope to the believers who are trying to keep their faith in this turbulent world. Even at a time when Christians were under severe persecution from the Roman government, God was in control over the universe. Through supreme glory and authority, the rule of God over His whole creation is finally going to come to end the power of the world. The book of Revelation is divided into three magnificent parts: "things which you have seen, things which are and will take place" (Revelation 1:19) - past (witnessed Christ-Revelation 1:1-20); present (message to the seven churches in Asia-Revelation 2:1-3; 3:22) future (tribulation, judgment, advent of the eternal world-Revelation 4:1-22:21) A layman believer may read the book of Revelation and receive grace, but I recommend you to get some help of sermons or bible study guide books. If the book of Genesis shows the 'beginning' (source) of all worldly creation (universe), the book of Revelation represents the 'end' (final judgment) of the world. The Lord God said to John, "I am the Alpha and the Omega, who is and who was and who is to come, the Almighty." (Revelation 1:8)

Revelation is also an apocalyptic prophecy. Plagues of wrath appear each time the seven seals are opened, seven trumpets are blown and seven bowls are poured. For unbelievers it may sound like judgments at the end of the world, but for believers it is a promise of hope for a new heaven and earth. "According to His promise we are looking for new heavens and a new earth, in which righteousness dwells." (2 Peter 3:13) In the book of Revelation, Apostle John tells us that the prophecy of Isaiah's "new heavens and the new earth" (Isaiah 66:22) will be fulfilled at the 2nd coming of Christ. The conclusion of the 66 books of the Bible is that all the sanctified believers will be called upon to participate in the wedding of the young lamb and will rule over the new heaven and earth, living a life in eternal paradise. "Then I saw a new heaven and a new earth; for the first heaven and the first earth passed away, and there is no longer any sea. And I saw the holy city, new Jerusalem, coming down out of heaven from God, made ready as a bride adorned for her husband." (Revelation 21:1-2)

The ultimate goal of Christians is to look forward to the new heaven and earth upon the 2nd coming of the Son of God (Jesus the Little Lamb) who will come from the seat of the heavenly throne. In the new heaven and earth, believers will participate in the heavenly festive wedding of the Little Lamb and will receive a crown of righteousness according to their deeds in the world. With this hope Christians who have overcome all persecution, tribulation, suffering and temptation will be made a pillar in the temple of God and will also receive a great blessing of God the Father and Son's name engraved on them. "He who overcomes I will make him a pillar in the temple of My God, and he will not go out from it anymore; and I will write on him the name of My God, and the name of the city of My God, the new Jerusalem, which comes down out of heaven from My God, and My new name." (Revelation 3:12)

The book of Revelation is a message of hope. After Genesis 3, God promised to recover His kingdom on this earth, and in order to fulfill His promise, has worked patiently for a long time. It is a moving message of God's final purpose for the world that is about to be accomplished on this earth.

Understanding and Benefit of the Tongue

The 'Word of God' can be learned from a pastor but, unfortunately, there are not many pastors who teach us how to pray. Reflecting on my own personal experience, it was difficult to learn to pray on one's own. (a prayer that is moved by the Holy Spirit to feel the presence of the Lord).

There may be different prayers that each believer prays to experience the Holy Spirit, but I am confident that there is no better way to pray other than to pray in tongues to fully experience the powerful presence of the Holy Spirit. I would like to share my experience with the readers here at this last portion of the 'Threading the Bible' of what I personally learned and benefited from praying in tongues.

Many people have researched on the Holy Spirit and the spiritual gifts of the Holy Spirit but the characteristics of prayer of tongue and its benefit have not really been properly made known to believers. My attempt is to assist and help those who have already received the spiritual gift of praying in tongues but have no idea why it is necessary to continue to pray in such way. It is also for those who are earnestly yearning for the gift of praying in tongues. Bear in mind though that what I'm about to say is not absolutely 100 percent perfect or correct. Spiritual gifts are partial and temporary until the 2nd coming of Christ. At that time it would be like just uncovering the towels and finally seeing each other. So until then, things that appear through the Holy Spirit are only partial. Again, the spiritual gifts are not the essence of the Christian life since the Holy Spirit is given to make us effective for Christ. My life has personally benefited enormously through praying in tongues and would like to introduce a method to enjoy the paradise in whatever environment or circumstances a person may be in. (Notes: Chun Soo Lee's "Understanding and Benefit of the Tongue" "Ministry of Spirituality"- 1999)

The Holy Spirit in Us

As previously mentioned, the conclusion of the Old Testament is not only the promise of the coming Messiah but also the promise of the "Holy Spirit to be put inside us." (Ezekiel 36:26) We have already gone over the flow of the Old Testament with similar prophecies such as the following verses: "It is the Spirit who gives life; the flesh profits nothing; the words that I have spoken to you are spirit and are life." (John 6:63) "A new spirit will be put within you." (Ezekiel 36:26) "I will put My law (Word) within you." (Jeremiah 31:33) The prophecies of the two prophets Ezekiel and Jeremiah were that the Messiah will come to take over the work of the redemption of the cross and that His Spirit will dwell within us. It is because the Word is Spirit. (John 6:63) Jesus died, resurrected, and as promised, the Holy Spirit was sent to whoever received the Word.

Then, how can we tell that the Holy Spirit has come in us? Paul spoke to the church members of Corinth, "Do you not know that you body is a temple of the Holy Spirit who is in you, whom you have from God?" (1 Corinthians 6:19) Our body is the temple of the Holy Spirit. But how did God's Spirit come inside us? The Bible witnesses that the Spirit comes when we believe the Word in our hearts and acknowledge through your lips.

The Holy Spirit basically attacked us. "For by grace you have been saved through faith and that not of yourselves, it is the gift of God." (Ephesians 2:8) We are full of sin, filth and of Satan, but with the Holy Spirit's interference, the Spirit of God came into us. "We have this treasure in earthen vessels" (2 Corinthians 4:7) As fragile as we are, a remarkable treasure, the Holy Spirit, has been put inside us.

Why did God put the Holy Spirit in this breakable vessel as us? The Holy Spirit wants us to realize that it is only God who has the supreme power and made us into an earthen vessel and put the treasure of the Holy Spirit inside us. "Now we have received, not the spirit of the world but the Spirit who is from God so that we may know the things freely given to us by God." (1 Corinthians 2:12) It is the grace of God that the Holy Spirit has been put inside us. The believers of God do not receive the spirit of the world or Satan's spirit but the Spirit of God.

But unfortunately, it is not only God's power that has been put inside the earthen vessel. God has given us freewill and asks us to make a choice: whether to follow the Spirit of God (eating from the tree of life) or to follow Satan's spirit (eating from the tree of the good and evil).

If we receive the gospel with Amen, the Spirit of God comes into us. The Holy Spirit which is the greatest power of Spirit, Spirit of love, and the Spirit of life (character) come into our hearts. The Spirit that has come inside us wishes to work within our hearts.

Signs of the Holy Spirit

Surprisingly enough, there are many unbelievers and even believers who say, "What Holy Spirit? There's no such thing. I can believe in God or Jesus but I cannot believe in the Holy Spirit because it appears to be some kind of a ghost or some weird spirit." Actually intellectuals are the most skeptical of them all.

The Bible not only testifies the Holy Spirit that works within us, but God also has given us a sign. For example, oxygen is invisible but we know that it exists. If there was no oxygen we cannot breathe, not even for a moment. And we indicate the invisible oxygen as O and water as H_2O which are signs and marks.

Along the same lines, God is also invisible but He makes the Holy Spirit within us appear visibly. Boiling water in a tea kettle produces energy and makes the water overflow. When the Holy Spirit works vigorously within us, our body reacts. With the energy of the Holy Spirit that inspires us, a part of our body is affected by it.

In reality, when the Holy Spirit works strongly in us believers, just like the energy from the boiling water, the energy of the Holy Spirit also appears visibly. In the Bible, this is referred to as signs. "These signs will accompany those who have believed: in My name they will cast out demons, they will speak with new tongues; they will pick up serpents, and if they drink any deadly poison, it will not hurt them; they will lay hands on the sick, and they will recover." (Mark 16:17-18) Why is it mentioned as new tongues? Originally, languages of different countries are referred to as tongues, so it is not referring to a foreign language but a 'new language' that comes from the guidance of the Holy Spirit.

So why is it difficult to believe such fact? It is written in the Bible, "Things which eye has not seen and ear has not heard, and which have not entered the heart of man, all that God has prepared for those who loved Him. For to us God revealed them through the Spirit for the Spirit searches all things even the depths of God." (1 Corinthians 2:9-10) We give presents to our loved ones on birthdays or anniversaries. Likewise, God has also prepared a lot of gifts to those who love Him. The spiritual gifts are something we humans cannot even fathom with our imagination. But amazingly, once you receive them, the Word of God becomes totally new and you find yourself asking, "Was there such a verse in the Bible?" Contrary to the past, you start to hear the voice of God!

This is a miracle. The things you couldn't imagine doing you start to do it. A person whom you couldn't love in the past you start to love; a person whom you couldn't forgive you forgive. "How can I humble myself in front of that person when I'm so much superior?" You become humble. God asked you, "I know that you have saved up tens of thousands of dollars. I want you to give it away." This would have been impossible in the past but you share it with others. This is not your doing and certainly impossible with your own will. It is through the spiritual gifts that God has prepared, which enabled you to do the things that you considered impossible. Anything is possible when the Spirit of God is poured into us.

The Types of Spiritual Gifts

There are various gifts of the Holy Spirit. In the New Testament there are approximately 21 gifts mentioned and it states clearly that the Holy Spirit has distributed a variety of effects according to each person as it sees fit. (1 Corinthians 12) As we are made to be in one body in Christ, each person with different spiritual gifts needs each other to become full. So you must not think of yourself as special just because you have received a spiritual gift.

Also, God gives us spiritual gifts according to our character. A person with a warm heart receives a gift of prophecy. A person who boldly says "Amen" when others are unbelieving receives a gift of faith. What this means is that one person does not receive all the spiritual gifts but the Holy Spirit adequately distributes the gifts to each individual according to the person's faith, ability, life experiences.

A person who has received a gift on the hand serves others. This person is warm-hearted and shares love with others. A person who has received a gift of healing is able to heal people by laying hands on them. A person who has received a gift on the head is able to teach the Word of God. A person who has received a gift on the feet wears the shoes of the gospel and evangelizes. "Having shod your feet with the preparation of the gospel of peace." (Ephesians 6:15) These people cannot stay at one place so they need to move around. A person who has received a gift of speech has the ability to praise and pray inspired by the Spirit, which is the gift of tongue. And as the person progresses in prayer of tongue, this person receives the gift of interpretation of tongue and further the gift of prophecy.

God puts a new spirit, God's Spirit, in our hearts. The presence of the Holy Spirit is in our hearts, and tongue being the most intimate part connected to the heart, the gift of tongues comes through our tongue. For that reason, praying in tongues is not something we do with our own senses but it is strictly inspired by the Spirit. A prayer of tongue is when you totally surrender your tongue to God. Rather than saying "We pray that the Holy Spirit fill us today. We pray that the Holy Spirit will be with us this hour" in our own language, saying this in another tongue would make it easier for us to experience the works of the Holy Spirit within us. Moreover, whenever you want you will be able to feel the presence of the Holy Spirit.

Anyone Can Receive the Gift of Tongues

Many people think that they cannot receive the gift of tongues. Other spiritual gifts are distributed to each individual's character and their level of faith by the Holy Spirit but the gift of tongues is given to all believers. It is because the gift of tongues is an ability to praise God and pray as well as having an individual relationship with God. Those who believe in Jesus must all pray and give worship to Him. Note that there is no direct verse in the Bible that says "everyone will receive the gift of tongue." But Apostle Paul says, "I wish that you all spoke in tongues." (1 Corinthians 14:5) He does not say, "I wish that all of you receive the gift of healing." He says the following referring to himself, "I thank God, I speak in tongues more than you all." (1 Corinthians 14:18) Apostle Paul was a man of tears and humility. If he were boastful of his ability that others fellow workers didn't have, he might have been the most arrogant person in the world. All the other believers were able to pray in tongues and knowing how beneficial it was, Paul was thankful that he spoke in tongues more than they did.

The gift of tongues can be received by anyone but you need to surrender your tongue to the Holy Spirit, so that the passage of the Spirit is opened for the Holy Spirit to work. It is because "the word is spirit and life." (John 6:63) The reason why believers receive grace when they hear a sermon from a pastor is because the Word that is delivered by the pastor opens the passage of the Spirit. We can feel the Holy Spirit working within us in powerful ways when we receive the Word in sermons. The Holy Spirit does not work only when we listen to the Word passively. Those times when we experience the work of the Holy Spirit are as follows: First, when we read or listen to the Word; second, when we pray; and third, when we praise God with our lips.

The commonality of these three instances is the fact that one can experience the works of the Holy Spirit through spoken words when the passage of the Spirit is open.

BENEFIT OF USING TONGUES

Receive Guidance of the Holy Spirit

"Walk by the Spirit, and you will not carry out the desire of the flesh. For the flesh sets its desire against the Spirit, and the Spirit against the flesh; for these are in opposition to one another so that you may not do the things that you please.' (Galatians 5:16-17) 'For if you are living according to the flesh you must die; but if by the Spirit you are putting death the deeds of the body you will live." (Romans 8:13) We must be led by the Holy Spirit if we do not want to follow the fleshly desires. Then, how can we be led by the Spirit?

The Lord tells us to "pray at all times in Spirit." (Ephesians 6:18) We need to pray seeking the Spirit and being led by the Spirit. God wants to give something that is unseen, unheard and unthinkable to those who love Him. If we pray in our own words we end up praying something we have heard, seen or thought - such as necessity things like food, clothing, shelter and prosperity of our children, which are basically all worldly things. Occasionally there may be a glimpse of prayer seeking God's kingdom and His righteousness, but basically "we do not know how to pray as we should." (Romans 8:26) It is because whatever we seek and whatever God wants to give us are different.

Prayer is difficult, because we do not know what we should be praying for. That is why God has permitted a secret tunnel for us. "For one who speaks in a tongue does not speak to men but to God; for no one understands, but in His spirit he speaks mysteries." (1 Corinthians 14:2) Prayer of tongue is a communication in spirit with God, not with men.

People who pray in tongues do not know what they are praying about, so they often end up thinking it is senseless and useless. Whenever one prays in a tongue, the spirit of Satan interferes putting suspicion and strange thoughts into the heart of the person. One believer said, "Why is prayer of tongue so important when the Bible tells us five words are better to spread to others rather than ten thousand words in a tongue?" (1 Corinthians 14:19) Remember now, prayer of tongue is a secret communication with God, not man. It makes us repent the sins of our past - the secrets we have hidden so deeply in our hearts. If we repent with our own mind probably only 1/10th will be remembered if at all. But once we are led by the Holy Spirit, the repentance begins from the deeply rooted sins of the long lost past and memory. Just as Jesus says, "Blessed are those who mourn, for they shall be comforted," (Matthew 5:4) our deepest soul starts to mourn and tears are shed - which is a true repentance. Not knowing what we are saying could be a blessing.

A person does not disclose a secret unless you're intimate with the person. Prayer of tongue is just like telling your secret to God. It is strictly between you and God. You don't need to bother with the person next to you. God's love is so great that whenever speaking to others it should be clearly understood through interpretation (prophecy). "If the whole church assembles together and all speak in tongues, and ungifted men or unbelievers enter, will they not say that you are mad?" (1 Corinthians 14:23) But talking to God in spirit is a privilege given by God to those who love Him.

Give Worship in Spirit and Truth

The second benefit of praying in tongue is that it is a true worship given in spirit. Do you think you could worship in spirit and truth even if you wanted to? It can only be done through praying in tongues. Praying in tongues is "speaking in other tongues as the Spirit leads you" (Acts 2:4) a worship driven by the inspiration of the Holy Spirit.

It is through prayer of tongue that true repentance can be done.

Unknown praises come out - a familiar praise song and yet spoken in different language. Having surrendered our tongue, we give praise to God, and thankfulness flow out of our mouth. Prayer of tongue has all the elements of worship such as repentance, praise, thankfulness and glory.

Destroys the Spirit of Satan

The Holy Spirit is a consuming fire. Satan's spirit is consumed when prayers are lifted up in tongues and Satan fears it the most. Satan blocks or interferes with the prayer of tongue. We can actually experience Satan being consumed inside us when we pray in tongues.

First, worries and concerns disappear.

Jesus says, "Do not worry about tomorrow; for tomorrow will care for itself. Each day has enough trouble of its own." (Matthew 6:34) But realistically, is it possible not to have worries in our daily lives? Just because you say to yourself, "I'm not going to worry," it doesn't make you stop worrying. It will definitely not go away just like that. But if you pray in tongues, concerns, worries, anxieties and despair vanish away without you realizing it. The Holy Spirit works when you surrender your tongue. Through the works of the Holy Spirit, the worries and concerns given by the spirit of Satan disappear.

Worldly thoughts enter us through watching television and sometimes simply talking to people. Once that happens our faith deteriorates, and worries, concerns and uneasiness start to pile up, causing us not to pray. The less you pray, the more the doors of prayers get shut down. Then, worldly thoughts sneak up on you again, and your faith decreases. It is a vicious cycle.

Praying in tongues enables you to pour everything out to God in His secret language. In return, you are filled with His peace. "Peace I leave with you; My peace I give to you not as the world gives do I give to you. Do not let your heart be troubled, nor let it be fearful." (John 14:27) Have you heard this before? If so, are you experiencing the peace that the world cannot give? We must not read the Bible with our head. Invite the Holy Spirit into your life then you will experience the Word.

Second, your inner scars are healed.

When our sins are forgiven and our hurts are healed through the blood of Jesus, we refer to this as the healing of our inner scars. Prayer of tongue makes us confess our sins that are unknown to us as well as our inner pain. The spirit of Satan gets consumed by the fire and is replaced with peace which heals our inner self. Once you confess your hurts led by the Holy Spirit, a person you used to hate won't bother you anymore. On the other hand, a person who fails to repent through the inspiration of the Holy Spirit is unable to forgive and lives under suppression without being aware of it. Surprisingly, there are many believers of Jesus who live like this.

Third, the spirit of doubt is destroyed.

Satan makes you doubt the Word of God. Even though we believe in God there are certain parts in His word that we have a hard time believing. This comes from the doubtful spirit, and this constantly brings us down. However, once you pray in tongues continuously, the doubtful spirit disappears. Though you may not fully understand it, the Holy Spirit leads us in prayer with unimaginable lament.

We must also understand that the way the Holy Spirit works is not only through the gift of tongues. You can also experience the Holy Spirit while listening to the Word because it inspires us. But experiencing the Holy Spirit through listening to another person's sermons is a passive way.

Prayer of tongue is a treasure hidden in heaven. "As for you, the anointing which you received from Him abides in you, and you have no need for anyone to each you." (1 John 2:26) If we read the Bible through the guidance of the Holy Spirit, we start to understand things we haven't before. Prayer opens the channel of spirit. When we utter words in prayer, they are not whole, for they are of thoughts of what we know and what we have experienced On the other hand, praying in tongues is led by the Holy Spirit to help our weaknesses and help us to offer a true and complete worship.

A person I knew well was suffering from severe migraines. So I advised him to pray in tongues in the early dawn service. A week later he came to me and said, "You should put another title as Doctor in front of Ambassador." He was overjoyed for being completely healed after taking my advice. Worries and concerns disappear when we open the channel of spirit through words. There is no reason why one has to have a headache. Once the Holy Spirit works it wets you with amazing inspiration and joy, guiding you deeper into spirituality.

There was a man who used to be a drug addict but received Jesus and prayed in tongues. He visited a preacher and said, "Pastor, my very first prayer in tongues felt just like my first drug intake." Drugs lead to death but prayer in tongue leads you to life.

Fourth, the energy of the flesh is driven out.

The energy of the flesh through accumulated sins within our body starts to leave us when we pray in tongues led by the Holy Spirit. The reason our spirit is hard as rock is because of the accumulated energies in us over the years. Selfishness, ambition, jealousy, anger, resentments, greed and sense of superiority are all the elements that make our hearts hard as rock. This energy of the flesh can only be crushed through the works of the Holy Spirit. People equate this effect with denying one's self. Without crushing our inner self, we won't be able to feel the seed of life that is already in us. The heart remains hard in spite of praying at early dawn services.

Faith grows only when the energy of the flesh goes out of us. The deepest part of our soul must be crushed so that the seed of the Holy Spirit can grow. Those who mourn from their heart are able to bear fruit of thirty, sixty, hundredth-fold. The best remedy to get rid of the fleshly energy is praying in tongues. This is the gift that God has prepared for those who love Him.

Fifth, you are set free from physical pleasures.

Once you pray in tongues, the things that you used to enjoy become less attractive. It is difficult to cut off the ties of worldly pleasures. For instance, smokers or drinkers have a hard time getting rid of their habits by themselves. Also, there are people who consume their day by watching TV shows from the minute they wake up. Ups and downs of many relationships are the same as well. Alcohol, cigarettes, dancing, or karaoke bars are things of the world that consumes us. When a person sings with their eyes closed at karaoke bars is an act of shifting the channel of spirit and opening the doors of the worldly spirit. The more you activate it the more Satan's spirit fills your heart which results in accumulating the energies of the flesh. But if you pray in tongues, the physical interest and worldly thoughts become automatically terminated.

My youngest daughter used to enjoy singing at karaoke bars. But ever since she started praying in tongues she came up to me and said, "Dad, I've lost interest in karaoking" and stopped going. It is because she has found great inspiration and joy in the presence of the Holy Spirit instead of the worldly pleasures.

Sixth, human relationships begin to work out.

Social gatherings of people become less interesting once the Holy Spirit works within you. You start to distance yourself from the worldly people who gather to gossip or meet just to spend time to hang out. Without realizing it, you begin to lose interest in praying since lengthy conversations of worldly things have captured your heart. This applies to believers as well. Cell groups that have gathered to give worship may end up talking about things of the world and gradually forget the purpose of the meeting.

If we pray in tongues, the Holy Spirit guides our human relationships according to the Word. It enables us to have a proper relationship with one another based on the Word of God. Prayer in tongue also prohibits us from tests and trials relating to people in the church. Rather than finding faults in a person we find ourselves having a merciful heart instead. All the unnecessary people that we have around us are cleared away by the Holy Spirit and are replaced with those that would help us in faith. The joy and inspiration filled by the presence of the Holy Spirit must be experienced in us. Heavenly peace and joy await us. While praying in tongues, we are guided to a person who would help us out of the blue after having received the invisible spark of light from the Holy Spirit.

The Perfect Intercessory Prayer

When we pray in tongues, we receive amazing answers to our prayers. We may also receive answers to your ordinary prayers but they are not as consistent. However, once we pray in tongues led by the Holy Spirit, our spirit communicates the secrets that are made visible through angels who work at the command of the Holy Spirit. It means our prayer becomes real. "For the Word of God is living and active." (Hebrews 4:12) The Holy Spirit makes it real through the Word - a miracle happens. That is praying in tongues makes a perfect intercessory prayer. God receives our prayer and works. The reason why God is not working is because we are asking for unnecessary things of the world. When we conduct intercessory prayer, God listens to our prayer in tongue rather than our prayer on our list of items. Usually our intercessory prayers are done through the things we have seen or heard which limits our prayer topics.

We intercede for our families, children, grandchildren, friends, deacons, church or even missionaries sent abroad. But don't forget that God is the Master of the entire world. "All the earth is Mine." (Exodus 19:5) God has interests in all the things in the world and wants to work for all mankind. That is why He makes us do things we were not aware or capable of. A prayer that is done without knowing what you're praying for is a blessing. If you were to know what you were saying, would you pray for a dying soul in Siberia or pray for an unknown missionary who is suffering in Africa? Most likely not. But a prayer led by the Holy Spirit would be a prayer that God wants. The time spent going back and forth to the church for the early dawn service is so precious to me.

Somebody said, "It takes me 30 minutes to get to church so it's too far for me to go." But if that person only knew how precious the time would be when he prays in tongues while driving and how great an intercessory prayer could be, the distance would be a blessing in disguise and something to be thankful for. I received an email one day from a foreign country which read, "Dear Elder, thank you very much for praying for our family. Something that is unimaginable has happened. Our kid who was divorced has re-united with the spouse." How did the person know what I prayed? It was the Holy Spirit that informed the person that I was praying for them. In another incident a Chinese person sent me a letter. He told me that one night he was sleeping and suddenly the Holy Spirit woke him and said, "Ambassador Moon is praying for you now, so wake up immediately and pray." Obviously I have not prayed for that person consciously. But the person said, "It was the most crucial time when I desperately needed prayers but I didn't pray. Your intercessory prayer woke me up and made me pray. As a result, the personnel problem was smoothly resolved. I thank you deeply." This kind of situation arises when prayers are led by the Holy Spirit. It is really fascinating. So whenever I receive a request for an intercessory prayer, I openly give my promise to pray. Even if I may have forgotten it, I truly believe the Holy Spirit remembers to pray for that person when I pray in tongue.

When we pray in tongues, it is just like us providing God a blank check with our signature on it for Him to use wherever necessary. We may not know where God will use it - it may be for a dying child in Iraq, or for leaders of the underground Chinese church who are being persecuted. Wherever God deems necessary, it will be used, and how thankful we are to participate in His work in such a way!

In New York I used to raise one hand and continuously intercede in tongues while passing through the apartment buildings in early dawn. Then, the Holy Spirit spoke to me, "During your days of intercessory prayer I will protect New York never to experience an incident of the 9.11 terror again."

Distinct Proof of the Lord's Resurrection

How can we believe in the blood of Christ on the cross and His resurrection? How can we believe that He has risen from the dead and is now sitting on the right side of God's throne? For three years, the 12 disciples followed Jesus and listened to His sermon but once He died on the cross they all ran away. After Jesus' ascension, the disciples gathered to pray in Mark's attic and they became apostles after receiving the power of the Holy Spirit. From that point on, the disciples risked their lives to witness Jesus. "You will receive power when the Holy Spirit has come upon you; and you shall be My witnesses both in Jerusalem and in all Judea and Samaria and even to the remotest part of the world." (Acts 1:8)

They did not believe Jesus was the Son of God at first. The Bible must not be read or understood literally. The Word must have the witness of the Holy Spirit, because without it one cannot believe. It is only when the Holy Spirit testifies that true faith is born in us. You may understand the witness of the Holy Spirit when listening to the Word of God, but the actual experience of the presence of the Holy Spirit happens when we open the channel of the Spirit through our words.

I personally feel frustrated when believers say, "I have experienced the Holy Spirit in the past. It was great then but now I have lost my first love." This kind of remark is spoken because they are not aware that the Holy Spirit, who loves us, is in us right now. The Holy Spirit is knocking on the door to meet us. "Behold, I stand at the door and knock; if anyone hears My voice and opens the door, I will come in to him and will dine with him and he with Me." (Revelation 3:20) Please pray in tongues. The Holy Spirit will work inside you when you pray in tongues, and because of it, your heart will be opened. Imagine yourself in the embracing arms of God. You will feel the heartbeat of God, His breath, and you will surely shed tears of joy. And also, when you pray in tongues, God fills your heart with goodness. "The good man brings out of his good treasure what is good." (Matthew 12:35)

Keep Praying Even Though You Don't Understand

Be persistent in praying even though you have no idea what you're praying about. Just carry on by saying, "God, I don't understand it but the Holy Spirit in me tells me that this is the way to worship You." You will not be sorry. Why? Because this is a true worship given in spirit even though you don't understand what you're saying. A new creation is created through worship. You may not know what you're praying for but be assured that through it you will be given amazing power and wisdom for a new creative day. I challenge my readers to go deeper in worship of spirit so that you may experience the presence of the Holy Spirit.

Desire for Prayer of Interpretation and Prophecy

When you first start praying in tongues you don't understand the meaning of it but once you continue to do so you will begin to interpret your own prayer. Apostle Paul said to desire earnestly for spiritual gifts, especially the gift of prophecy. (1 Corinthians 14:1) Once you pray in tongues, you first start with the interpretation of prayer and then the gift of prophecy will follow next. Prophecy is a gift to interpret other peoples' prayers in tongues. Since the Holy Spirit in us is only one spirit, the person who interprets is able to see the spirit of the other person.

People start to hear the voice of God after receiving the gift of the interpretation. They can personally communicate with God. They are able to hear God's voice as the channel of spirit is opened through the prayer in tongue. A true relationship is formed with God. This is exactly the secret of success which Jesus said, "abide in Me and I in you." Love is not a one-way street. It must be a two-way street. I urge my readers to desire for the gift of interpretation.

I had the blessing of receiving the gift of interpretation in a month, but it all differs from every individual. The most important thing is that even though you have received the gift to interpret 100 percent, it is not necessary to interpret 100% of everything. It is more essential to give worship than knowing and understanding the content of your own prayers. "One thing I have asked from the Lord, that I shall seek; that I may dwell in the house of the Lord all the days of my life, to behold the beauty of the Lord and to meditate in His temple." (Psalms 27:4) There is no need for interpretation when you give worship. The best worship and the best intercessory prayer happen when we surrender all our thoughts, emotions, and will to the Lord. Therefore, we do not be need to be discouraged when we do not understand our prayers prayed in tongues. It is actually a great blessing not to know and a short cut to go in deeper in spirit for a true worship, which is what God wants us to do. But then again, I want the readers to desire for the gift of interpretation. It is because when you are able to interpret, you will hear the voice of God and understand your own prayer and ultimately have a personal relationship with the Lord.

Be Guided by the Word of God

After experiencing the Holy Spirit and hearing the voice of God, the Word (Jesus) might gradually disappear. Once that happens sermons preached by ministers cannot be received properly. Because a heart of pride starts to sprout. "I can hear the voice of God directly so the pastor's message is not important." With the great spiritual gifts you received, you might even challenge God with them, if you are not led by the Word. You might get to the point of denying Jesus. This is one of the reasons why people with spiritual gifts fall (corrupt) and heresy arises. Also, some pastors have a tendency to be skeptical towards believers when they express that they had received the gifts of tongues and prophecy at a Christian retreat. The problem with people with the gift of tongues and prophecy is that they may easily fall into the trap of mysticism.

Therefore, a person who prays in tongues must receive the guidance from the Word of God. For instance, if you prayed in tongues for one hour, you must also spend (digest) the same amount of time reading the Word. The Word is like a corrective handle for believers. When you do not have the right grip of the handle, you can get into an accident or even hurt various people. We must be led by the Word with the power of the Holy Spirit (energy & movement)

Build Up the Church

The reason why the Holy Spirit gives us great power is for us to build up the church. In order to edify the church, we must be obedient to our pastors. People who have received spiritual gifts and do not obey respective pastors will fall one day. The rules and regulations of a church must be observed. Even if you have received the gift of tongues, you must be thoughtful of others as not to interfere with the atmosphere of the prayer time at church. It is important to control yourself according to the rules of your church. The difference between an insane person and a person who prays in tongues is that the crazy person cannot control himself but a person who prays in tongue can.

Two Types of Tongues: Tongue of Men and Tongue of Angels

Apostle Paul says, "If I speak with the tongues of men and of angels, but do not have love, I have become a noisy gong or a clanging cymbal." (1 Corinthians 13:1) Even if one may have received the spiritual gifts of tongue or prophecy, it means nothing if there is no love. All spiritual gifts are given for the sake of love. According to this verse, Apostle Paul is informing us that there are two types of tongues.

First, there is the tongue of men which refers to as languages spoken in various countries in the world. For instance, when a person speaks in a tongue it could be in Spanish, Arabic or any other language used in different regions, which means that it can be interpreted.

Second, there is the tongue of angels which is an unknown language that we cannot understand. The important fact is that we should not be focused on the actual sound that comes out of the mouth. The sound itself has no significant meaning. It may appear that a person interpreting the tongue is simultaneously translating word by word, but actually this is not the case. The interpretation of the tongue is entirely revealed by the Holy Spirit to our spirit so the actual sound is not important.

Be Persistent in Receiving the Gift of Tongues

Apostle Paul said, "Desire earnestly for the spiritual gifts." (1 Corinthians 14:1) There is an interesting parable in Luke 11. "Suppose one of you has a friend and goes to him at midnight and says to him, 'Friend, lend me three loaves; for a friend of mine has come to me from a journey, and I have nothing to set before him.' And from inside he answers and says, 'Do not bother me; the door has already been shut and my children and I are in bed; I cannot get up and give you anything.' (Luke 11:5-7) What did the friend say after reluctantly giving the bread? He said, "I'm not giving you the bread because you're my friend but because of your persistence."

After telling the parable Jesus said, "I tell you, even though he will not get up and give him anything because he is his friend, yet because of his persistence he will get up and give him as much as he needs. So I say to you, ask and it will be given to you; seek, and you will find; knock, and it will be opened to you." (Luke 11:8-9) It means that if you really want to receive the gift of tongue then ask for it persistently. "If you then, being evil, know how to give good gifts to your children, how much more will your heavenly Father give the Holy Spirit to those who ask Him?" (Luke 11:13)

That is why Apostle Paul said, "I want all of you to speak in tongue." When Peter was delivering the Word to Cornelius, he knew that the Holy Spirit was present when Cornelius started to speak in tongues. Similarly, while listening to the Word or praying, you may also speak in tongues through the strong presence of the Holy Spirit.

Those who have an earnest desire in receiving the gift of tongues have already received it in their hearts. On the other hand, it can be said that those who have not yet received it have no desire for it primarily due to lack of knowledge of the benefit of the gift of tongues or have negative thoughts about it. You may miss your opportunity by thinking like: "It can't be me yet." "One day it will be given to me."

Concluding the Book

LET'S READ THE BIBLE, KNOW THE FATHER'S WILL AND HIS LOVE

Ever since the creation, God's main interest has been in recovering (expand) His Kingdom on this earth. Upon God's creation, He put Adam and Eve in the Garden of Eden (His Kingdom) and immediately after the fall of man, God cursed the serpent and promised that He will crush the head of the serpent through the descendent of a woman. (Genesis 3:15) It is a promise that the Messiah who is to come as the descendant of a woman will demolish the power of Satan and bring forth new heaven and new earth in this land. Abraham, Moses, Elijah, John the Baptist, Jesus, and many apostles have endlessly proclaimed of the Kingdom of God that is to come on this earth.

We have learned through the Bible the providence of God and the Kingdom of God and how it is gradually being fulfilled. (Parable of the seed - Matthew 13:1-23; Promise of future form - 1 Corinthians 15:36-38, etc.) History of the Old Testament (Abraham's promise; Exodus; Conquer of Canaan; Kingdom of David; Temple construction; Re-building of the temple and city wall after return from exile) supports this.

The Kingdom of God began to appear on earth through the works of Jesus. The Holy Spirit is working until the 2nd coming of Christ, so that we may experience the kingdom of heaven through our daily lives and look forward to the glorious new heaven and earth. The Kingdom of God is fulfilled steadily through the present and future. Starting right now from within ourselves, the Lord will give us a glorious world at the time that only God the Father knows. Jesus said, "Therefore be alert for you do not know which day your Lord is coming." (Matthew 24:42-43) "Be on the alert for you do not know the day nor the hour." (Matthew 25:13) And the apostles encouraged us, "Therefore be patient, brethren, until the coming of the Lord. The farmer waits for the precious produce of the soil, being patient about it, until it gets the early and late rains." (James 5:7) "He who has an ear, let him hear what the Spirit says to the churches. To him who overcomes, I will grant to eat of the tree of life which is the Paradise of God." (Revelation 2:7)

We have understood the fundamental teachings that when we respond to God's love (the Word) the Kingdom of God starts from our hearts. As believers of God, we must be sanctified. "Therefore if anyone cleanses himself from these things, he will be a vessel for honor, sanctified, useful to the Master, prepared for every good work" (2 Timothy 2:21) until the 2nd coming of Christ.

With the help of the power of the Holy Spirit, I wish upon my readers to read the Word of God and pray daily to enjoy the kingdom of heaven and look forward to the presence of the Lord's glorious kingdom in the future ahead. I also pray in the name of Jesus that we become God's predestined children to fulfill the dream of the sacred hope (salvation of all mankind) and the plan of the Father and the Son before creation.

This book is a compilation of my own personal study materials of past 10 years while reading, learning and research of various related books. It also includes my personal inspiration of the Holy Spirit during my daily prayers at dawn break. As a layman with no theological education, I have tried to organize them in my own way. These are the contents of the lectures I gave each Sunday at different places that God had sent me to over the years. I realize that there are many areas that need to be supplemented, but I feel strongly that there are people out there like myself who thirst for the knowledge of the Father's will while reading the Bible. In order to help them to become intimate with the Bible, I felt compelled and passionate to share the grace that I have received and wrote this book. I urge many people to keep this book close to the Bible. I wish and pray that all of you may experience the same wonderful grace and love that I have experienced while studying the Word. At the same time, I welcome any feedback or input from you so that I may make a note for future reference. (bjmoon49@naver.com) I offer this book on the altar of the Lord.

October 2007
B.J. MOON